D0122232

THE DARK DOVE

The Sacred and Secular in Modern Literature

BY EUGENE WEBB

UNIVERSITY OF WASHINGTON PRESS
SEATTLE AND LONDON

Printed in the United States of America

Library of Congress Cataloging in Publication Data

Webb, Eugene, 1938-
The dark dove.

Bibliography: p.
Includes index.
1. Holy, The, in literature. I. Title.
PN49.W33 809'.933'8 74-28210
ISBN 0-295-95377-2

For Alix, my daughter,
who is not yet old enough to read this book,
but over whose whole life, I pray, its subject
may brood "with warm breast and with ah! bright wings"

Preface

"It is in literature," said Alfred North Whitehead, "that the concrete outlook of humanity receives its expression. Accordingly, it is to literature that we must look, particularly in its more concrete forms, if we hope to discover the inward thoughts of a generation."[1] This is especially true of this book's subject — the study of the sacred and its transformations in modern thought, and the transformations of the secular in relation to it. More than just a concept, the sacred involves affective attitudes; it therefore receives its most direct and adequate expression not in philosophical, theological, or psychological treatises, but in works of imaginative literature, where imagery can combine its intellectual and emotional elements and communicate both, fused in a single cognitive experience.

The sacred may be higher or lower than reason, or it may be true or false, beneficent or menacing — and this book will consider all of these possibilities — but it has a power in men's lives that is inescapable. It may happen that many men in a given generation will scarcely feel its power, but there will probably be few among them who do not at least feel its absence, and there will always be some who will feel that acutely enough to want to know what it is that is missing or, in some cases, to want to rediscover

1. *Science and the Modern World* (Cambridge: Cambridge University Press, 1929), p. 106, quoted in Joseph Anthony Mazzeo, "Some Interpretations of the History of Ideas," *Journal of the History of Ideas,* 33, no. 3 (July-September 1972): 389.

it. And there will also be some, among whom I would list the authors studied here, who know its calling and its power but who have had to find a new symbolic language in which to understand it and to speak of it. These are the true explorers of their generation, for it is to them more than to any others that we owe the possibility of depth in our lives.

I would like to take this opportunity to express my gratitude to the following friends and colleagues who have read parts of this work in manscript and have aided me with their comments: Professors David C. Fowler, Otto Reinert, Harold P. Simonson, and Richard Blessing of the University of Washington; Professor W. Ward Gasque of Regent College, University of British Columbia, Vancouver; and Professor Fredrick C. Candelaria of Simon Fraser University, Burnaby, B.C.

Acknowledgments

Permission to quote from the following works of W. H. Auden has been granted by Random House, Inc.: *The Collected Poetry of W. H. Auden* © 1945, *Collected Shorter Poems 1927-1957* © 1966, *About the House* © 1965, and *City Without Walls* © 1969. Excerpts from the poetry of T. S. Eliot are reprinted from his volume *Collected Poems 1909-1962* by permission of Harcourt Brace Jovanovich, Inc.; copyright, 1936, by Harcourt Brace Jovanovich, Inc.; copyright © 1963, 1964, by T. S. Eliot. Excerpts from the following works of Rainer Maria Rilke are quoted by permission of W. W. Norton and Company: *Duino Elegies* by Rainer Maria Rilke, translated by J. B. Leishman and Stephen Spender, copyright 1939 by W. W. Norton & Company, Inc., copyright renewed 1967 by Stephen Spender and J. B. Leishman; *Sonnets to Orpheus* by Rainer Maria Rilke, translated by M. D. Herter Norton, copyright 1942 by W. W. Norton & Company, Inc., copyright renewed 1970 by M. D. Herter Norton. Excerpts from the following works of Wallace Stevens are quoted by permission of Alfred A. Knopf: *The Collected Poems of Wallace Stevens* © 1923, 1931, 1935, 1936, 1937, 1942, 1943, 1944, 1945, 1946, 1947, 1948, 1949, 1950, 1951, 1952, 1954, *Opus Posthumous* © 1957. Excerpts from the following poems of William Butler Yeats are quoted by permission of Macmillan Publishing Company, Inc.: "To the Rose upon the Rod of Time" (copyright 1906 by Macmillan Publishing Company, Inc., renewed 1934 by Macmillan Publishing Co., Inc.), "Byzantium" (copyright 1933 by Macmillan Publishing Co., Inc., renewed 1961 by Bertha Georgie Yeats), "Vacillation" (copyright 1933 by Macmillan Publishing Co., Inc., renewed 1961 by Bertha Georgie Yeats), "Among School Children" (copyright 1928 by Macmillan Publishing Co., Inc., renewed 1956 by Georgie Yeats), "The Magi" (copyright 1916 by Macmillan Publishing Co., Inc., renewed 1944 by Bertha Georgie Yeats), "Ego Dominus Tuus" (copyright 1918 by Macmillan Publishing Co., Inc., renewed by Bertha Georgie Yeats).

Contents

The Dark Dove

The Sacred and Secular in Modern Literature

CHAPTER I

The Paradox of the Sacred

A general tendency toward secularization, widely recognized as one of the distinctive features of the present age, is often linked with the idea of a general decline in concern with the sacred. The death or disappearance of the sacred, in so far as it is connected with conceptions of the divine, has become a commonplace of modern cultural criticism, both on its highest and on its lowest levels. Popular journalism proclaims the death of God one year, when a book like J. A. T. Robinson's *Honest to God* presents in an easily comprehensible form from some of the speculations of Paul Tillich and Rudolph Bultmann, then in another year proclaims His return as translations of subsequent thinkers such as Jürgen Moltmann and Wolfhart Pannenberg become available. On the highest level, a careful and discriminating scholarly study such as J. Hillis Miller's *The Disappearance of God* discusses the entire postmedieval European tradition in literature as a record of "the gradual withdrawal of God from the world."[1]

That a profound change has taken place during the last few centuries in the religious thought and sensibility of

1. *The Disappearance of God: Five Nineteenth Century Writers* (Cambridge, Mass.: Harvard University Press, 1963), p. 1.

modern man is fairly obvious. What this consists of, however, is only gradually becoming clear, and discussions formulated in the language of traditional theology, references to the "death of God," for example, often only generate further confusion. Miller is well aware of this danger; after opening his study with the statement of his theme cited above, he goes on to warn that "such a statement must not be misunderstood. It does not mean blank atheism, the 'God is dead' of Nietzsche as it often is interpreted." What it does mean for many, he says, is that although God still lives, He lives high above our heads in a different world: ". . . God exists, but he is out of reach." To put the issue another way, what the situation Miller and others describe means, whether "blank atheism," deism, or any other variant of traditional attitudes, will depend to a large extent on what one means by "God," "disappearance," and so on. It will also depend — and here we touch on an important aspect of the problem that may open up new avenues for its interpretation — on attitudes and feelings that are not altogether conceptual and that may be distorted or obscured if formulated in a terminology that forces them into an inappropriate conceptual mold.

The sacred is only in part an intellectual concept: it is also a mode of experience. And its opposite is not, properly speaking, the secular, but the profane. The secular, which is to say, the world of life in time, may be experienced as either sacred or profane; and secularization, though it may indeed involve desacralization, may also involve transformations in the concepts of both the secular and the sacred — transformations that in some cases may bring them closer together rather than forcing them apart. The sense of the sacred is far older than theology and, because it is not an idea but an experience, it is also more fundamental; theology, like ritual and all other aspects of religion, arises from a sense of the sacred and takes shape around it. Consequently, although theology as a rational discipline may be governed by the laws of logic, its developments, including the explicit theological attitudes involved in the world-view of a given period, may also take place according to changing patterns in experiences that are intrinsically nonrational.

To understand the role of the sacred in the thought and sensibility of a given period it is necessary to attend to both of its aspects, the conceptual and the experiential. These cannot be altogether separated, but they can be distinguished to some extent, and it may even happen in some cases, as we shall see in the third chapter of this study, that a thinker who expresses himself in language that would normally be thought of as conceptually atheistic may also express, even in that very language, a strong sense of reverence for a sacred dimension in being.

Although the history of theology as a theoretical discipline goes back thousands of years, the study of the sacred as a mode of religious experience is quite recent; it began in 1917 with the publication of Rudolf Otto's *Das Heilige,* translated in 1923 as *The Idea of the Holy.*[2]

Approaching the subject of the sacred from the point of view of the comparative study of religions, a discipline which itself did not come into being until the mid-nineteenth century, Otto traced the common features of the sense of the sacred as it appears in a variety of religious traditions, though his focus was primarily on the Judaeo-Christian tradition. Subsequent studies, among which those of Mircea Eliade are especially notable, have gone

2. Rudolf Otto, *The Idea of the Holy: An Inquiry into the Non-rational Factor in the Idea of the Divine and its Relation to the Rational,* trans. John W. Harvey (2d ed.; London: Oxford University Press, 1950).

on to apply the same approach to a large number of primitive and nonwestern religions. According to this school of thought, the sense of the sacred has certain features that are constant to it wherever it appears: a feeling of awe, even of terror, before the sacred, which is experienced as something unfathomable and incomprehensible, that simply overwhelms the intellect (*mysterium tremendum*); a sense of the majesty (*majestas*) of its vast superiority of power; a fascination with its fullness of being (*mysterium fascinans*); a sense of its total otherness, that it is like nothing else, human or cosmic, and that all analogies fall infinitely short of it; a feeling of total ontological dependence, of "creature-feeling," in Otto's phrase; and a feeling of abysmal deficiency or unworthiness — in religious terms, of "sinfulness."[3]

Another important feature of the sacred is the manner in which it manifests itself. In various traditions it appears in a great variety of forms, but always in a form that is particular, that is, in some element of the secular world, as Eliade puts it, "in objects that are an integral part of our natural 'profane' world." This constitutes a paradox; the sacred, by its very nature as outlined above, transcends everything finite, and yet it reveals itself only in and through the finite: "It is imposible to overemphasize the paradox represented by every hierophany, even the most elementary. By manifesting the sacred, any object becomes *something else,* yet it continues to remain *itself,* for it continues to participate in its surrounding cosmic milieu. A *sacred* stone remains a *stone*. . . ."[4] Or to adapt

3. This treatment of the subject of the sacred is presented in Chapters III-VII of Otto, *The Idea of the Holy*. For a brief, summary statement of the main points see Mircea Eliade, *The Sacred and the Profane: The Nature of Religions,* trans. Willard R. Trask (New York: Harper and Brothers, 1961), pp. 8-10.

4. Eliade, *The Sacred and the Profane,* pp. 11, 12.

the language of St. John the Evangelist, a particular manifestation of the sacred simultaneously is in the world but not of it, and of the world but not entirely in it; it is an uneasy union of finite and infinite and points in both directions at once.

To put it in other terms that may be helpful in illuminating the dynamics of the sacred as an experience and as a source of the patterns of thought that inform our tradition, the sacred, however it is formulated conceptually, is always apprehended experientially as simultaneously transcendent and immanent, and its transcendent and immanent aspects may serve as poles between which the experience moves. When one pole is more prominent than the other, this will affect the character of the experience. When the transcendent pole dominates, the experience will be characterized relatively more strongly by the sense of terror and of sinfulness; when the immanent pole becomes more prominent the sense of terror and sinfulness will give way to other feelings, perhaps a sense of salvation and forgiveness, perhaps a sense of rebirth and of participation in sacred being.

If the sense of the sacred is to retain its vitality, in fact if there is to be any experience of sacredness at all, both poles must be present, and the force of both must be felt. If, from the point of view of the experience, the whole of being were to come to seem completely contained within the finite, the awe, which is a function of the sense of transcendence, would evaporate, and the experience would be one of a pure, which is to say a profane, secularity. If, on the other hand, the fullness of being, conceived of as the being of God or the gods, were to come to seem exclusively transcendent, completely beyond the world, it would also seem utterly remote, in Miller's phrase, "out of reach," and ultimately of no value to man;

both man and the universe would have been abandoned, forced to suffice to themselves. Either path out of the polar tension of the sacred, whether through what might even at first appear a glorification of nature or through an extreme emphasis on the majesty of God at the expense of creation, leads to the same place, a desacralized universe.

Examples of both tendencies are to be found in many religious traditions, so many in fact that they almost seem to be governed by some sort of law whereby transcendent deities must gradually refine themselves out of existence, or at least out of man's universe, and immanent divinity must gradually lose itself in nature. Sky gods for example, as Eliade describes them, are pre-eminently transcendent, by way of the natural symbolism of height and celestial vastness, and also characteristically remote, even to the point of being nonfunctional: "Celestially structured supreme beings tend to disappear from the practice of religion, from cult; they depart from among men, withdraw to the sky, and become remote, inactive gods (*dei otiosi*)."[5] Their characteristic function is creation, and once they have performed that, there is nothing left for them to do, unless the community is threatened with destruction so that there is a new need for the creative power:

> If the High God is still remembered, he is known to have created the world and man, but this is almost all. Such a Supreme God seems to have ended his role by achieving the work of creation. He plays almost no role in the cult, his myths are few and rather banal, and, when he is not completely forgotten, he is invoked only in cases of extreme distress, when all other divine beings have proved utterly ineffectual.[6]

5. Ibid., pp. 121-22.
6. Mircea Eliade, *The Quest: History and Meaning in Religion* (Chicago: University of Chicago Press, 1969), pp. 81-2.

As the High God withdraws into the sky, his place in the economy of the sacred is largely taken over by the forces of immanent divinity:

> Through his concern with hierophanies of life, through discovering the sacral fertility of the earth, and through finding himself exposed to religious experiences that are more concrete (more carnal, even orgiastic), primitive man draws away from the celestial and transcendent god. The discovery of agriculture basically transforms not only primitive man's economy but also and especially his *economy of the sacred.* Other religious forces come into play — sexuality, fertility, the mythology of woman and of the earth, and so on.[7]

These seem more accessible than the sky deity, and perhaps vastly more pleasant, but they are limited in their power,[8] and ultimately, like the cosmos they animate, they depend on the transcendent for the quality of sacredness that they enjoy:

> What are called vegetation cults do not depend on a profane, "naturistic" experience, connected, for example, with spring and the reawakening of vegetation. On the contrary, the religious experience of renewal (= rebeginning, re-creation) of the world precedes and justifies the valorization of spring as the resurrection of nature. It is the mystery of the periodical regeneration of the cosmos that is the basis for the religious significance of spring. Then, too, in vegetation cults the emphasis is not always on the natural phenomenon of spring and the appearance of vegetation but on the prophetic *sign* of the cosmic mystery.[9]

One might say that it is the transcendent pole of the sacred that is the source or ground of its sacral quality and that the immanent is its vehicle, the means by which it becomes accessible to man. If either were missing, the

7. Eliade, *The Sacred and the Profane,* pp. 125-26.
8. Ibid., p. 127.
9. Ibid., pp. 150-51.

sacred would vanish from human experience. Of course, in primitive cultures this does not happen. The radical desacralization of the universe is a recent, characteristically modern, and largely western development. In most traditions what has happened is that even when the creative deities become remote, they still remain active through symbolism; the imagery of height — mountains, the heavens, and so on — continues to represent transcendence and to impress it, however dimly, upon man's vision of the universe.[10]

The common pattern has not been a movement out of the sacred, but an alternation between less extreme positions within it, between a somewhat greater prominence of the transcendent pole and a somewhat greater prominence of the immanent pole. In either case, the force of both is felt and the universe remains a divinely founded and inspirited cosmos.

The experience of the modern West, however, has been more complicated. It has had and in various ways still has its sense of the sacred, but it has seen this sense increase, diminish, and transform in different periods and in the minds of different men. It has also seen it vanish — and not on a small scale or briefly, but in a way that touches to a greater or lesser extent the life of every person in the modern world. Those who seek to hold on to the traditional sense of the sacred can do so only by fighting the demons of doubt, and even the most triumphant faith has a Waste Land as its background, a "tusked, ramshackling sea,"[11] and the "Bad Lands" where "All landscapes and all weathers freeze with fear."[12] Those who do not seek this, or

10. Ibid., pp. 128-29.

11. Dylan Thomas, "Poem on his Birthday," *The Collected Poems of Dylan Thomas* (New York: New Directions, 1953), p. 193.

12. W. H. Auden, "The Quest," in *Collected Shorter Poems, 1927-1957* (New York: Random House, 1966), p. 179.

do not win their way through to it, are left in a desacralized wilderness. Different people respond to this in different ways. Some, like Milton's fallen angels, explore their new world and try to build a home in it; some, like Eliot's Fisher King, either out of habit or out of hope, continue fishing on the shore of the "arid plain."[13]

The chapters that follow will examine some representative works by modern poets, novelists, and playwrights who have explored the possibilities of this situation. The chapter on the ambiguities of secularization in Nietzsche, Ibsen, Beckett, and Stevens will discuss the manner in which these four writers, who present a radically secularized and in conventional terms even perhaps atheistic vision of life, both criticize traditional concepts of the sacred and probe toward new ones. The next three chapters treat the manner in which William Butler Yeats, Rainer Maria Rilke, James Joyce, and Thomas Mann draw on various kinds of traditonal imagery of the sacred to resacralize the secular in terms of what may be called, with some reservations, a pantheistic vision. The chapters on T. S. Eliot and W. H. Auden discuss the manner in which these two Christian writers have reformulated and renewed the orthodox religious tradition of the West in a way that adapts it to the challenges that secularization offers.

For the sake of historical perspective, the following chapter will take a brief and necessarily rather general look at a few aspects of the tradition underlying these modern developments.

13. T. S. Eliot, "The Waste Land, *The Complete Poems and Plays, 1909-1950* (New York: Harcourt, Brace and World, 1952), p. 50.

CHAPTER II

The Tradition of the Sacred in the West

The root of our traditions of feeling and thought about the sacred is the religion of the Hebrews. The general importance of the Greek civilization to our culture is obvious, and no one could dispute it, but its specific influence on the shape of our experience of the sacred has been relatively small. Classical thought may have given us categories with which to interpret the sacred on an intellectual level, but the classical sensibility of the sacred, embodied in a heterogeneous mass of local genii,Olympian sky gods, fertility gods, auguration, and mystery rites, largely died out after the fall of Rome, or was transformed by the absorption of its particulars into the Christian cult.

What the Hebrew religion contributed that was uniquely important was a powerful, and eventually highly refined, version of the transcendent creator deity. This evolved out of a long process of interactions between the traditions of a variety of Semitic and Canaanite deities, most importantly El, Baal, and Yahweh.[1] Gradually Yahweh became pre-eminent among the Israelites and took over the functions, and even in most cases the names, of his rivals.

1. Edmond Jacob, *Theology of the Old Testament,* trans. Arthur W. Heathcote and Philip J. Allcock (New York: Harper and Row, 1958), pp. 43-48.

Most of these were what comparative religion calls "high gods," though some, such as Baal, had fertility associations as well. Yahweh became the "high god" *par excellence*, the only one among the ancient gods to remain fairly constantly over a long period of time both transcendent and active. One reason for this may have been that the Yahwistic creation myth was unique among primitive myths of the kind in involving a Fall. Other myths of its type, of which there were many, were affirmative, rather than critical, of life and involved no sense of sin or exile,[2] and as Rudolf Otto pointed out, the sense of sinfulness is one of the characteristic features of the experience of the transcendent sacred.

Of course the pre-eminence of Yahweh was only *fairly* constant; the Hebrew sense of the sacred fluctuated between the transcendent and the immanent poles as did that of other people, and when it veered toward the immanent pole, it became, by their own later standards, rather debased. The ancient Hebrews seem to have suffered two principal temptations. One was to abandon Yahweh for various fertility gods, the Baals and Astartes their prophets so frequently had to recall them from. The other was to reduce the transcendent *majestas* of Yahweh to a magical force subject to their control. An example of this tendency can be seen in their use of the Ark of the Covenant as a secret weapon in war as described in 1 Samuel, chapter 4. Fortunately for their subsequent contribution to our civilization, they lost that battle. Fortunately also they lost enough other battles, and wars, to recall them again and again to a more critical conception of the divine transcendence.

The important contribution of the Hebrews to the

2. Joseph Campbell, *The Masks of God: Occidental Mythology* (New York: Viking Press, 1964), pp. 104-5.

later religious tradition of the West was a strong sense of the *majestas,* the *mysterium tremendum et fascinans* of the transcendent sacred and the absolute dependence and deficiency of man in relation to it. Much of the later history of the Judaeo-Christian tradition and of the modern civilization that has grown out of it has been the story of attempts in various ways to balance this intensely felt transcendent pole of the sacred with a similarly intense immanent pole. To move away from the transcendent pole toward the immanent is quite common, but the attempt to balance a strong sense of the transcendent sacred with a strong sense of the sacred as immanent is unusual. It is also extremely difficult. Their power pulls the heart in two different directions at once, and when their union or conjunction is conceptualized, it seems only confusion to the logical intellect. Because of the difficulty of keeping the two poles in balance, the normal pattern has been for one to become stronger than the other.

If we consider the course of the western religious tradition as a whole from the point of view of this problem, what we find, is that from the time that Yahwism became pre-eminent in the Hebrew religion until approximately the time of the European eighteenth century, the dominant pole has been the transcendent, with at times more or less strong development on the side of the immanent. In the modern period, on the other hand, wherever the sense of the sacred is still alive, the immanent pole seems relatively the stronger, particularly outside the context of religious orthodoxy, but even to a large extent within it. Let us consider how this has developed.

The Christian movement, in its origins within the Jewish tradition, may be considered as, among other things, a major realigment of the poles of transcendence and immanence. The coming of the divine power in the person of a man, the redemption of man from his abasement and exile in sin, and the gift of the same divine power to men as the Holy Spirit was the transformation of what had often seemed a very remote transcendent deity into a powerful presence, simultaneously transcendent and immanent, and both to a very high degree of intensity. To compare the Hebrew and Christian scriptures in much detail with regard to this development would be an unwieldy task, and probably superfluous, but comparison of a few key images may make the nature of the transformation more concrete and more vivid.

A particularly good example is a comparison of the Hebrew and Christian Pentecosts, with their imagery of wind and fire. When God first called Moses to his mission as prophet and leader of the Israelites, He appeared to him in the form of a supernatural fire in the "burning bush," which, significantly, was not consumed: it is an important aspect of the paradox of the sacred, and one that later became one of the key elements of the Christian doctrine of the Incarnation, that in a manifestation of the transcendent in the particular, the particular retains its identity intact. Later at the giving of the Law on Mount Sinai — commemorated in the Jewish feast of Pentecost — He appeared once again as fire: "Mount Sinai was all smoking because the Lord had come upon it in fire; the smoke went up like the smoke of a kiln; all the people were terrified . . ." (Exod. 3:18-19).[3] Thunder and lightning are mentioned as well. The image seems to be a combination of storm and volcanic eruption, suitable symbols for the majesty of the *mysterium tremendum*.

Here the emphasis is on God's transcendence. The people remain at the foot of the mountain in terror, and

3. Except where otherwise indicated all Biblical quotations are from the *New English Bible* (Oxford University Press and Cambridge University Press, 1970).

Moses acts as mediator between them and a presence they would not be able to endure — in fact, his face afterward is so dazzling that he has to wear a veil to protect them from the sight of it. Of course, as the story goes, they also during this episode turned away from the transcendent God to the calf of gold and had to be called back from it, but they did return, and the experience of Sinai and the giving of the Law, together with the miracles of the Exodus, became for them one of their most important continuing symbols of the majesty of their God.

In a later age, when God seemed to have abandoned Israel, and when prophets began to look for a return of His power, the pentecostal imagery reshaped itself around a new, eschatological hope. Isaiah, for example, prophesies another, final coming in wind and fire:

For see, the Lord is coming in fire,
        with his chariots like a whirlwind,
    to strike home with his furious anger
        and the flaming fire of his reproof.
The Lord will judge by fire,
        with fire he will test all living men,
        and many will be slain by the Lord;
    those who hallow and purify themselves in garden-rites,
        one after another in a magic ring. . . .
[Isa. 66:15-17]

This coming, Isaiah goes on to say, is not to be only for judgment, but also for redemption, the transformation of Israel and the world into a sacred kingdom in which God Himself will live as an indwelling presence:

Then I myself will come to gather all nations and races,
        and they shall come and see my glory;
        and I will perform a sign among them.
I will spare some of them and send them to the nations . . .

distant coasts and islands which have never yet heard of me
  and have not seen my glory;
 these shall announce that glory among the nations. . . .
For, as the new heavens and the new earth
which I am making shall endure in my sight,
 says the Lord,
so shall your race and name endure. . . .

[Isa. 66:18-22]

The development of the Christian religion was one expression of this hope. Again the ancient imagery of the Mosaic Pentecost was transformed to become a vehicle for the new experience and vision. As the Acts of the Apostles tells the story, God descended again as wind and fire in a new Pentecost parallel to the earlier one.[4] Just as He had come to Moses, the representative of Israel, on Mount Sinai on the fiftieth day after the Exodus from Egypt, so now He came to the apostles — twelve of them, as an analogue to the patriarchs of the twelve tribes of Israel — on the fiftieth day after a new miraculous Exodus, the resurrection of Jesus from the dead and with him, potentially at least, all of Israel and mankind from sin and darkness. And this time He came as an indwelling presence, which like the supernatural fire in the burning bush, transfigured without destroying them:

While the day of Pentecost was running its course they were all together in one place, when suddenly there came from the sky a noise like that of a strong driving wind, which filled the whole house where they were sitting. And there appeared to them tongues like flames of fire, dispersed among them

4. Cf. Alan Richardson, *An Introduction to the Theology of the New Testament* (New York: Harper and Row, 1958), pp. 116-19. It is interesting that Saint John's account of the conferring of the Holy Spirit on the apostles is completely different from Saint Luke's and involves none of the pentecostal imagery; it appears probable that Luke was consciously constructing his version of the story in such a way as to emphasize the parallels between the two events.

and resting on each one. And they were all filled with the Holy Spirit and began to talk in other tongues, as the Spirit gave them power of utterance. [Acts 2:1-4]

Here each of the representatives of the new Israel has become himself a holy mountain, an epiphany in life of the divine power. That they believe this will be true not only of them but also of the entire people is made clear by Peter's speech to the crowd a few lines later on (referring to Joel 2:28-29): ". . . this is what the prophet spoke of: 'God says, "This will happen in the last days: I will pour out upon everyone a portion of my spirit; and your sons and daughters shall prophesy . . ." ' "(Acts 2:16-17).

Much of the New Testament, especially the epistles of St. Paul, is a working out of the implications of this idea. The implications were enormous. If every Christian was now a living Sinai, then the law given by Moses was no longer a necessary guide, but each was a living law, or to put it another way, each was free to follow the movements of the Holy Spirit within him — in fact, not only free, but obliged, for to do otherwise would be to fall back into the life of the old Adam. Obviously this is a belief that would lead to difficulties in practice for Christians, and it did and always has. Despite the efforts of St. Paul and many of his successors to reconcile freedom and law, the tension between the two has always persisted in the Christian tradition.

This, the problem of the Chrisian life, was one of the forms that the tension between the immanent and transcendent poles of the sacred took on in the new religion. It also took on ontological and epistemological forms. The ontological problem was that of the nature of God as a Trinity of Father, Son, and Holy Ghost, and of the relationship between Jesus Christ, as man, and the Son as second person of the Trinity. The controversy over an adequate formula for this worked out over a period of approximately four hundred years. It was settled, in formulae that proved satisfactory for at least another millennium, with the ratification at the Council of Chalcedon in A.D. 451 of the Nicene Creed and the Chalcedonian Definition of the Faith. The former of these documents formulated the doctrine of three persons in one God, of which the Son was "of one substance" (*homoousios*) with the Father, and the latter defined the person of the Son as comprising two natures, divine and human, in one person. This meant that the transcendent divine being (*ousia*) was fully immanent in the Incarnation (*homoousios*), and also immanent, through the gift of the Holy Spirit, in the new Israel, the *ekklesia* of those "called out" of profane secularity into the transfigured, sacred secularity of the incarnate divine life.

This was, of course, in explicit language, the same idea that had been, in the famous words of St. Paul, a scandal, that is, a stumbling block, to the Jews and foolishness to the Greeks (1 Cor. 1:23) — a scandal to the Jews because it seemed to threaten with a new return to golden calves and garden rites the divine transcendence their tradition of the sacred had had to sruggle so hard to preserve, foolishness to the Greeks because if it made any sense at all, it was a sense that transcended rational categories.

The epistemological problem was closely related to the ontological one as well as to the logical problem of a truth transcending reason. There have been two important approaches to it: the apophatic and the cataphatic. These are different types of theological methodology. The former, which became the dominant method in the

Orthodox East, emphasizes the inadequacy of all concepts applied to God.[5] The problem that the apophatic method tries to deal with is that while all concepts are finite, God Himself is infinite. We can apply concepts to Him analogically, but must alway remember that, in the maxim of the medieval scholastics, *analogiae claudicant,* analogies limp. This approach to theology was developed in its most extreme form in the treatise *Of the Divine Names* by Dionysius the Pseudo-Areopagite, a work that was very influential through the Middle Ages because it was believed to have been written by the Dionysius converted to Christianity by St. Paul in Athens. For Dionysius, God is beyond even the name "existent": ". . . or rather He doth not even exist, but is the Essence of existence in things that exist. . . ."[6] The apophatic method is in essence a way of negation; it speaks of the transcendent by way of simultaneous affirmations and denials of the terms that may be analogically applied to it and considers the denials as more adequate to truth than the affirmations.

The cataphatic method, which emphasizes the partial adequacy of analogy and consequently tends to trust affirmation to a relatively higher degree, has been dominant in the West, though the apophatic method has been important in mystical writings, especially after the translation of Dionysius from Greek into Latin in the ninth century by Erigena.

All of these problems, the ethical, the ontological, and the epistemological, are versions of the problem of the relationship between the immanent and transcendent aspects of the sacred. All derive from the intrinsic paradox

5. An excellent study of this aspect of Eastern Orthodox theology is Vladimir Lossky, *The Mystical Theology of the Eastern Church* (London: James Clarke, 1957).

6. C. E. Rolt, trans., *Dionysius the Areopagite On the Divine Names and the Mystical Theology* (London: SPCK, 1920), p. 135.

of the sacred, that it can be known only in and through finite manifestations, whether these are golden calves, Tables of the Law, or theological creeds and treatises. Any traditions of the sacred, to remain viable, must work out a strategy for handling this tension — not for resolving it, for that would probaly involve a reduction of the sacred to the profane, but for enabling the participants of the tradition to live with it.

The strategy that did this for western Christendom was that worked out by Saint Augustine in *The City of God*. This divides the human situation into two elements: the city of God (*the sacred*) and the earthly city (*the profane*). The separation between these originated with the fall of the evil angels and will continue until the Second Coming of Christ. During this interim period, God's transcendent power is perfect, but His immanent presence in Christians is incomplete. Only at the end of this age will the participants in redemption be lifted up into it fully, and the immanence of the transcendent God be made perfect:

> But, in that final peace to which all our righteousness has reference, and for the sake of which it is maintained, as our nature shall enjoy a sound immortality and incorruption, and shall have no more vices, and as we shall experience no resistance either from ourselves or from others, it will not be necessary that reason should rule vices which no longer exist, but God shall rule the man, and the soul rule the body, with a sweetness and facility suitable to the felicity of a life which is done with bondage. And this condition shall there be eternal. . . .[7]

The implication of Augustine's theory is that until the end of historical time God must remain primarily a tran-

7. *The City of God*, part 19, par. 27, trans. Marcus Dods, in *Great Books of the Western World*, (Chicago: William Benton, 1952): 18: 529.

scendent authority, rather than an immanent source of spiritual freedom. Luther and Rome later had different ideas as to what the implications of Augustine were for the relationship between the hierarchy and the laity, but from the time of Augustine until that of Luther the effect of the theory of the two cities was probably greatly to support the centralization of ecclesiastical authority in Rome, and this in turn served to make the authority of Augustine's theory almost immune to challenge. When an important challenge did appear, in the twelfth century, it was strongly suppressed.

This challenge was the theory developed by Joachim, Abbot of the Monastery of St. John at Fiore, that history would have three stages prior to the Second Coming, corresponding to the persons of the Trinity.[8] Each age, according to Joachim, had or would have its leader (*dux*) and its preparers. The first age was that of the Hebrew dispensation, and the leader was Moses. This first age made known the transcendent glory of the Father. The second had as its *dux* Saint John the Baptist; this was the age of the Church and had as its function the making known of the Son. This, Joachim thought, was a transitional period in which the way was being prepared for the full entry of God into human life as an immanent presence in the third period, the age of the Spirit. The principal preparers of the third period were Saint Paul and the

8. Joachim's principal statement of his ideas on this subject appears in his *Expositio in Apocalypsim* (Venice, 1527). A brief summary of his main points may be found in Karl Löwith, *Meaning in History: The Theological Implications of the Philosophy of History* (Chicago: University of Chicago Press, 1949), pp. 145-59. The most extensive study in the English language of the Joachimite movement as a whole is Marjorie Reeves, *The Influence of Prophecy in the Later Middle Ages: A Study in Joachimism* (Oxford: Clarendon Press, 1969). The latter contains a complete bibliography of Joachim's writings as well as of spurious works attributed to him.

founders of monastic orders, such as Saint Anthony, Saint Benedict, and Saint Bernard of Clairvaux (Joachim was himself a Cistercian and a participant in the reform movement begun by Saint Bernard). The age of the Spirit was to be inaugurated by a *dux* — the Elijah prophesied in the last lines of the Hebrew Bible (Mal. 4:5-6)—who would appear, according to Joachim's calculations, in the year 1260 and who would abolish both the feudal and the ecclesiastical hierarchies, which would no longer be necessary since all men would be inspired directly by the Holy Spirit.

As one would expect, there were those who took up this idea with enthusiasm, and as one would also expect, it became anathema to those in authority. The most prominent spokesman for the Joachimite movement, Gerard of Borgo San Donnino, whose *Introduction to the Eternal Gospel* (1254) had enjoyed great popularity, was condemned to imprisonment for life, while a variety of candidates for *dux* were roasted or dismembered piecemeal. Although Joachim himself died in good standing with the church and was later placed in Paradise by Dante as one "through whom the spirit prophesied" (*Paradiso,* XII, 140),[9] his theory of history and his writings were condemned by the Church and his following was proscribed. The suppression of the movement was fairly effective, though its hope enjoyed recrudescences, mostly in secularized forms, from Cola di Rienzo in the fourteenth century through Gotthold Ephraim Lessing in the eighteenth. In the Renaissance, although it would probably have seemed unrecognizable to the austere Abbot Joachim, Rabelais's Abbey of Theleme, with its motto,

9. The translation of Dante that I will be using throughout is that by Laurence Binyon in *The Portable Dante* (New York: Viking Press, 1947).

"FAY CE QUE VOULDRAS" ("Do as you please"), stood in the direct succession of the Joachimite movement.[10] After Joachim's idea of the three stages of history was rediscovered and adapted in a new form by Lessing, it had a profound, far reaching influence, a subject that will be taken up in greater detail in Chapters III and V.

Another seminal thinker for the transformation of the theory and sensibility of the sacred in the modern world has been the fifteenth century German theologian, Nicholas of Cusa. Cusanus was seminal in the sense that many important currents of thought from the ancient and medieval worlds — Dionysius, Erigena, Hermetic philosophy, and the mysticism of Meister Eckhart, for example — flowed into his thought and writings, combined there in new ways, and flowed out again to influence, directly or indirectly, such influential subsequent figures and movements as Renaissance and modern science, Giordano Bruno, Spinoza, Leibniz, the German idealists, and William Butler Yeats.

The key element in Cusanus' thought was the idea that God is a *coincidentia oppositorum*, an absolute simplicity of being that transcends and yet includes the distinct perfections of all creatures.[11] From this it follows that God is the infolding (*complicatio*) of all finite being and that finite being is the unfolding (*explicatio*) of God. The

10. For some other Renaissance versions of Joachimism see Werner Kaegi, "The Transformation of the Spirit in the Renaissance," trans. Ralph Manheim, *Spirit and Nature: Papers from the Eranos Yearbook* (New York: Pantheon, 1954), pp. 284-87.

11. A brief summary of the thought of Cusanus may be found in the introduction by D. J. B. Hawkins to Nicholas Cusanus, *Of Learned Ignorance*, trans. Germain Heron (New Haven, Conn.: Yale University Press, 1954), pp. ix-xxviii. See also John Herman Randall, Jr., *The Career of Philosophy* (New York: Columbia University Press, 1962), 1:177-91; Frederick Copleston, *A History of Philosophy* (Westminster, Md.: Newman Press, 1953), 3:231-47; and Ernst Cassirer, *The Individual and the Cosmos in Renaissance Philosophy*, trans. Mario Domandi (New York: Barnes and Noble, 1964), pp. 7-72.

world is therefore a theophany, a kind of created version of God (*quasi Deus creatus*). There is only one Being, not a series of different types of being in a graded hierarchy — the "great chain of being" of the mainstream of neo-Platonism and of medieval thought generally.[12] This one Being is God, *complicative*, and creation, *explicative*. God, as *coincidentia oppositorum*, is, in a geometric analogy of a kind Cusanus was fond of, simultaneously the center and circumference of the universe in that He is fully present everywhere, yet contained nowhere. God is the soul of the world (*anima mundi*), the informing principle shaping it and giving life to it from within. The Incarnation in Christ is the point of union between the relative and the absolute, and the destiny of man is to be incorporated into this highest manifestation of the *coincidentia oppositorum* through union with Christ.

Every form of *coincidentia oppositorum*, of course, and especially that of the Incarnation, is beyond the comprehension of discursive reason (*ratio*) with its laws of opposites, but they can be apprehended, even if not comprehended, by a higher, intuitive faculty (*intellectus*, in Cusanus' terminology) that leaps beyond contradictions to their ineffable source in the heart of being. This intuitive higher wisdom, or "learned ignorance" (*docta ignorantia*), cannot, by its very nature, be expressed in language, which is the creation and instrument of *ratio;* rather it must be communicated indirectly by suggestion and analogies, such as that of the infinite circle which would have its center everywhere and its circumference nowhere, and which would, moreover, be identical with an infinite straight line and an infinite triangle.

12. For a study of the traditional idea see Arthur O. Lovejoy, *The Great Chain of Being: A Study of the History of an Idea* (Cambridge, Mass: Harvard University Press, 1936).

A heady brew. That it skirts pantheism is obvious, though Cusanus, who as cardinal, bishop, and papal legate was a bulwark of orthodoxy, was careful to insist on its distinctness from pantheism, and he seems to have had reasonable grounds for claiming a difference: although his God is immanent in creation He can still be interpreted as transcending as *complicatio* the finite beings that are his *explicatio*.

Giordano Bruno, about whom there will be more to say in the chapter on Joyce, drew heavily on some of the elements of Cusanus' theories to construct what seems a genuinely pantheistic vision. For Bruno, as for Spinoza later, there is only one infinite substance, which, considered under different aspects, is both the universe and God.[13] God is the world soul pervading all of nature, and his causality is that of the informing nature of all things. Considered as *natura naturans* the universe is God; considered as *natura naturata* it is creation. But both are simply different aspects of a single reality. This concept of the world soul led eventually to the development of the idea of the cosmos as a living, quasidivine organism in the Romantic movement, where the immanent pole of the sacred finally began, throughout European thought, to gain a dominant position over the transcendent.

The process by which this took place was aided by a parallel withdrawal of the figure of the transcendent deity. Transformations in the sense of the sacred can take place

13. A brief summary of the thought of Bruno may be found in the introduction to Giordano Bruno, *The Expulsion of the Triumphant Beast*, trans. and ed. Arthur D. Imerti (New Brunswick, N.J.: Rutgers University Press, 1964), pp. 29-46. See also Dorothea Waley Singer, *Giordano Bruno: His Life and Thought with Annotated Translation of His Work On the Infinite Universe and Worlds* (New York: Henry Schuman, 1950). For a dissenting opinion on the question of Bruno's pantheism see Copleston, *History of Philosophy*, 3:260-61.

so gradually that it is impossible to specify the point at which, as in the case of the deism that became so widespread in Western Europe in the seventeenth and eighteenth centuries, a transcendent God becomes a *deus otiosus*. How can one identify, even in the thought of a single individual, the moment when God, the Great Artisan manifesting his majesty in his handiwork, becomes the remote Great Watchmaker who left his watch to go on ticking by itself? It might seem that the famous "breaking of the circle," the collapse of the Ptolemaic cosmology and of other aspects of the medieval world picture that went with it,[14] would have been the crucial point of transition, but it did not work that way. For Copernicus and his immediate successors, such as Galileo and Johannes Kepler, far from desacralizing the cosmos, the new astronomy had the effect of exalting man and the earth into the sacred heavens.[15] Similarly the discovery of mountains on the moon, rather than simply lowering the celestial realm into the profane, seems in the long run to have had the effect of lifting the curse of profanity from the mountains of the earth. When Thomas Burnet published his *Telluris Theoria Sacra* (*Sacred Theory of the Earth*) in 1681, recording along with his theories of the origin and geology of the earth his feelings of mingled awe and horror on crossing the Alps ten years earlier, a shift was taking place not only in the aesthetics of nature, but also in the morphology of the sacred.[16] In the Middle Ages mountains were thought to be excrescences thrown up on the face of the earth by the convulsions consequent

14. Marjorie Hope Nicolson, *The Breaking of the Circle: Studies in the Effect of the "New Science" upon Seventeenth-Century Poetry* (rev. ed.; New York: Columbia University Press, 1960).

15. Randall, *Career of Philosophy*, 1:309.

16. Marjorie Hope Nicolson, *Mountain Gloom and Mountain Glory: The Development of the Aesthetics of the Infinite* (Ithaca, N.Y.: Cornell University Press, 1959), pp. 184-224.

on the Fall of Man and therefore a symbol of the horror of man's profane state after Eden. The abhorrence Burnet felt was an expression of the medieval attitude, but his sense of the sublime was the expression of a different complex of attitudes that was beginning to take shape and that had the effect of rendering the earth sacred again in a new way. The sense of the sacred transformed to fit these changes of sensibility — just as it withered with regard to the Divine Watchmaker. As the primarily transcendent God drew further away, the immanent divine presence in creation, both on the earth and in the infinite interstellar spaces, began to call to man.

To some, Wordsworth for example, the call was relatively clear — though for him clearer sometimes than at others — and relatively positive:

> Ye Presences of Nature in the sky
> And on the earth! Ye Visions of the hills!
> And Souls of lonely places! can I think
> A vulgar hope was yours when ye employed
> Such ministry, when ye, through many a year
> Haunting me thus among my boyish sports,
> On caves and trees, upon the woods and hills,
> Impressed upon all forms the characters
> Of danger or desire; and thus did make
> The surface of the universal earth
> With triumph and delight, with hope and fear,
> Work like a sea?[17]

There were also others to whom the call and its meaning, whether from heaven or hell, to glory or to emptiness, were ambiguous. An illustration from Goethe seems particulary appropiate, because in portraying a new Pentecost it brings us full circle from the Hebrew and Christian Pentecosts with which this chapter opened. At the beginning of

17. William Wordsworth, "The Prelude," Bk. I, 11. 464-75, *Selected Poetry,* ed. Mark Van Doren (New York: Random House, 1950), p. 191.

Faust II, after having suffered a complete collapse as a result of his betrayal and loss of Gretchen in *Faust I*, and after being restored to health and sanity, significantly enough by the beneficent spirits of nature, Faust sets out to win a position of power at the court of the Emperor. To accomplish this, he and Mephistopheles devise an allegorical masque for the Feast of Carnival, which the court is about to celebrate. Carnival, a pagan rite of spring integrated into the Christian calendar as Shrove Tuesday, is a festival of misrule, in which the energies that have previously been under restraint — by winter in nature, by convention in man — are released to regenerate human and natural life. In this case the festival is definitely more pagan than Christian. The Emperor has visited the seat of classical civilization and has brought back, not only a grant of secular authority from the Pope, but also a token of the immanent divine forces celebrated in pagan traditions. The Herald that announces the festivities tells us:

> Don't think ye'll here see German revels,
> A Dance of Death, of Fools and Devils!
> A cheerful festival awaits you here.
> Our ruler, when to Rome he went campaigning,
> His profit and your pleasure gaining,
> The perils of the Alps disdaining,
> Won for himself a realm of cheer.
> First, at the holy feet bowed down,
> A grant of power he besought,
> And when he went to fetch his crown,
> The fool's-cap too for us he brought.
> Now we are all new-born in years,
> And every well-sophisticated man
> Happily draws it over head and ears.
> Akin to crazy fools he now appears,
> Under it acting wisely as he can.

[Denkt nicht, ihr seid in deutschen Grenzen
Von Teufels-, Narren- und Totentänzen;
Ein heitres Fest erwartet euch .
Der Herr, auf seinen Römerzügen,
Hat, sich zu Nutz, euch zum Vergnügen,
Die hohen Alpen überstiegen,
Gewonnen sich ein heitres Reich.
Der Kaiser, er, an heiligen Sohlen
Erbat sich erst das Recht zur Macht,
Und als er ging, die Krone sich zu holen,
Hat er uns auch die Kappe mitgebracht.
Nun sind wir alle neugeboren;
Ein jeder weltgewandte Mann
Zieht sie behaglich über Kopf und Ohren;
Sie ähnelt ihn verrückten Toren,
Er ist darunter weise, wie er kann.]
[Ll. 5065-87][18]

In the masque Faust takes the role of Plutus, god of wealth and the underworld; Faust is going to use the man-made gold of paper money as the basis of power which will in the long run have ambiguous results, both for Faust and for the empire. As befits his role as the representative of the secular world as a whole, the Emperor appears as Pan. The most important of the other figures in the allegory is a boy charioteer, who announces that he represents Poetry:

I am profusion, I am Poesy!
The poet who's attained his goal
When he's poured out his inmost soul.
I too am rich with untold pelf
And value me the peer of Plutus' self,
Adorn, enliven, make his revels glow;
And what he lacks, that I bestow.

18. German quotations from *Faust* are from *Goethes Faust: Der Tragödie erster und zweiter Teil, Urfaust,* with a commentary by Erich Trunz (Hamburg: Christian Wegner, 1963). The translation is that by George Madison Priest in *Great Books of the Western World,* vol. 47.

[Bin die Verschwendung, bin die Poesie;
Bin der Poet, der sich vollendet,
Wenn er sein eigenst gut verschwendet.
Auch ich bin unermesslich reich
Und schätze mich dem Plutus gleich,
Beleb' und schmück' ihm Tanz und Schmaus,
Das, was ihm fehlt, das teil' ich aus.]
[Ll. 5573-79]

The relationship between Poetry and Plutus is rather like that between spirit and flesh, or perhaps like that between quintessence and nature in alchemy. Poetry grows out of nature's abundance, but also transcends it and in its own turn raises it to a higher level of life. Plutus appreciates the complementary relationship between himself and this embodiment of inspiration, and he is appreciative as well of his own subordinate position:

I say with joy: Thou art spirit of my spirit!
Thy deeds are ever after my own will;
Rich as I am, thou art richer still.
Thy service to reward in fitting measure,
The laurel more than all my crowns I treasure.
This truth in all men's hearts I would instil:
In thee, dear son, I have much pleasure.

[So sag' ich gern: Bist Geist von meinem Geiste.
Du handelst stets nach meinem Sinn,
Bist reicher, als ich selber bin.
Ich schätze, deinen Dienst zu lohnen,
Den grünen Zweig vor allen meinen Kronen.
Ein wahres Wort verkünd ich allen:
Mein lieber Sohn, an dir hab' ich Gefallen.]
[Ll. 5622-29]

"Geist von meinem Geiste": the quasi-divine spirit of Poetry, even though it transcends nature, is here primarily an immanent energy emerging from within nature's own depths. All men are potential vehicles of its

power, although there are few in whom it blossoms into full actuality. The boy charioteer scatters flames, like those at the Christian Pentecost, upon the heads of those assembled in the hall:

> The greatest gifts my hand deals out,
> Lo! I have scattered roundabout.
> On this head and on that one too
> There glows a flamelet that I threw.
> From one to other head it skips,
> To this one cleaves, from that one slips;
> It seldom flares up like a plume,
> And swiftly beams in transient bloom.
> Ere many its worth recognize,
> It burns out mournfully and dies.
>
> [Die grössten Gaben meiner Hand,
> Seht! hab' ich rings umher gesandt.
> Auf dem und jenem Kopfe glüht
> Ein Flämmchen, das ich angesprüht;
> Von einem zu dem andern hüpft's,
> An diesem hält sich's, dem entschlüpft's,
> Gar selten aber flammt's empor,
> Und leuchtet rasch in kurzem Flor;
> Doch vielen, eh' man's noch erkannt,
> Verlischt es, traurig ausgebrannt.]
> [Ll. 5630-39]

The end of the masque makes clear the ambiguity of this "great gift" of the fire from nature's depths. When the Emperor in the role of Pan bends too far over a well of fire so that his beard ignites, evidently a symbol of his natural vitality being caught up and enflamed by the spirit of inspiration, the resulting conflagration nearly burns down the palace before Faust extinguishes it:

> He stoops down low to look inside. —
> But now his beard is falling in! . . .
> The beard flies backward, all ablaze,

And kindles wreath and head and breast;
Turned into sorrow is the jest. —
To quench the fire they race and run,
But free from flames there is not one,
And as they slap and beat it too,
They only stir up flames anew;
In fiery flames entangled, caught,
A masker's group is burned to naught.

[Dann sinkt sie wieder hinab zum Grund. . . .
Er bückt sich tief hineinzuschaun. —
Nun aber fällt sein Bart hinein! . . .
Nun folgt ein grosses Ungeschick:
Der Bart entflammt und flieg zurück,
Entzündet Kranz und Haupt und Brust,
Zu Leiden wandelt sich die Lust. —
Zu löschen läuft die Schar herbei,
Doch keiner bleibt von Flammen frei,
Und wie es patscht und wie es schlägt,
Wird neues Flammen aufgeregt;
Verflochten in das Element,
Ein ganzer Maskenklump verbrennt.]
[Ll. 5923-43]

Here is a *mysterium tremendum et fascinans,* but one which springs up from the depths rather than coming down from on high and which replaces the Tables of the Law with a force that has the power to destroy as well as to liberate. The fire is real, and so is the inspiration it symbolizes, but what it leads to is difficult to tell. The question points in several directions, some of which we will explore in the chapters that follow.

CHAPTER III

The Ambiguities of Secularization: Modern Transformations of the Kingdom in Nietzsche, Ibsen, Beckett, and Stevens

> The palm at the end of the mind,
> Beyond the last thought, rises
> In the bronze decor,
>
> A gold-feathered bird
> Sings in the palm, without human meaning,
> Without human feeling, a foreign song.
>
> You know that it is not the reason
> That makes us happy or unhappy.
> The bird sings. Its feathers shine.
>
> The palm stands on the edge of space.
> The wind moves slowly in the branches.
> The bird's fire-fangled feathers dangle down.
>
> WALLACE STEVENS, "Of Mere Being"

The *heitres Reich* which Goethe's Emperor was supposed to have brought back from his Roman journey may have been related to the *drittes Reich,* the Third Kingdom, that became such a popular theme in German thought after Lessing rediscovered the ideas of Joachim of Fiore and proclaimed a "new eternal gospel" in his *Education of the Human Race* in 1780:

. . . perhaps certain enthusiasts of the thirteenth and fourteeth centuries . . . have only erred in so far as they proclaimed its advent too early. . . . Perhaps this doctrine of three world-ages was not at all an empty whim of these men; and certainly they did not have any bad intentions when they taught that the new covenant would become as antiquated as the old one already was. Even so, they maintained the same economy of the same God, or, to let them speak my own language, the same plan for a common education of the human race. They only hastened it too much, believing that their contemporaries, who had just grown out of their childhood, could suddenly be made into adults, worthy of the third age, without proper preparation and enlightenment.[1]

From Lessing this idea passed into the thought of Fichte, Schelling, and Hegel, Comte, Marx, and countless others who have been influenced by them.[2] In all of these cases it was a secularized version of Joachim's age of the Holy Spirit, but there may be, and were, different kinds of secularity.

The secularization of a religious vision may have basically two different effects: either to desacralize what had been sacred in that vision, or by the application of traditional imagery and patterns of feeling to the new world-view, to raise the secular to a sacred level. As it was formulated by Lessing, the revived Joachimism pointed in both directions. The new age was to be an age of reason and human self-realization, the adulthood of humanity, but it was also to be characterized by spontaneous benevolence: men would no longer require the external rewards and punishments promised by the earlier ages' belief in an afterlife, but would do good for its own sake. This was a charismatic element in the new gospel, a secularized version of the Christian *agape* or *caritas*; and secularized as it was, it still involved enough of a transcendent

1. Quoted in Löwith, *Meaning in History,* p. 208. The original can be found in Gotthold Ephraim Lessing, *Werke,* ed. Paul Stapf (Berlin and Darmstadt: Tempel Verlag, 1961), 2:995-96.

2. See Löwith, *Meaning in History,* pp. 208-13.

ideal, since this spontaneous benevolence remained something surpassing man's ordinary capacity, to confer on it qualities of the sacred.

Those who later adopted this theory of history developed its implications variously. Some, like Schelling in his *Philosophy of Revelation,* made it into a new stage in the development of the Christian religion.[3] Others, like Auguste Comte in his three stages of human intellectual and social development — theological, metaphysical, and positivist — saw it as an age of scientific humanism, with sociology the queen of the sciences. It is significant, however, that in the later development of his thought, though he was strongly antitheological, Comte began to see his positivist sociology as culminating in a new Religion of Humanity, complete with all the traditional vehicles of the sense of the sacred — rituals, prayers, and festivals.[4]

The reason some version of the traditional sense of the sacred or an attempt to cultivate it reappears in various modern secularized world-views is probably that a radically desacralized vision of life is extremely difficult to maintain. If it is true that, as Eliade says, "desacralization pervades the entire experience of the nonreligious man of modern societies,"[5] it is also true that, as he goes on to say,

> . . . such a profane existence is never found in the pure state. To whatever degree he may have desacralized the world, the man who has made his choice in favor of a profane life never succeeds in completely doing away with religious behavior. . . . even the most desacralized existence still preserves traces of a religious valorization of the world.[6]

3. Ibid., pp. 209-10.
4. Randall, *The Career of Philosophy,* 2 (New York: Columbia University Press, 1965): 481.
5. *The Sacred and The Profane,* p. 13.
6. Ibid., p. 23.

There are many reasons, both intellectual and emotional, why such desacralization of vision is difficult to carry out consistently. Perhaps many modern men have thought they were doing this when in fact all they were doing was drifting, like Dante's "trimmers," avoiding the genuine rigors of either the sacred vision or the profane.[7] The few who have made a serious effort to live in full conscious clarity in a universe without God have been heroic, and even they have usually suffered divided minds.

The thought of Friedrich Nietzsche is especially interesting in this respect. The theoretical difficulties he discovered in his attempt to develop a consistent atheism and the strategies he worked out to deal with them have been very influential, even among many who have not sought that vision, and they tell us much about the arduousness of the enterprise.

In the first of his speeches after the Prologue in *Thus Spoke Zarathustra,* Zarathustra tells of the "three metamorphoses of the spirit": "how the spirit becomes a camel; and the camel, a lion; and the lion, finally, a child."[8] The reason it becomes a camel is that it demands the most difficult burdens in order that it may prove and exult in its strength. After it experiences many different kinds of burden, which generally have an ascetic character, such as "humbling oneself to wound one's haughtiness," it withdraws into the loneliest of deserts, where it transforms into a lion. The lion wishes to "conquer his freedom and be master in his own desert," and therefore he seeks out his last master and god, the "great dragon," whose name is "Thou shalt." The scales of the dragon are "values, thousands of years old." "All value of all things shines on me,"

7. Dante, *Inferno,* Canto III.

8. *The Portable Nietzsche,* trans. Walter Kaufmann (New York: Viking Press, 1954), pp. 137-39. Subsequent page references will be given in parentheses.

says the dragon. "All value has long been created, and I am all created value. Verily, there shall be no more 'I will.' " The lion "once loved 'thou shalt' as most sacred," but now, in order to win freedom from his own tendency as a strong and reverent spirit to love his burdens, "he must find illusion and caprice even in the most sacred." But even if he can win his "I will" from "Thou shalt," to create new values is not within his power. For that the third metamorphosis is needed:

> But say, my brothers, what can the child do that even the lion could not do? Why must the preying lion still become a child? The child is innocence and forgetting, a new beginning, a a game, a self-propelled wheel, a first movement, a sacred "Yes." For the game of creation, my brothers, a sacred "Yes" is needed: the spirit now wills his own will, and he who had been lost to the world now conquers his own world.

The relation of this schema to that of the Joachimites is clear. In a characteristically German psychological format, with its picture of an inner evolution through conflict between thesis and antithesis towards a higher synthesis, it recapitulates the familiar pattern of development from subordination to the transcendent sacred, through a transitional period of partial freedom, to full autonomy based on an immanent sacred power. In *Beyond Good and Evil* Nietzsche even calls this culmination "the free spirit" and speaks of himself in the Joachimite manner as its herald and forerunner.[9] Like his Zarathustra, he intends to play the role of prophetic preparer for the man of the age to come, the *Uebermensch*. Although he had little use for the idea of doing good for the sake of goodness — since it was so tainted by Christian associations of self-abnegation — Nietzsche imagined his

9. *Beyond Good and Evil,* trans. Helen Zimmern, in *The Philosophy of Nietzsche* (New York: Random House, 1927), p. 428.

ideal man as being characterized by a secularized version of spontaneous benevolence, the gratuitous generosity of the strong to the less fortunate, "an impulse generated by the super-abundance of power."[10] Nietzsche's version of the Holy Spirit is the Will to Power, which, in the strong and noble man, wells up from within as "a feeling of plenitude, or power, which seeks to overflow, the happiness of high tension, the consciousness of a wealth which would fain give and bestow."

Nietzsche's use of the dragon image in his parable of the three metamorphoses is especially interesting in relation to this. Whereas the Will to Power is life itself according to Nietzsche,[11] the dragon of external, transcendent authority is the ultimate embodiment of the forces of death. As the representative of a fixed, immutable absolute, it stands outside the dynamic becoming that is genuine life and tries to impose its fixity upon it. It is not merely, as might appear from its relation to a tradition of values, a false or superseded cosmos as such. This is a traditional association of the dragon as an image and one that occurs in many cultures: as Eliade describes it, "the dragon is the paradigmatic figure of the marine monster, of the primordial snake, symbol of the cosmic waters, of darkness, night, and death. . . . The dragon must be conquered and cut to pieces by the gods so that the cosmos may come to birth."[12] In this case the third stage of history, the metamorphosis into the "new beginning" of the child, the "self-propelled wheel," is the birth of the first true and genuinely sacred cosmos.

The defeat of the dragon of "Thou shalt" will be the consummation of the death of God that Zarathustra

10. Ibid., pp. 579-80.
11. Ibid., p. 395.
12. *The Sacred and the Profane,* p. 48.

announced in the Prologue, the death, that is, of the sacred conceived as a transcendent external authority. From Nietzsche's point of view this victory is necessary for two reasons. One is that it is the only way for man to win authenticity of vision; he must demystify or demythologize his vision in order to liberate himself from the illusion that there are transcendent absolutes of truth and value. The second grows out of the first: only by liberating himself from the claims of external authority — both intellectual and moral — can man become free to recognize and affirm his own will as the Will to Power.

It may seem extreme that Nietzsche denies not only external claims of value, but also of truth, but he means it quite seriously: "*To recognize untruth as a condition of life*: that is cetainly to impugn the traditional ideas of value in a dangerous manner, and a philosophy which ventures to do so, has thereby alone placed itself beyond good and evil."[13] It is, in fact, essential to his position. The truth or falsehood of an opinion is not even an important question, he says, "the question is, how far an opinion is life-furthering." What matters ultimately is the Will to Power, and all other claims of truth and value are subordinate to it. Knowledge is not a good in itself, nor is true knowledge necessarily superior to false. Rather the value of an opinion, whether true or false, is as an instrument to further the Will to Power.

The Will to Power is life itself. It is the universe. It is everywhere, in everything. As God was for Bruno, it is a kind of *natura naturans,* the dynamic aspect of the world. It is fully immanent; it and the world are simply two ways of looking at the same reality. It is its own source and goal, simultaneneously free and necesssary, self-causing

13. *Beyond Good and Evil,* p. 384.

and self-justifying. And man as *Uebermensch,* in Nietzsche's Third Kingdom of the cosmic child, is called to share in this freedom and life.

What this means, of course, is that Nietzsche has replaced the traditional idea of the transcendent God with an immanent sacred that is itself a new absolute value. This is quite clear, and Nietzsche would have ackownledged it himself; this is why he draws on pagan imagery of the sacred, such as the figure of Dionysus, whom he praises throughout his works, from *The Birth of Tragedy* to the last aphorism of *The Will to Power* — not just to counter Christian piety, but to express his own.

There was a great danger for him in this, however, and he sensed it and fought against it with the most powerful weapon he could devise. Wherever there is a sense of the sacred, there must always be some sense of it as transcendent. The immanent pole may overshadow the transcendent, but it cannot eclipse it without itself vanishing. The danger for Nietzsche was that the pull of the transcendent pole, which was very much alive in him under the cover of the pagan imagery, might bring back the old God under the name of the universe. The parallel of the Will to Power in his thought to that of the *anima mundi* in Bruno's makes this clear, but for Nietzsche the danger was even greater than this parallel would indicate. The son of a Lutheran pastor and raised in a household of pious women, he was steeped in Christian attitudes and patterns of feeling and he carried these with him into his neo-paganism; the ancient Greeks he tried to model himself on had felt awe before Fate, but Nietzsche tried to love it.[14] And he did so, with a genuine devotion that sacrificed everthing else in his life to that

14. Cf. Löwith, *Meaning in History,* p. 221.

love. With his mind, he did the best he could to desacralize the Will to Power, but to his heart, as is evidenced in every page of his rhapsodic writings, it said "I am the Lord thy God, and thou shalt have no other gods before me."

Nor was the attraction of transcendent deity only an emotional danger; it was also a conceptual one. This is apparent in the "*zuletzt*" of his parable: "finally, a child." That the Will to Power has a beginning of its operations and a goal makes it perilously similar to a Creator, and that this could be a final goal, not only the high point, but the terminus of its creative activity, would make it practically Augustine's God under a new name.

Augustine is an important point of comparison in this respect, because it was Augustine who revised the classical conception of time in his apologetic for belief in the Christian vision. The prevalent attitude of the ancient Greeks was a belief in endless cyclical time, forever repeating itself with neither a beginning nor an end. The Hebraic idea of God as choosing a people and preparing them for a destiny, whether for an earthly promised land or an eschatological Kingdom, was the opposite of the belief in cyclical time, and after it passed into Christianity it became an important countercurrent to the Hellenic view. Augustine's *City of God,* by managing to unite classical traditions of learning and eloquence with Christian eschatology, succeeded in converting the western world to belief in linear time. This has proven a more durable victory in its way than that of any other aspect of the Christian vision. Even among completely secularized *philosophes* and Romantic theorists of history it persisted as a belief in evolution and progress.[15]

15. See Carl L. Becker, *The Heavenly City of the Eighteenth-Century Philosophers* (New Haven, Conn.: Yale University Press, 1932).

Nietzsche saw clearly that this was a halfway house to theism and set himself against it. The weapon he used was his doctrine of eternal recurrence.

Although eternal recurrence is not an explicit theme until part III of *Zarathustra,* it is implicit in the image of the cosmic child as a "self-propelled wheel, " and its significance is implied in the definition of the "sacred Yes" as the spirit willing its own will. All that follows in the work may be considered an explication of the opening parable. If there is no God to begin time and direct it toward an end, then it is infinite and circular. Without recognition of this there can be no consistent atheism, and without affirmation of it there can be no sacred Yes.

The idea first occurs to Zarathustra in a vision. Walking alone at dusk up a mountain path, "a path that ascended defiantly through stones, malicious, lonely, not cheered by herb or shrub" (p. 268), he meets a dwarf, representing the spirit of gravity pulling him downward from his ascent. To defeat this impediment he tries confronting him directly with a conscious recognition of the most difficult truth man has to face,[16] that time is an infinity in which all possibilities are actualized an infinite number of times:

Behold this gateway, dwarf! . . . It has two faces. Two paths meet here; no one has yet followed either to its end. This

16. It is significant that Nietzsche would see the vision of cyclical time as hard to face; it had not been for the Greeks. Cf. Löwith, *Meaning in History,* p. 221: "To the Greeks the cyclic motions of the heavenly spheres manifested a universal rational order and divine perfection; to Nietzsche the eternal recurrence is 'the most frightful' conception and 'the heaviest burden' because it bears upon and conflicts with his will to a future redemption." Cf. also Eliade, *The Sacred and the Profane,* pp. 203-4: " . . . nonreligious man descends from *homo religiosus* and, whether he likes it or not, he is also the work of religious man; his formation begins with the situations assumed by his ancestors. In short, he is the result of a process of desacralization. . . . But this means that nonreligious man has been formed by opposing his predecessor. . . . In other words, profane man cannot help preserving some vestiges of the behavior of religious man, though they are emptied of religious meaning."

long lane stretches back for an eternity. And the long lane out there, that is another eternity. . . . Must not whatever *can* walk have walked on this lane? Must not whatever *can* happen have happened, have been done, have passed by before? And if everything has been there before — what do you think, dwarf, of this moment? Must not this gateway too have been there before? And are not all things knotted so firmly that this moment draws after it *all* that is to come? Therefore — itself too? For whatever *can* walk — in this long lane out *there* too, it *must* walk once more. [Pp. 269-70]

After this, the dwarf vanishes and Zarathustra sees a young shepherd writhing on the ground with a snake stuck in his throat, its head hanging out of his mouth. The man's face is filled with nausea and dread. Zarathustra cries out to him to bite the snake's head off, and when he does so, he leaps up reborn:

. . . he bit with a good bite. Far away he spewed the head of the snake — and he jumped up. No longer shepherd, no longer human — one changed, radiant, *laughing*! Never yet on earth has a human being laughed as he laughed! O my brothers, I heard a laughter that was no human laughter; and now a thirst gnaws at me, a longing that never grows still. My longing for this laughter gnaws at me. . . . [P. 272]

Although Zarathustra himself may be said to have bitten off the head of this snake by facing and formulating this vision, it is a long time before he is free from nausea and trembling at what he calls the "abysmal thought" (p. 274). As his animals, who find the eternal circle easier to face than he, tell him some time later, to preach the doctrine of recurrence is both his highest destiny and his greatest challenge (p. 332), the ultimate test of his strength and clarity of mind and his affirmation of the Will to Power. If the life of the Will of Power is an endless necessity of repetition, then Zarathustra has to learn an *amor fati,* not only to accept but to love the necessity of having to struggle again and again through the same battle with human smallness, both in himself and in others:

> Naked had I once seen both, the greatest man and the smallest man: all-too-similar to each other, even the greatest all-too-human. All-too-small, the greatest! — that was my disgust with man. And the eternal recurrence even of the smallest — that was my disgust with all existence. Alas! Nausea! Nausea! Nausea! [P. 331]

To face this would be to see and will that the *"zuletzt"* of the transformation into the child would not mean "finally" in the sense of a termination that would bring a lasting satisfaction, but only in the sense of the high point of a cycle, with both the zenith and the nadir of the cycle unending. For Zarathustra to will this would be for the Will to Power, consciously manifest in him as his own spirit, to will its own will.

Eventually Zarathustra wins his way through the bitterness and nausea to this triumph, the sacred Yes that he sings in his "Yes and Amen Song": "Oh, how should I not lust for eternity and after the nuptial ring of rings, the ring of recurrence? . . . *For I love you, O eternity*! " (pp. 340 ff.). He sings it again, recapitulating the whole cycle of vision, struggle, and triumph — an imitation in another figure of the burden of the camel, the defiance of the lion, and the innocence and affirmation of the child — in the last pages of the book in his "Drunken Song," which he calls his "round" (*Rundgesang*), "whose name is 'Once More' and whose meaning is 'into all eternity' ":

> O man, take care!
> What does the deep midnight declare?
> "I was asleep —
> From a deep dream I woke and swear:

The world is deep,
Deeper than day had been aware.
Deep is its woe;
Joy — deeper yet than agony:
Woe implores: Go!
But all joy wants eternity —
Wants deep, wants deep eternity.
[P. 436]

[O Mensch! Gib acht!
Was spricht die tiefe Mitternacht?
"Ich schlief, ich schlief——,
"Aus tiefem Traum bin ich erwacht:—
"Die Welt ist tief,
"Und tiefer, als der Tag gedacht.
"Tief ist ihr Weh —,
"Lust — tiefer noch als Herzeleid:
"Weh spricht: Vergeh!
"Doch alle Lust will Ewigkeit —,
"— will tiefe, tiefe Ewigkeit!"][17]

Cyclical time is a recurrent theme of various cultures. It can be found in Asia, especially in India, as well as in the classical west.[18] Normally it is seen from a religious point of view, and in such a context it has an affirmative quality. The potential death of the sacred year at the winter solstice is seen as a threat that can be fought with prayers and sacrifices, and its rebirth is an occasion for rejoicing. If the cycle loses its sacred character, however, as it did for many people in ancient India, then doctrines of salvation by extinction or deliverance from time begin to develop.[19] Eliade says that "repetition emp-

17. *Also Sprach Zarathustra* (Wiesbaden and Berlin: Emil Vollmer, n.d.), p. 289.

18. See Mircea Eliade, "Time and Eternity in Indian Thought"; Henry Corbin, "Cyclical Time in Mazdaism and Ismailism"; Helmut Wilhelm, "The Concept of Time in the Book of Changes"; and Henri-Charles Puech, "Gnosis and Time," all in *Man and Time: Papers from the Eranos Yearbooks,* trans. Ralph Manheim (New York: Pantheon, 1957).

19. Eliade, *The Sacred and the Profane,* pp. 107-9.

tied of its religious content necessarily leads to a pessimistic vision of existence . . . when it is desacralized, cyclic time becomes terrifying."[20]

It threatened to become that for Nietzsche. To free himself and the vital force he valued so religiously from the hostile external authority of a dead transcendent God, he had to try to become an atheist —and the effort brought him dangerouly close to succeeding. In the end, however, if we can take his Zarathustra's triumph as his own, he managed to break through to a new religous vision of the immanent sacred. Fortunately for his sacred Yes, his sense of the immanent sacred retained about it, despite his efforts, enough of the transcendent to keep it sacred. This can be seen in the quality of his personal dedication, in his constant tendency to look toward the future for a satisfaction of his hopes, in his reverence and awe before the Will to Power, and in his desire to efface himself before the *Uebermensch* to come. It is significant that he says of his eternal cycle, "The center is everywhere" (p. 330) — like the immanent and transcendent God Nicholas of Cusa imaged as an infinite circle.

Nietzsche's Zarathustra looked for "laughing lions" (p. 395) to succeed him and perpetuate the sacred Yes and Amen. He has had successors, and some of them have been lions in their way, but not all have come laughing, and when they have, it has not usually been with the same laughter.

Henrik Ibsen had his own version of the Kingdom, but much of the time he was less optimistic than Nietzsche about its possibilities of realization, and the quality of his laughter was consequently more bitter than joyous. He first presented the idea in fully developed form in his long epic drama, *Emperor and Galilean*. The pattern is thesis,

20. Ibid., p. 107.

antithesis, and synthesis: pagan energy and freedom, Christian self-control, and a higher synthesis of energy freely directed. The idea is interestingly similar to Nietzsche's idea of the necessary balance between Dionysian energy and Apollonian control, presented by Nietzsche in *The Birth of Tragedy* in 1872, the year that Ibsen was writing *Emperor and Galilean* in Dresden. Since Ibsen first thought of the possibility of a play about Julian the Apostate during a visit to Rome in 1864,[21] it is not likely he conceived his idea of this particular synthesis under Nietzsche's influence, but when he did read Nietzsche he found his thought congenial and once defended him against the charge of Satanism.[22] The reason for the parallel was probably the common shaping influence of German thought; Ibsen said that *Emperor and Galilean* was the first work he wrote under German intellectual influence.[23]

The play is about Julian's attempt to inaugurate a new age that would be founded on a synthesis of paganism and Christianity. At the opening of the play, he is a Christian, but he is restless in his faith. Later he goes to Athens to study the pagan religion, but he eventually becomes disillusioned with that too. Both are only partial answers to life. Finally he finds the true vision of wholeness, of harmony between flesh and spirit, freedom and control in the teaching of a mystic named Maximus. After becoming emperor he tries to bring about the conditions for the synthesis by proclaiming a regime of tolerance so that

21. Michael Meyer, *Ibsen: A Biography* (Garden City, N.Y.: Doubleday, 1971), p. 223.

22. Ibid., p. 796.

23. In a letter quoted in M. C. Bradbrook, *Isben the Norwegian: A Revaluation* (new ed., Hamden, Conn.: Archon Books, 1966), p. 66. Bradbrook thinks these influences were primarily Schopenhauer and Hegel. Schopenhauer was also the principal influence on the early thought of Nietzsche.

both paganism and Christianity may flourish and grow closer together. The Christians, however, resist the return of paganism and destroy the temples. Julian is consequently forced to a bloody persecution. At the end he is killed by a Christian who had been a former friend. The result of all of this is ironic; his tyranny has stirred the Christians from their relative slumber, thereby forcing the development, not of the third age, but of the second in its full form. This is necessary for the eventual arrival of the third. Julian was right about the eventual outcome of the historical dialectic, but wrong about its timing. When he dies, he acknowledges that the Galilean has triumphed, but at the end Maximus prophesies a final triumph for his and Julian's dream:

> Oh my beloved — all signs deceived me, all auguries spoke with a double tongue, so that I saw in thee the mediator between the two empires.
>
> The third empire shall come! The spirit of man shall re-enter on its heritage. . . .[24]

Fifteen years later, at a banquet in Stockholm, Ibsen spoke in a similar manner of his own hope for the eventual birth of this synthesis:

> I believe that an epoch is about to dawn when our political and social conflicts will cease to exist in their present forms, and that the two will grow together into a single whole which will embody for the present the conditions making for the happiness of mankind. . . . Particularly and specifically do I believe that the ideals of our age, in passing away, are tending toward that which in my drama *Emperor and Galilean* I have tentatively called the Third Empire.[25]

24. Henrik Ibsen, *Emperor and Galilean: A World-Historic Drama*, trans. William Archer (New York: Schribner's 1911), p. 536.

25. Speech of 24 December, 1887, quoted in Maurice Valency, *The Flower and the Castle: An Introduction to Modern Drama* (New York: Macmillan, 1963), p. 188.

The hope for this, or the question of its possibility, became a constant theme in his plays. It is "the most wonderful thing of all," hoped for by Nora in the last line of *A Doll's House,* and it is the responsible participation in "the joy of life," sought by Osvald Alving and his mother in *Ghosts,* by Johannes Rosmer and Rebecca West in *Rosmersholm,* and by the central characters of most of Ibsen's other plays. In more cases than not, however, the quest led to defeat, as in the case of Osvald and Mrs. Alving, or to the kind of ambiguous victory Rosmer and Rebecca achieved in suicide.

Looking at his works generally, instead of at his words in the profession of faith cited above, one gets the impression that Ibsen's Third Kingdom was more an occasion of heartbreak than of hope. In one play at least, he considered the possibility that it might be an unrealizable dream — in *Hedda Gabler.*[26]

Hedda Gabler presents a forceful picture of what the universe must look like to a person who has hoped for the Third Kingdom, even if in this case a rather vaguely conceived version of it, and then has lost hope of its realization. Significantly enough, this play presents us with another treatment of the theme of cyclical time, but without Zarathustra's eventual joy in it. The principal image used to represent both the ideal synthesis of freedom and control and the vision of cyclical time is that of the god Dionysus. But whereas Nietzsche used this imagery in a positive way to express his reverence

26. *Hedda Gabler* was written in 1890 and first produced in 1891. An earlier version of my interpretation of the play appeared as "The Radical Irony of *Hedda Gabler*" in *Modern Language Quarterly,* 31, no. 1 (March 1970): 53-63. The original article has more secondary references and quotes the Norwegian text in footnotes. The translation used is that by Otto Reinert in *Drama: An Introductory Anthology,* Alternate Edition, ed. Otto Reinert (Boston: Little Brown, 1961). Page references will be given parenthetically in the text.

for life, Ibsen uses it critically, to express a completely desacralized vision. He accomplishes this by the most destructive of all possible methods — not by expunging the traditional imagery of the sacred, but by reducing it to triviality. When the play is finished, the divine forces are still divine, and even triumphant, but they are no longer awesome. Their transcendent grandeur is vanished, with the awe it might have been able to generate, and nothing is left but boredom.

This aspect of the play was not appreciated, or even clearly understood by its earliest audiences. Reviews of the first English production in 1891 spoke of the play as "motiveless" and of Hedda herself as "a monstrous specimen."[27] G. B. Shaw, in his *Quintessence of Ibsenism,* 1891, trying to read Ibsen as a social reformer interested in the emancipation of women, interpreted Thea Elvsted as the true emancipated woman and Hedda as simply a decadent who lacked both the courage and the intelligence to become truly free.[28]

During the twentieth century, a different view of Ibsen has gradually emerged. The desire to read Ibsen as a fairly straightforward social reformer has slowly given way to the idea that Ibsen tended, especially in his later years, toward a basic pessimism with regard to man and man's place in the universe. Robert M. Adams, writing in 1957, praised Ibsen in terms that would have seemed condemnatory to the early Ibsenites: Ibsen, said Adams, was actually "a perfectly destructive author" expressing a "discontent with the human condition itself."[29]

The difficulty that early critics had with *Hedda Gabler*

27. See Miriam Alice Franc, *Ibsen in England* (Boston: Four Seas, 1919), pp. 89, 40.

28. New York: Brentano's, 1905, pp. 118-27, 135, 139.

29. "Henrik Ibsen: The Fifty-first Anniversary," *Hudson Review,* 10 (1957): 422.

derived from the fact that they wanted to impose on Ibsen and on his play a humanistic and fundamentally optimistic point of view. They wanted to interpret Hedda as a demonic villainess who is justly destroyed in the end by the triumphant forces of goodness and light. In reality, however, the play neither condemns Hedda nor extols her opponents. There is an opposition in the play, but it is not as simple an opposition as one of good versus evil. The play is radically ironic. As in the traditional pattern of comedy from Aristophanes onward, the forces of life triumph over the forces of destruction, but in this case the life that triumphs is represented as something of questionable value, and the nihilism that motivates Hedda is shown as deriving, although it moves her to cruel and destructive acts, from a kind of thwarted idealism with which the audience is forced to feel a certain sympathy.

The key to the understanding of Hedda Gabler as a person and of the world she lives in is the symbolism around which Ibsen has so carefully constructed the play. Numerous symbolic motifs combine into an over-all structure which embodies the meaning of the work. The unifying principle of this structure is the myth of Dionysus Zagreus.

In the ancient world, the cult of Dionysus expressed a worship of vitality, especially in the form of cyclical fertility. Dionysus himself was the symbolic personification of the forces of life, and the legends of his birth, death, and resurrection were a mythic representation of the struggle in nature between life and death, between winter and spring. As the worship of Dionysus was widespread in the various regions of the Hellenic and Near Eastern world, the myth appears in many forms. In the Zagreus ("torn to pieces") form, Dionysus, son of Zeus and Demeter or Persephone, is torn apart soon after his birth by the Titans, who then either roast or boil the fragments of his body. There are several different versions of the sequel, though all have in common the resurrection of the god.[30] According to some, the pieces of his body are reassembled and restored to life by Rhea, a goddess of fertility. In some other versions, the fragments are taken to the temple of Apollo at Delphi, where, partially through the prayers of the Maenads assembled there, they are restored to life by Apollo. In most of the versions that have come down from ancient authors, the myth of Dionysus Zagreus is explicity spoken of as an allegory of the annual renewal of vegetation, usually with special reference to the vine. The general point of the myth is the resilience of life, the ability of the forces of vitality to withstand the forces of decay and death and to renew themselves even when they appear to have been completely defeated.

The classical worship of Dionysus expressed reverence for a cycle of life which included both decay and renewal. The worshiper could see and revere a type of eternal life in the cycle if he was willing to tolerate the necessity of decay and death as concomitants to birth and growth. Similarly, he could find in it a kind of personal immortality, but only through acceptance of his own displacement by the children who would succeed him.

In *Hedda Gabler,* Hedda thinks of herself as a devotee of a Dionysian ideal, the ideal she alludes to so often during the play by her use of the image of vine leaves in the hair, a traditional symbol of the Dionysian. Her ideal, however, is quite opposed to the cyclical pattern of fertility and vitality which has been the traditional center of the cult of Dionysus. She is disgusted by both decay and the cycle of renewal in life, and what she hopes for is a transcendent grandeur that would transfigure the

30. Cf. Ivan M. Linforth, *The Arts of Orpheus* (Berkeley and Los Angeles: University of California Press, 1941), pp. 311 ff.

trivial round of ordinary life into something beautiful and incorruptible. As the play goes on, she comes to realize that her ideal is only a dream, that it will never have any power in the real world. When she understands this fully, she turns her fury against life itself. The basic pattern is ironic: although Hedda wishes to be a cultist of Dionysus, the god who symbolically embodies the forces of life, she actually becomes, through the extreme idealism of her demands on life, the enemy of the very god she claims to worship.

Early in the play, Hedda's sense of the ideal is actually not much more than a vague feeling for material elegance, evidently derived in large part from the influence of her childhood environment. In the first scene, Miss Tesman makes it clear that Hedda has lived in a world of finer style than that of the Tesman household: "Just think of the kind of life she was used to when the General was alive. Do you remember when she rode by with her father? That long black riding habit she wore? And the feather in her hat?" (p. 390).

For all of the elegance of that life, however, the General seems to have left her little besides memories and the pistols. She married Tesman out of economic necessity, evidently in the hope that he would be able to support her in the manner to which she had been accustomed. As the play opens, we find that Hedda has begun her marriage with a series of extravagant purchases — the boxes of clothing brought back from the honeymoon trip — and with an elaborate program of future expenditures which are aimed at re-establishing her former way of life: she wants a new piano, a horse, a footman, and the ability to entertain in style. She has given little thought to how such a program would be financed and, in fact, feels scornful of Tesman for his being the sort of person who has to be concerned with "how people are going to make a living" (p. 409). As the plot becomes complicated by the return of Eilert Løvborg, who might win the professorship Tesman has been counting on, mundane economic reality forces itself on her attention. A marriage she entered into only as a means to a certain way of life becomes a disappointment: "The agreement was that we were to maintain a certain position — entertain . . ." (p. 411). And as it disappoints her, it comes to seem a prison or a trap, a permanent condemnation to a trivial bourgeois life: "Yes! There we are! These shabby circumstances I've married into! That's what makes life so mean. So outright ludicrous!" (pp. 418-19).

This is Hedda's analysis of her situation, but as she is only barely aware of the true character of her problems, it is only partially accurate. Her true enemy is reality itself, something she has long been trying to escape — she told Løvborg that the reason she threatened him with the pistol years before was that "reality threatened to enter our relationship" (p. 426). Hedda's real world, the world she gradually realizes she is going to be forced to live with whether she likes it or not, is the world of cyclical time in which all beauty, not only that of her former artisocratic way of life, flowers only to decay and in which she herself will eventually age and be succeeded by her children. Her desire to transfigure her world, first by covering it with a veneer of elegance, later by making a Dionysian superman of Løvborg, grows out of her basic desire to escape from life's inevitable cycles of decay and renewal. As she says in Act III when she refuses to go visit the dying Aunt Rina, "I don't want to look at death and disease. I want to be free from all that's ugly" (p. 437).

Hedda's antagonism to the natural world with its cycles of growth and decay is indicated at the beginning of the play by her dislike of flowers. When she comes downstairs, she finds Miss Tesman in a room filled with sunlight, fresh air, and flowers, among them the bouquet just sent in, significantly, by Thea Elvsted. Both Thea and Miss Tesman like flowers and children and the world of which they are a part. To Hedda, on the other hand, all of these are abhorrent. Thus at the very opening, the opposition is drawn up between the true worshipers of Dionysus, Miss Tesman and Thea, who rejoice in fertility and who are willing to accept decay as a necessary element of the cycle of life — Miss Tesman even makes a positive good of it, finding a purpose in life by nursing invalids — and Hedda, who rejects the cycle in its entirety.

It is also important that at the time of the action the cycle of life is not only an object of scorn and disgust in the abstract to Hedda, but also an immediate personal threat. When Judge Brack asks her in Act II why she married Tesman, she answers, "I had danced myself tired, my dear Judge. My season was over" (p. 414). She no sooner mentions this idea, though, than she tries to repress it: "No, no — I don't really mean that. Won't think it either." These are thoughts Hedda will not allow herself to face consciously, but throughout the play they are immediately below the surface of her consciousness, and every now and then they begin to intrude themselves into her awareness. In Act I after Tesman accompanies his aunt to the door, he returns to find Hedda looking out the window at the autumn leaves. "They are so yellow," she says, "and so withered" (p. 398). The season is already turning cold at the time the action of the play occurs — the prudent and adaptable Judge Brack carries a light overcoat — and Hedda undoubtedly sees in the yellow leaves a reminder that her own life is approaching its autumn. Old age and death are inescapable elements of life in this world. Even Hedda's new house, which Miss Tesman, in expectation of the children Hedda will give birth to in it, calls "the house of life" (p. 446), is also a house of death. The smell of lavender and rose sachets which belonged to "the late lamented Secretary's wife" lingers in all the rooms. "It smells of mortality," says Hedda, ". . . like corsages, the next day" (p. 418).

The thought of renewal through her progeny is no consolation to her. When she tells Tesman she is pregnant, she feels mortified by his enthusiasm and by his desire to tell Berte, their maid, the good news: "I'll die in all this. . . . In all this ludicrousness" (p. 449). For Hedda, reproduction, like sexuality in general, lacks chic. Throughout the play, whenever anybody mentions the possibility of her having children she tries to avoid the subject. When Tesman speaks of her in Act I, even before he knows she is pregnant, as being in bloom, to Hedda it means only disfigurement and the burden of unwanted responsibilities.

To those who revere it, the cycle of life is a type of immortality, an eternally self-renewing source of joy. To Hedda, however, the cycle is an eternal monotony, a source only of boredom and repulsion. "Everlasting" is a word she uses often, but always in a pejorative sense. She tells Judge Brack that the most unbearable thing about marriage is that it requires one "everlastingly to be in the company of the same person" (p. 414). When Brack agrees, "Both early and late — yes. I can imagine — at all possible times," Hedda insists, "I said everlastingly." Over and over in the play she speaks of how boring she finds this life. At one point she even says, with unintentional irony, that she has talent for only one thing in life: "To be bored to death" (p. 419).

By the time Løvborg arrives at the Tesman house in the middle of Act II, Hedda has already suffered her initial disappointment in finding that she and Tesman will not be able to afford the style of life she had hoped for, and she is already beginning to feel trapped in a trivial world of "everlasting aunts" (p. 417). Her attempt to find her Dionysus in Løvborg is her last desperate effort to make her world habitable for her.

What she hopes to find in him is a liveliness that can serve as an antidote to her boredom. "Lively" is another word Hedda uses often, as Judge Brack explicitly points out. She may use it ironically to describe "that lively crowd of summer guests" (p. 425) she and Tesman met in the village below the Brenner Pass on their honeymoon. At other times she uses it positively to describe a kind of glamour and vitality that she hopes will lift her world out of its humdrum routine and transfigure it with a vital beauty that is even beyond elegance. This is what she is thinking of when she speaks of the "unadulterated liveliness" (p. 431) she imagines will prevail at the Judge's bachelor party, the party she sends Eilert Løvborg to in order that he may come back "with vine leaves in his hair." In Act II, Løvborg still looks to Hedda like a person capable of fulfilling the dreams she cannot hope to live up to herself. She senses that Thea Elvsted's reforming influence may have subdued him to some extent, but believes that she will be able to liberate his energy once again if only she can break Thea's hold over him and establish her own. What she wants to see in her Dionysus is a combination of energy, courage, freedom from convention, and self-control — in short, Ibsen's Third Kingdom. This is what she is referring to when she tells Thea that when Løvborg comes back from the party "with vine leaves in his hair," "he'll have mastered himself. And be a free man for all the days of his life" (p. 431).

Hedda's vision of her Dionysus, however, is only "a pretty illusion" (p. 453), as Judge Brack informs her later. In the world of the play, there can be no such Dionysus, no such exotic glamour, no such divine freedom. The world of *Hedda Gabler* is a trivial one, populated by quite ordinary people. It has no heroes. Hedda is not capable of the heroic, nor is Løvborg. Ironically, the Dionysian element in this world is the very fertility that Hedda despises: the sexual fertility in herself that would produce real children, and the spiritual fertility of Thea's influence on Løvborg, which has produced their figurative child, the book that contains the future. It is the vitality of the ordinary.

As it turns out, Løvborg at the party has a great deal of energy, but no self-control. His frenzy is far from Hedda's conception of the divine. He goes berserk and ends up in the custody of the police. This last detail finishes him in Hedda's eyes: to be detained by the police is ludicrous and vulgar. After this, Hedda abandons all hope of ever finding the Dionysus of her dreams. When she gives Løvborg the pistol and asks him to kill himself beautifully, she only means that he should do it in the artistocratic style, with a bullet through the temple. He thinks she means something more: "Beautifully? With vine leaves in the hair, as you used to say" (p. 444). "Oh no," she replies, "I don't believe in vine leaves any more. But still beautifully! For once" (p. 445). She is no longer asking for heroic grandeur. Despairing of the divine, she is willing to settle once again for mere elegance.

At this point, having lost hope of transforming her world, Hedda turns against what she has vaguely sensed all along to be her real enemy, life itself. The nihilism she ends with is more than a desire to escape from existence; it is an active commitment to nonbeing. Her burning the book is an attempt to destroy life as such: "Now I'm burning your child, Thea. You — curlyhead! Your and Eilert Løvborg's child" (p. 445). The book is, in a sense, a child, the fruit of the spiritual union of Thea and Løvborg. Thea and Løvborg themselves frequently refer to it as their child. But the book is more than just the joint creation of these two people, and in burning it, Hedda is trying to do more than just destroy the symbol of their relationship. Like the infant Dionysus, the book embodies the vitality of the universe. It contains the future. It is more than just a work of scholarship, the sort of book Tesman would produce. It seems to contain a creative power of its own: it is the seed from which the future will grow. Hedda, in trying to destroy it, is trying, like Macbeth, to exterminate "nature's germens,"[31] the very sources of being, the energy behind the cycles of time.

As Hedda tears up the book and stuffs handfuls of it into the fire, she explicitly associates it with another symbol of the same energy — Thea's hair: "You — curly-head!" According to the stage directions, Hedda's hair is "not particularly abundant" (p. 395) while Thea's is "unusually rich and wavy" (p. 399). Hedda has always envied her this; even when they were in school together she had threatened to burn Thea's hair. Now she associates it with the power Thea has over Løvborg. In Act II she said, in envy of Thea's relationship with him, "Oh, if you knew how poor I am! And you got to be so rich! I think I'll have to burn your hair off after all!" (p. 432). Now, as Hedda burns the book, she is symbolically tearing to pieces and roasting the child that embodies the energy of life, and she is symbolically destroying Thea's hair, the symbol of the fecundity that gives rise to life.

The parallel to the myth of Dionysus Zagreus is obvious. Hedda, burning the book, is like the Titans tearing to pieces the infant god of vitality. Disappointed in her own dream of a Dionysus, she has turned against the true Dionysian and against those who, like Thea, and like Løvborg in his calmer hours, are its true worshipers and servants. The Dionysian is there in Hedda's world; it just

31. *Macbeth,* 4. 1. 58.

is not what she expected or wanted it to be.

As the myth of the resurrection of Dionysus Zagreus suggests, life will not be defeated. Hedda's destructive act is only an attack on the power of life, no real victory over it. As Act IV progresses, she realizes this. For one thing, she is pregnant, and pregnancy, for Hedda, is not only a fall from an ideal of elegance, it is also the mocking, ironic presence of the power she has tried to destroy. She cannot help realizing that she is the prisoner of her own physical fertility.

What is more, the one battle she thinks she has won turns out to have been lost after all. Like the classical Bacchantes assembling the fragments of the slain god, Thea and Tesman turn to the reconstruction of Løvborg's book from the notes Thea has preserved. Tesman even says that he feels Thea will inspire him the way she did Løvborg. It may be more than a coincidence that Thea's name (which itself means "goddess") so closely resembles that of Rhea, the goddess of fertility who, in one of the versions of the myth, restored Dionysus to life.

The final blows come to Hedda when Judge Brack tells her the true story of Løvborg's death and tries to use his knowledge of it to blackmail her. Hedda has, until this point, been enjoying the "pretty illusion" that Løvborg died, if not heroically, at least with dignity. She even tries to think of it as "an act of free courage . . . beautiful by its very nature" (p. 453). The Judge disillusions her; he informs her that Løvborg shot himself, not in the temple, nor in the chest, but "in the guts" (p. 454). And even this may not have been by choice; it may only have been the accidental result of a brawl in a house of prostitution. "What is this curse," exclaims Hedda in despair, "that turns everything I touch into something ludicrous and low!" (p. 454). If the judge were to make it known that Løvborg had used Hedda's gun, she would become involved in the sort of scandal she has always feared. When the Judge attempts to blackmail her with this in order to force her to enter into a sordid relationship with him as his virtual prisoner, Hedda knows that the world has defeated her. There is nothing left for her to do but either submit to this world or withdraw from it.

She chooses suicide. Her death is a final protest against her world. She dies according to her ideal of conduct, with a bullet through the temple, destroying along with herself the seed of life, the unborn child within her.

Even this is not a victory, however. In the world of this play, the cycle of life has the resilience to go on in spite of apparent setbacks. The book will be resurrected, and Miss Tesman will probably someday have children as well as new invalids to busy herself with. Thea and Tesman had courted some years before: she is even said to have been "an old flame" of his (p. 399). Now that they are united by their common concern with the reconstruction of the manuscript, it would seem likely that their mutual enthusiasm will develop into love and marriage. Although Thea's marriage with Sheriff Elvsted has produced no children, there is nothing to indicate that she cannot have them. For Thea someday to bear Tesman's child would put a symbolic finishing touch on Hedda's defeat.[32]

Does this mean, then, that Ibsen has presented a play in which the awesome forces of life, *tremendum et fascinans,* triumph over a nihilistic villainess? Not really. Hedda is defeated, but the life that defeats her is not

32. It is true that Thea has borne no children to Sheriff Elvsted, but this is not necessarily an indication that she is to be interpreted as sterile. Isben may have made that marriage childless simply to avoid the distracting complications of having to explain what becomes of her children when she leaves her husband to follow another man: to have had her accompanied by her children would have been clumsy, if not ludicrous; to have had her abandon them would have made her a less sympathetic figure than she has to be to contrast with Hedda.

tremendum et fascinans. This is the radical irony at the heart of the play. Thea is a colorless person at best, and in her own way she is as timid as Hedda. Tesman is a pedant and a bore. If they ever were to marry they would be a perfect match for each other. The implication of the ending is that the life they worship, for all its inexorable power, deserves exactly such worshipers as these.

Nor is Hedda really a mere villainness. Of course one cannot admire her; she is a petty, mean person. Her tormenting Miss Tesman about the hat at the beginning of the play makes this side of her character quite clear from the start. But if we allow the play to draw us into its vision, we cannot help sympathizing with her. The demands she makes on life do have a certain grandeur about them, and the world she rebels against really is dull. The gods are there, but they are small; the cycles of time are an endless round of trivia.

This is not to say, of course, that *Hedda Gabler* was Ibsen's last word on life, or even Ibsen's word at all, in any definite sense. Even in the most directly self-expressive forms of literature there is probably always an element of hypothesis, and drama is one of the least directly self-expressive. What it is is a dramatic enactment of one way of looking at life, probably the most effective presentation in drama of this particular, radically desacralized, way of looking at it until the appearance of our own century's theater of the absurd in the 1950's.

The supreme exemplar of the latter school is Samuel Beckett. There is probably no other writer, in any period, who has worked out so thoroughly the implications of the desacralized vision. Some of his works concentrate primarily on analyzing the elements of that vision — especially cyclical or formless time, human isolation, and the moribundity of the idea of God — but there are also others that explore possible avenues of exit from it, and when they do, the new vision toward which they probe, though it is never directly pictured, begins to take on some of the qualities usually associated with the sacred.

Waiting for Godot, one of the plays that concentrate on analysis, has the simplest of plots, and the plot it has is circular.[33] Two vagabonds, Vladimir and Estragon — who call each other Didi and Gogo — are waiting for a specific event, the arrival of a local landowner named Godot, who they hope will give them jobs. The action of the play covers two days, but days that are basically similar and seem to be a fair sample of what all their other days are like. In the morning they begin their day's waiting; during the day they spend their time "blathering about nothing in particular," as Gogo puts it at one point (p. 42a), with the occasional distraction of a visit from Pozzo and Lucky, another landowner and his servant; in the evening a boy arrives with the message that Godot "won't come this evening but surely tomorrow" (p. 33a, see also p. 58a).

The drama of the play is in the gradual realization of some of the characters, especially Pozzo and Vladimir, that time has no goal, but is an endless cycle of hope and frustration, and that it consequently has no significant shape, but is a single infernal moment, perpetually repeated. "Have you not done tormenting me with your accursed time'" exclaims Pozzo as he is driven to a full realization of its torment by the questions of Vladimir, who is ironically only trying to get assurance that time does have a shape and that it moves in a straight line.[34] When! When! One day, is that not enough for you, one day

33. *Waiting for Godot* (New York: Grove Press, 1954). Page references will be given in parentheses. Since only the left-hand pages are numbered, to indicate that a quotation is from the right-hand page I will insert the letter "a" after the page number.

34. For a fuller discussion of this idea see Eugene Webb, *The Plays of Samuel Beckett* (Seattle: University of Washington Press, 1972; London: Peter Owen, 1972), pp. 34-40.

> he [Lucky] went dumb, one day I went blind, one day we'll go deaf, one day we were born, one day we shall die, the same day, the same second, is that not enough for you? . . . They give birth astride of a grave, the light gleams an instant, then it's night once more. [P. 57a]

That evening, the second in the play, when the messenger arrives from Godot, Vladimir is able to anticipate every detail of the message, realizing that it has always been the same and will continue to be. He also realizes that the Godot they are waiting for, like the traditional God, whose name Godot's is a diminutive of,[35] would be an empty hope even if he came.

Lucky, who is the most elaborate thinker of the group, devotes his one long speech of the play to the problem of the relation of God to the world. As Lucky describes Him, He seems a classic example of the *deus otiosus.* He is defined as impervious to feelings of any kind and insensible to impressions from His creation, which is languishing without Him. His only relation to man seems to be an imaginary one growing out of man's need to believe in it, and even the belief is hard to maintain in view of the effects of the divine remoteness on human life:

> Given the existence as uttered forth in the public works of Puncher and Wattman of a personal God . . . with white beard . . . outside time without extension who from the heights of divine apathia divine athambia divine aphasia loves us dearly with some exceptions for reasons unknown but time will tell. . . . [P. 28a]

We have already seen what time tells to Pozzo and Vladimir by the end of the play. It seems to be telling something of the same kind to Lucky:

35. Although the ending "-ot" is a French diminutive and "God" is English, it does not prevent "Godot" from being a diminutive of God. It is not surprising that Beckett should make a bilingual play on words, since he is bilingual himself and also had some previous experience in working with multilingual verbal play in his work as one of the translators of Joyce's *Finnegans Wake.*

> . . . it is established beyond all doubt that in view of the labors of Fartov and Belcher left unfinished for reasons unknown . . . that man in brief in spite of the strides of alimentation and defecation wastes and pines wastes and pines. [P. 29]

And what is more, he says, "concurrently simultaneously . . . for reasons unknown" a "great cold" is settling down upon the air, the sea, and "the earth abode of stones" (pp. 29-29a).

The personal God with white beard, even if Puncher and Wattman are correct in their calculations and He does exist, is of no real use to the world.

In his final realization Vladimir sees the parallel between Lucky's God and his own Godot. When he asks the boy, "What does he do, Mr. Godot?" (p. 59), the boy answers, "He does nothing, Sir." He then asks, "Has he a beard, Mr. Godot?", and when the boy answers that Godot does and that he thinks it's a white one, Vladimir cries out, "Christ have mercy on us!" Evidently he realizes that although Godot, of course, is only a local landowner, he and Gogo have been using him in the manner in which tradition has used God, to give time the semblance of a linear shape moving toward a goal.

To rest in this realization, however, would be impossible for him; it would be more than either his mind or his heart could endure. Instead he turns to reviving as best he can, both for himself and for Estragon, the hope that eventually Godot will come and that when he does, "We'll be saved" (p. 60a).

Waiting for Godot simply analyzes this situation, the necessity of perpetually rekindling a false hope in an empty God or God-substitute and of using this to impose an artificial pattern on a life that is, if not absolutely shapeless, then devoid of the shapes men usually look for in it. *Endgame* is the first of Beckett's works to seriously consider the possibility that beyond the limited horizon of traditional concepts there may be more to life than man has supposed and that it is his clinging to them that cuts him off from what could be the source of genuine vitality.

The two main characters are Hamm, the master of the household, and Clov, who seems to be both his servant and a sort of adopted son. Every day — if day is still the appropriate word for what in this play seems to have so little shape — Clov uncovers Hamm's face at the beginning and covers it up at the end. The interim is spent with the usual sort of blather. Here, too, time seems a circle in which the same hollow moment is endlessly repeated. When Hamm asks what time it is, for example, Clov answers, "The same as usual."[36] That it could be more, however, is hinted at in the dialogue that follows shortly after:

> Hamm: Have you not had enough?
> Clov: Yes! . . . Of what?
> Hamm: Of this . . . this . . . thing.
> Clov: I always had. . . . Not you?
> Hamm (gloomily): Then there's no reason for it to change.
> Clov: It may end.
>
> [P. 5]

There seem to be two important reasons why time does not move for these characters, and both of them are inner, moral reasons. One is that Clov's life has not yet developed to a point at which disgust could be followed by departure from Hamm's circle of power. The other is that both of them cling to the concepts that imprison them. "You've asked me these questions millions of times," says Clov at a later point (p. 38). "I love the old questions," answers Hamm with fervor. "Ah the old questions, the old answers, there's nothing like them!"

36. *Endgame* (New York: Grove Press, 1958), p. 4. Subsequent page references will be given parenthetically in the text.

One of the old concepts Hamm is fond of is that of God. Although God shows no signs of presence or power, and although Hamm himself says, "The bastard! He doesn't exist!" (p. 55), Hamm insists that the whole household — Clov, Hamm, and Hamm's parents, Nagg and Nell — join him silently in the Lord's Prayer, a routine that Clov's exclamation, "Again!", indicates is frequently repeated. It would appear that in the universe Beckett sets up in his plays, to break through to a new vitalizing vision man would have to see through the old concept of a transcendent deity and leave it behind. None of his characters ever succeeds in this breakthrough, but some come close to it.

Clov seems to be approaching it towards the end of *Endgame.* Instead of asking for new words to replace the old ones that are wearing out, as he did with regard to the word "yesterday" somewhat earlier (pp. 43-44), he finds a new independence developing, both from words and from the teachers of words. Once "they" taught him words like "friendship," "beauty," and "order," but now he seems to be almost ready to leave all words behind: "Then one day, suddenly, it ends, it changes, I don't understand, it dies, or it's me. I don't understand that either. I ask the words that remain — sleeping, waking, morning, evening. They have nothing to say. . . . I open the door of the cell and go" (p. 81). He doesn't know what he is going toward, nor whether it will be of any value to him. "It's easy going," he says, but adds, "When I fall I'll weep for happiness." Nor is it even clear that he goes; the ending of the play is ambiguous on this point, leaving him standing in his traveling clothes looking at Hamm. What is important, however, is the idea of departure as a possibility — that, as Hamm suggests earlier, perhaps the sterility of life is only in their lives as they now live them: "Did you ever think of one thing? . . .

That here we're down in a hole. . . . But beyond the hills? Eh? Perhaps it's still green. . . . Flora! Pomona! . . . Ceres!" (p. 39). Since he seems basically a pessimist, this is probably not a serious suggestion on Hamm's part, despite his ecstatic tone, but it serves to remind the audience that what he talks about is at least possible.

Something else that suggests its possibility is the one real event of the play, the sighting of a small boy outside in the distance. This is evidently not just part of the usual round, since Hamm and Clov seem genuinely surprised by it, and it is probably significant that the change in Clov and his resolve to leave follow immediately after it.

Not much is said about the child in the English version of the play, but the French original made quite a bit of him. When Clov first sights the boy through the telescope in the French version, Hamm says, "*La pierre levée*" ("the lifted stone"), recalling the stone moved from the mouth of Christ's tomb. Then when Hamm asks if he is looking toward their house "*avec les yeux de Moïse mourant*" ("with the eyes of the dying Moses") recalling Moses looking from the heights of Mount Pisgah toward the Promised Land, Clov answers that the child is contemplating his navel.[37]

The use of the child image here is especially interesting in relation to Nietzsche's somewhat similar use of it in his parable of the cosmic child. In both cases, the child seems to present the possibility of a new beginning — not just a starting all over again, but a regeneration that would raise life to a higher level. It seems, in other words, to hint at a new version in Beckett of the motif of the Third Kingdom. At the same time, however, it seems to have been advanced rather tentatively by Beckett and later to have been judged partially inadequate by him, since he dropped all but the boy himself from the

37. *Fin de partie* (Paris: Editions de Minuit, 1957), pp. 103-5.

English translation. If we were to speculate about what Beckett was trying to formulate symbolically in his original image, we would probably come up with the idea of some sort of synthesis of qualities associated with the Judaeo-Christian and Buddhist religious traditions. Not pagan freedom and Christian control as in Ibsen's version of the Third Kingdom, but something like detachment and involvement. The symbolism seems rather clumsy and unclear, however, and Beckett may also have felt that the associations of the Christian and Buddhist traditions were too specific and limited and not really adequate to his meaning. He was probably wise to drop these elements from the image when he prepared the English version.

Still, even if we drop as Beckett did the idea of a conjunction of Buddhist and Christian values, the question of what the child points to in Beckett's thought is an interesting one. He still sits there, even in the English *Endgame,* hinting at the possibility of a new life. Perhaps the reason Beckett may have decided that the Christian and Buddhist allusions were inappropriate is that the new life he seems to be driving some of his characters toward would grow not out of a combination of ideas of any sort, but out of an inner transformation. His later plays seem to be pointing toward something of this kind, a renewal of vision that would consist in a change not in the way of conceptualizing what is seen, but in the way of seeing.

It is significant that some of the characters of these plays are being pursued by eyes that seem to represent their own deepest level of consciousness or their potential for a clear vision of their moral or existential reality, unfalsified by the artificial framework of the old questions and the old answers. Winnie, for example, in *Happy Days,* speaks of the "strange feeling" she gets sometimes that someone is looking at her: "I am clear, then dim, then gone, then dim again, then clear again, and so on, back and forth, in and out of someone's eye."[38] These could be any eyes, of course, at this point in the play, in the first act. They could be the eyes of the God she addresses her morning prayers to, for example. To come to the realization that the eyes that matter are one's own, one has to pass through a complete disillusionment with all the artificial patterns of meaning man imposes on his experience. Beckett's characters rarely seem to be seeking this sort of disillusionment; on the contrary, they usually avoid it as long as they can. They do not seek the desacralized vision; rather, it pursues them as all the concepts that they have used to hide the true absurdity of the universe evaporate one by one, leaving them defenseless. The belief in a transcendent God is one of the most common of their defenses, but also one of the most vulnerable. Most of Beckett's characters find it slips away from them fairly early in their careers, though it may linger as a habit long after it has ceased to be believable. At the beginning of Act II of *Happy Days,* Winnie seems relatively less dependent on the theistic system of defenses, since she does not begin her day with a prayer this time, though she still wants to think that "someone" is looking at her and caring for her still (p. 49). A few moments later, she reflects on the fact that she no longer prays and that this constitutes a large and rather mysterious change in her. Then the image of eyes recurs to her, this time in a manner that makes them sound as if they are offering her a possibility of new vision: "Eyes float up that seem to close in peace . . . to see . . . in peace" (p. 51). If they are offering this, nevertheless she rejects it: "Not mine. . . . Not now . . . No no." Evidently she prefers to retain her illusions as long as she can, if not the illusion of a God, then at least the illusion of a "happy day."

38. *Happy Days* (New York: Grove Press, 1961), p. 40.

The central character of Beckett's *Film* is less fortunate. He is a bipartite character, divided into object (O) and eye (E). O is the protagonist as an object of knowledge to himself; E is his true inner vision, which is in pursuit of him. The plot is the story of O's flight from and eventual capture by E. We never see E until the end, when he confronts O face to face. When we do see him, "It is O's face . . . but with very different expression, impossible to describe, neither severity nor benignity, but rather acute *intentness*."[39] Here we seem to be given a glimpse, if rather an external one, of the true vision itself, and as the allusions associated with the child image in the French *Endgame* hinted, it seems to embody a paradoxical combination of detached serenity and concern. O's reaction in this case is horror; he has been fleeing the true vision too long to accept union with it as a good.

There is one of Beckett's characters, however, who seeks clarity of vision, at least by telling a story about the quest for it, and who seems at the end of the play to be almost about to arrive at it. This is in *Cascando*.[40] The protagonist is a voice telling the story — one of the "thousands and one" he has told (p. 9). This time he thinks he may have "the right one," the one that will accomplish his quest for silence: ". . . this one . . . it's different . . . I'll finish it . . . then rest . . . it's the right one . . . this time I have it . . . I've got it . . . Woburn." The story is of Woburn's departure in a small boat from land and the lights of land, past the islands, out into the "vast deep" (p. 17). As the voice tells the story, the musical accompaniment, which had been playing independently, joins him, and he takes this for a sign of a developing unity of being: "From one world to another,

39. *Film,* in *Cascando and Other Short Dramatic Pieces* (New York: Grove Press, 1968), p. 83.

40. Included in *Cascando and Other Dramatic Pieces.* Page references will be given parenthetically in the text.

it's as though they drew together. We have not much further to go. Good" (p. 15). Previously "they" have told him his stories were simply fictions in his head, but he says this story is his very life, and now he does not protest against their charges any more, he just goes on. The last we see of Woburn, he is out on the sea with the lights of land far behind him, but he is clinging to the gunwales of his boat, his face in the bilge. The voice says that if he turned over, he would see the other lights, those of the sky, shining on him, but at the end he still has not changed quite enough to do this — "nearly" (p. 19), but not quite — unless the silence the play ends in indicates that the transformation has occurred.

As Beckett's characters draw closer, whether voluntarily or involuntarily, to the true vision, they have to leave behind every traditional concept of order or authority. This means, naturally, that all traditional imagery of the sacred, along with any analogues to it, such as Mr. Godot, must be deflated, and the characters' vision thoroughly secularized. Hamm, in the period prior to Clov's development of a new independence toward the end of *Endgame,* was another Godot-like figure; he and the words he has taught have been sacred in a sense to Clov, and it is only when Clov begins to become free from his need for these words and from what has been a compulsion to obey Hamm that he approaches the possibility of departing for a new life.

Yet, even as they leave the traditional sense of the sacred behind along with the concepts and images that had served as its vehicles, a new sense of the sacred begins to take shape around the new vision. Since Clov and Winnie do not especially wish it, and since O in *Film* is in such desperate flight from it, it could hardly be said to be a *mysterium fascinans* to them, but since they all, especially O, generally tend to fear it in proportion as it comes closer, it could be called a *mysterium tremendum.* And for one character at least, the narrator of *Cascando,* it definitely seems *fascinans.*

Why would this be? What is there in a universe so thoroughly reduced to secularity that can give rise to such feelings of terror and fascination? The answer would seem to be reality, or true being seen clearly and directly without the protective veil of artificial concepts. This, at least, is what seems to terrify, and sometimes to attract, Beckett's characters. Reality is what would shine down upon them in the light of the stars if they could look up to see them, and reality is what would face them if they could face themselves. And it is the unveiled vision of their reality they are running from when, like O and even the other characters in *Film,* they flee from any eyes that could see them clearly and pierce their defenses to transfix them with an "agony of perceivedness."[41]

It is easier, however, to understand why reality would be terrifying to Beckett's characters than why it would be fascinating. It would, after all, threaten to destroy the only self they seem able or willing to identify with, the self that is a tissue of illusions. But it does also fascinate many of Beckett's characters, not only the narrator of *Cascando,* but also Watt, Molloy, Malone, and the Unnamable, and perhaps most of his other characters as well to some extent.[42] Perhaps also Beckett himself, whose relation to all his characters seems rather like that of the narrator of *Cascando* to Woburn; it is he who drives all

41. *Cascando and Other Short Dramatic Pieces,* p. 78.

42. See *Watt* (New York: Grove Press, 1959; London: Calder, 1963); *Molloy,* trans. Patrick Bowles in collaboration with Samuel Beckett (New York: Grove Press, 1955; London: Calder, 1959); *Malone Dies,* trans. Samuel Beckett (New York: Grove Press, 1956; London: Calder, 1958); *The Unnamable,* trans. Samuel Beckett (New York: Grove Press, 1958; London: Calder, 1959). See also Eugene Webb, *Samuel Beckett: A Study of His Novels* (Seattle: University of Washington Press, 1970; London: Peter Owen, 1970).

of them on through various patterns of light and darkness, clarity and illusion.

Why would reality, being, be fascinating? There may be no clear, conceptual answer to this question. Perhaps it must simply be recognized as a datum of the experience of many people. It does seem to be a recurrent pattern of experience, not only for characters in novels and plays by Samuel Beckett, but in human life generally. Eliade describes it as one of the fundamental features of the sacred: ". . . where the sacred manifests itself . . . *the real unveils itself*. . . . religious man can live only in a sacred world, because it is only in such a world that he participates in being, that he has a *real existence*. This religious need expresses an unquenchable ontological thirst. Religious man thirsts for *being*."[43] Although Beckett's characters are hardly what we would speak of as religious men in a conventional sense, they seem to apprehend being as something that can be termed sacred, with the fascination of the sacred's call and the terror of its challenge.

The challenge is that it demands of them a kind of death, the death of the identity constructed of defenses, and a rebirth in the new mode of vision of eyes that could "close in peace . . . see . . . in peace," O and E joined in a new unity of being. If this rebirth were to happen, the cycles of time would probably cease to seem, as they do to Beckett's Unnamable, a "labouring whirl" in which "the seconds" are "all alike and each one is infernal."[44] Rather it would probably receive a new sacred value as something like the "self-propelled wheel" of Nietzsche's cosmic child. Beckett does not take us that far, however, and so to speak of what it would be for his characters is only to speculate. What he does do is present the chal-

43. *The Sacred and the Profane*, pp. 63-64.
44. *The Unnamable*, pp. 161, 152.

lenge and make us feel very forcefully its imperative.

There are also many other writers in the modern period who do this, and who do it, like Beckett, out of the very heart of a secularized vision. One of the most persistent and ardent explorers of that vision in the twentieth century was Wallace Stevens. Like Beckett, Stevens tried to penetrate through the mythic screen of traditional attitudes and beliefs to the raw rock of reality, and he too felt that reality transform from a profane to a sacred secularity.

In Stevens' earlier poems the desacralized vision tends to predominate, perhaps in part because of the heritage of the disappearance of God in nineteenth century thought, but also because for Stevens man's mythopoeic imagination is so powerful and needs to be strenuously opposed if the mind is to win through to genuine clarity. As he says in "The Sense of the Sleight-of-Hand Man," "It may be that the ignorant man, alone," the man who does not try to understand and therefore is not tempted to falsify, "Has any chance to mate his life with life," to unite, that is, his consciousness with real being.[45] Or as he put it in a more sombre tone in "The Snow Man," perhaps only one who is "nothing himself" would be capable of looking on the wintry Waste Land and seeing "nothing that is not there and the nothing that is" (*CP,* p. 10). Most people tend, like his "high-toned old Christian woman," to "take the moral law and make a nave of it / And from the nave build haunted heaven" (*CP,* p. 59). Or else they tend to "take / The opposing law and make a peristyle" and from the peristyle project a masque of bawdiness beyond the planets. Either, as the poem tells

45. *The Collected Poems of Wallace Stevens* (New York: Alfred A. Knopf, 1961), p. 222. Although this is one of Stevens' relatively later poems (1942), the attitude it presents is that which informs most of the earlier poems. Except where otherwise stated, page references for Stevens refer to *Collected Poems,* which will subsequently be abbreviated as *CP.*

the woman, is equally valid as a fiction, and equally invalid as truth, because both are imaginative interpretations projected onto the universe. Poetry, however, is "the supreme fiction," because it is only poetry that knows it is fictive; religions, whether Christian or pagan, when they mistake their visions for truth, fall short of poetry's clarity.

Still, to maintain this clear-sightedness is difficult even for poetry, as "The Sense of the Sleight-of-Hand Man" indicates — both because the mind is so fecund of fictions and because the universe in its essential barrenness seems so cold, desolate, and chaotic, in a word, so profane. Seen in its inhospitable reality, it is not a home for man, nor even a cosmos that could serve as the basis for a home. In "Domination of Black," for example, the poet sits at night watching the flames turning in the fire and thinks of the colors of bushes and leaves and of peacock's tails. As he sits remembering these images and the cry of the peacocks — a shriek that sounds like a man's or woman's cry for help — it seems that all of these elements of his experience are like leaves turning in the wind, a chaos sinking downward to death. In the last stanza he looks out the window and sees the heavens, too, absorbed into this vision of flux and mortality:

> Out of the window,
> I saw how the planets gathered
> Like the leaves themselves
> Turning in the wind.
> I saw how the night came,
> Came striding like the color of the heavy hemlocks.
> I felt afraid.
> And I remembered the cry of the peacocks.[46]

46. This appears in *CP*, p. 9, but the period after "hemlocks" is added in accordance with the correction in Wallace Stevens, *The Palm at the End of the Mind: Selected Poems and a Play*, ed. Holly Stevens (New York: Alfred A. Knopf, 1971), p. 15.

In "Sunday Morning" (*CP*, pp. 66-70) he sketches a possible way of making such a universe into a home. Here all of his major themes come together and unite their opposing tensions in what is one of the most powerful of Stevens' early poems. The challenge to clarity, the difficulty of maintaining this, the temptation to try to return to the Christian view, and the possibility of a supreme fiction that could restore value to human life in cyclical time all converge in the divided mind of a woman who sits in a peignoir enjoying late coffee and oranges in a sunny chair and wondering whether it would not perhaps be worthwhile after all to go to church. As she sits there musing, the oranges and the green wings of the cockatoo on her rug begin to seem to her like "things in some procession of the dead," mortal themselves and reminders of mortality, and so to lead her thoughts "to silent Palestine, / Dominion of the blood and sepulchre."

At the same time another line of thought, either her own or that of the poet in dialogue with her, springs up to argue against this sort of return to the traditional concept of the transcendent sacred: "Shall she not find in comforts of the sun, / In pungent fruit and bright, green wings . . . / Things to be cherished like the thought of heaven?" Real experience, even if it is only mortal, is preferable to a dream of immortality; and if there is to be any true "divinity" it is that which "must live within herself." If she cannot escape from the mind's need for a mythic vision, runs this argument, in a vein reminiscent of Nietzsche, then a pagan myth would be preferable because pagan myth is the expression of a primordial apprehension of nature's grandeur, not like Christian myth the imaginative fulfilment of relatively petty human desires:

> Jove in the clouds had his inhuman birth.
> No mother suckled him, no sweet land gave

Large-mannered motions to his mythy mind.
He moved among us, as a muttering king,
Magnificent, would move among his hinds,
Until our blood, commingling, virginal,
With heaven, brought such requital to desire
The very hinds discerned it, in a star.

To her objection that this does not satisfy her desire for permanence, the counterargument urges the perpetuity of time's cycles of decay and renewal in nature:

There is not any haunt of prophecy,
Nor any old chimera of the grave
. . . that has endured
As April's green endures; or will endure
Like her remembrance of awakened birds,
Or her desire for June and evening, tipped
By the consummation of the swallow's wings.

If April did not press on to June, or morning on to evening, time would no longer be vital and beautiful. "Death is the mother of beauty," not its enemy. She gives it birth even as she destroys it; although death "strews the leaves / Of sure obliteration on our paths," she also "makes the willow shiver in the sun."

Man's highest genuine possibility would lie not in an imaginative flight to a paradise of "insipid lutes" where ripe fruit never fell, but in transforming what is clearly recognized as "an old chaos of the sun, / Or old dependency of day and night" into a new vision of immanent sacredness by a supreme fiction that would celebrate the sun "Not as a god, but as a god might be." This would make it possible for man to accept the wilderness as wilderness and at the same time rejoice in the "sweet berries" that ripen there and the "spontaneous cries" whistled about us by the quail as deer walk upon our mountains, and it would make it possible for us to appreciate both implications — transitoriness and perpetuity

— of the ambiguous undulations made by "casual flocks of pigeons . . . as they sink, / Downward to darkness, on extended wings."

A beautiful idea and beautifully presented, but it was not to be Stevens' final answer to the problem. The effectiveness of its poetic expression gives it an appearance of greater cogency than it really possesses. Upon closer examination it seems logically paradoxical, if not contradictory — an attempt to make chaos into a home by projecting onto it a sacred quality that is simultaneously affirmed and disbelieved.

His later poems carry the effort forward in a different direction. They continue to strip away the traditional mythology of the sacred, but not for the sake of replacing it with an improved quasi mythology. Rather Stevens tries to purify his vision of all such embellishments in order to arrive at the essential real. As he said in a letter in May 1949, about his purpose in "An Ordinary Evening in New Heaven": ". . . here my interest is to try to get as close to the ordinary, the commonplace and the ugly as it is possible for a poet to get. It is not a question of grim reality but of plain reality. The object is of course to purge oneself of anything false."[47] Or as he put it poetically in "Credences of Summer":

> Let's see the very thing and nothing else.
> Let's see it with the hottest fire of sight.
> Burn everything not part of it to ash.
> Trace the gold sun about the whitened sky
> Without evasion by a single metaphor.
> Look at it in its essential barrenness
> And say this, this is the centre that I seek.
>
> [*CP*, p. 373]

47. *Letters of Wallace Stevens,* ed. Holly Stevens (New York: Alfred A. Knopf, 1966), pp. 636-37, quoted in A. Walton Litz, *Introspective Voyager: The Poetic Development of Wallace Stevens* (New York: Oxford University Press, 1972), p. 282.

There are several reasons why the imagery of the traditional sacred has to be stripped away. The main objection to Christianity in "Sunday Morning," however, is probably one of the least important — the objection that it lures its followers to a false hope for a paradise where ripe fruit will never fall. The Christian religion does not look primarily for hope of perpetuation of life on the same plane of existence; rather it looks for a new quality of life. Dante's Beatrice reminds him, for example, during their ascent through the heavenly spheres, ". . . non pur ne' miei occhi é paradiso" (*Paradiso,* XVIII, 21, "Not only in my eyes in Paradise"),[48] and it is a lesson he learns well as he mounts toward the still point of shining light that is the source of her eyes' brightness. A more serious objection is that whatever its hope may be, the falsehood of its myth is simply a fact, a part of the "plain reality" that must be accepted: "The tomb in Palestine / Is not the porch of spirits lingering. / It is the grave of Jesus, where he lay." Another that is probably equally important is that to penetrate through all imaginative accretions from the past, one has to break free from every traditional voice of authority. The voices of religious authority are among the most potent of these, and consequently a symbol of the threat in all of them. As Stevens puts it in "The Old Lutheran Bells at Home": "These are the voices of the pastors calling / And calling like the long echoes in one long sleep, / Generations of shepherds to generations of sheep" (*CP,* p. 461). When these voices, and all the voices of the past, are left behind, the explorer into reality can awaken from the long sleep to find himself in sunlight:

48. This and all subsequent references to the Italian text of Dante are to *La Divina Commedia,* ed. Natalino Sapegno (Milan and Naples: Riccardo Ricciardi, 1957). The translation is that by Laurence Binyon cited above (Chapter II, note 9).

The figures of the past go cloaked.
They walk in mist and rain and snow
And go, go slowly, but they go.

The greenhouse on the village green
Is brighter than the sun itself.
Cinerarias have a speaking sheen.
["Poesie abrutie," *CP*, p. 302]

Paradoxically, however, Stevens' goal in his later poems is not simply to break through to a clear, unembellished vision of natural objects; it is to arrive at a vision, or at least a glimpse, of their ground, of being as such.[49] It is paradoxical in two ways. One is that as he approaches this insight into being in its bareness, being begins to take on, all by itself, a sacred quality for him; probably his deepest objection to traditional religion is that its heritage of emphasis on the transcendent pole of the sacred is a distraction from the immanent sacred Stevens discovers in the being that discloses itself in the secular world. The other is that his method of exploration is very like that of traditional mystical theology. If the early Stevens is reminiscent of Nietzsche's proclamation of the death of God and his effort to revive in an atheistic framework a pagan sense of the sacred, the later Stevens is more reminiscent of the dialectical tension between cataphatic and apophatic theology. Being and nothingness are two of the most prominent motifs in the later poems, and in Stevens' use they are actually two aspects of one reality. Being is in all things, yet never contained in them; and although it is evanescent in them, it is only in them that it can be apprehended. Consequently to approach it in poetry, one must use both positive analogies and their negations. This is why, in "A Primitive like an Orb," Stevens uses the image of a "giant of nothingness . . .

49. See J. Hillis Miller, *Poets of Reality: Six Twentieth-Century Writers* (Cambridge, Mass.: Harvard University Press, 1966), pp. 277-84.

ever changing, living in change" (*CP*, p. 443), and in "Chocorua to Its Neighbor," of a giant whose body

> . . . seemed
> Both substance and non-substance. . . .
>
> Without existence, existing everywhere. . . .
>
> Cloud-casual, metaphysical metaphor,
> But resting on me, thinking in my snow,
> Physical if the eye is quick enough,
> So that, where he was, there is an enkindling, where
> He is, the air changes and grows fresh to breathe.
>
> The air changes . . .
> And to breathe is a fulfilling of desire,
> A clearing, a detecting, a completing,
> A largeness lived and not conceived, a space
> That is an instant nature, brilliantly.
> [*CP*, pp. 297-98, 301]

This is also why he says in "Less and Less Human, O Savage Spirit," that if man must think in theistic imagery, he should purify his image of God of all finite attributes, reducing it to a nothingness commensurate with the purity of being:

> If there must be a god in the house, let him be one
> Saying things in the rooms and on the stair,
>
> Let him move as the sunlight moves on the floor,
> Or moonlight, silently, as Plato's ghost
>
> Or Aristotle's skeleton. . . .
> He must be incapable of speaking, closed,
> As those are: as light, for all its motion, is. . . .
>
> If there must be a god in the house, let him be one
> That will not hear us when we speak: a coolness,
>
> A vermilioned nothingness. . . .
> [*CP*, pp. 327-28]

In Stevens' new version of the paradox of immanence and transcendence, being is simultaneously "the visible rock, the audible," of "Credences of Summer" (*CP*, p. 375), and the underlying blankness of "An Ordinary Evening in New Haven": "A blank underlies the trials of device, / The dominant blank, the unapproachable" (*CP*, p. 477). An ontophany in stone, and an ontophany in void.

That which cannot be contained in any metaphor must be pursued through a simultaneous negation of metaphor as such and the use of numerous successive metaphors to complement each other. This is interestingly similar to Dante's method of describing God in the *Paradiso* through a succession of images that finally surpass the powers of human speech and understanding — a point of light in the distance; a radiant white rose, representing the Mystical Body of Christ; a bound volume, of which the leaves are all finite beings; a single, simple flame, representing the unity of the divine being as the ground of all beings; and finally three circles, the Holy Trinity, two like rainbows and the third of fire, with the Incarnation the ultimate mystery that defeats him:

> But these my wings were fledged not for that flight
> Save that my mind a sudden glory assailed
> And its wish came revealed to it in that light.
>
> [. . . ma non eran da ciò le proprie penne:
> se non che la mia mente fu percossa
> da un fulgore in che sua voglia venne.]
>
> [Paradiso, XXXIII, 139-41]

Stevens, too, runs through a succession of images to describe something that lies beyond comprehension, "The palm at the end of the mind, / Beyond the last thought,"[50] and even if he conceived his goal rather differently from Dante, it might not be inappropriate to say that his mind, too, as he drew near the ineffable innocence and purity of

50. Stevens, "Of Mere Being," *Palm at the End of the Mind*, p. 404.

being, was assailed by a sudden glory. In "A Primitive like an Orb" he likens being to a poem, "The essential poem at the centre of things" (*CP*, p. 440). In "Study of Images I" he likens it to a landscape, with our situation in the landscape an image of our participation in being:

> If the study of his images
> Is the study of man, this image of Saturday,
>
> This Italian symbol, this Southern landscape, is like
> A waking, as in images we awake,
> Within the very object that we seek,
>
> Participants of its being. It is, we are.
> He is, we are.
>
> [*CP*, p. 463]

In "The River of Rivers in Connecticut," it is "The river that flows nowhere, like a sea," (*CP*, p. 533). Or in another use of the river image, in "Metaphor as Degeneration," it is a river that is not a river, the being that is simultaneously being and not being, landless and waterless, on whose banks beings bloom:

> It is certain that the river
>
> Is not Swatara. The swarthy water
> That flows round the earth and through the skies,
> Twisting among the universal spaces,
>
> Is not Swatara. It is being.
> That is the flock-flecked river, the water,
> The blown sheen — or is it air?
>
> How, then, is metaphor degeneration,
> When Swatara becomes this undulant river
> And the river becomes the landless, waterless ocean?
>
> Here the black violets grow down to its banks
> And the memorial mosses hang their green
> Upon it, as it flows ahead.
>
> [*CP*, pp. 444-45]

It is also a "holiness." Although we can approach it only obliquely and we see it only in glimpses that are here an instant, then vanish, nevertheless it is there, real, abiding in itself even in perpetual change; and in the rare, brief moments in which we are able to live in it consciously, our life united with life, we are transfigured:

> There may be always a time of innocence.
> There is never a place. Or if there is no time,
> If it is not a thing of time, nor of place,
>
> Existing in the idea of it, alone,
> In the sense against calamity, it is not
> Less real. . . .
>
> It is like a thing of ether that exists
> Almost as predicate. But it exists,
> It exists, it is visible, it is, it is.
>
> So, then, these lights are not a spell of light,
> A saying out of a cloud, but innocence.
> An innocence of the earth and no false sign
>
> Or symbol of malice. That we partake thereof,
> Lie down like children in this holiness. . . .
>
> ["The Auroras of Autumn," *CP,* p. 418]

An innocence of the earth, a holiness in which the immanent sacred replaces the transcendent that would be a false sign or a "symbol of malice," and yet in which the immanent and transcendent remain in their characteristic tension as the paradoxical union of beings and being.

Here again, in a new figure, we find the cosmic child and the Third Kingdom of the divine immanence. For Stevens, of course, it is not a third, but the only kingdom, and of course he would say, with the narrator of Beckett's *Cascando,* that "kingdom," too, is "an image, like any other,"[51] but it is a version of the kingdom nonetheless,

51. Beckett, *Cascando,* p. 18.

and one that, like its predecessors, crowns its participants with tongues of fire:

> He was as tall as a tree in the middle of
> The night. The substance of his body seemed
> Both substance and non-substance, luminous flesh
> Or shapely fire: fire from an underworld,
> Of less degree than flame and lesser shine.
>
> Upon my top he breathed the pointed dark.[52]

52. Stevens, "Chocorua to Its Neighbor," *CP*, pp. 297-98.

CHAPTER IV

The One and the Many: The Ambiguous Challenge of Being in the Poetry of Yeats and Rilke

> The whole system is founded upon the belief that the ultimate reality, symbolized as the Sphere, falls in human consciousness, as Nicholas of Cusa was the first to demonstrate, into a series of antinomies.
>
> W. B. YEATS, *A Vision,* p. 189

> Du bist der Wald der Widersprüche.
>
> R. M. RILKE, *Das Buch vom Mönchischen Leben*

"You are the forest of contradictions"[1] — Rilke's words describe the universe that many descendants of the romantics found themselves in toward the end of the nineteenth century and the beginning of the twentieth. The words are addressed both to God and to the world because from the point of view that they express, the two are ultimately one, though the contrast between what is conceived of as the perfect simplicity and unity of Being and the complex multiplicity of beings could not be more emphatic.[2]

1. Rainer Maria Rilke, *Werke in drei Bänden, I: Gedicht-Zyklen* (Frankfurt: Insel Verlag, 1966), p. 39.

2. I should explain that in this chapter I will be using the word "being" in both capitalized and uncapitalized forms: the former when it refers to the special concept of Being as the Absolute in the tradition of philosophical idealism, the latter when it refers either to particular entities or to existence in a general sense.

Yeats was correct in tracing the source of this vision to Nicholas of Cusa. Cusanus' theory of the *coincidentia oppositorum* and of the *complicatio* and *explicatio* became the basis for the theories of Fichte and other philosophical idealists about the evolution of the One or the Absolute from a condition of unconscious self-unity through an inner division into subject and object, whereby it becomes conscious but fragmented. This line of thought had widespread influence in the nineteenth century. It passed into English romanticism through the writings of Coleridge, who himself traveled in Germany, read the idealists, and adopted much of their thought in his own philosophical and critical writings. From England it passed into American thought by way of Emerson. And of course in Germany it became the dominant school of philosophy at least until after World War I.

As the German philosophers developed it, the idealist theory assumed that the evolution that began in the unity of simple Being and passed through the disruption into conscious duality, self-alienation, and antinomy was also moving ultimately toward fulfillment in a new, luminous self-unity and self-possession: the self-realization of the Absolute. For some exponents of this tradition, one thinks especially of Schelling and Hegel, this prospect offered an occasion for serene optimism: man is the spearhead of the Absolute's process of self-realization, and the fulfillment of this process is taking place according to laws of being that are both inevitable and intelligible. As the nineteenth century moved on, however, much of the optimism faded, undermined by latent ambiguities within the idealist theory. These sprang from the idealists' identification of consciousness, and especially the human mode of consciousness, with the split of the One into subject and object, and ultimately into multiple subjects and objects.

This identification of consciousness with duality had several implications. For one thing, it meant that although Being, considered absolutely, might be one and simple, from the perspective of human consciousness it can be known only in fragments — logically as irresolvable contradictions, psychologically as the struggle of the subject to know or take possession of the object and to fight off, when necessary, the claims of rival subjects. It also meant that although the ultimate reality of the universe might be moving towards a perfect fruition as self-realized Absolute, man himself, being indissolubly bound up with duality, will not participate as man in that fruition. Rather, all of what man thinks of as knowledge is really only an illusion of perspective, a distortion in Being's experience of itself, and even man's very existence is an illusion that Absolute Being must eventually outgrow. From this point of view, the universe will attain fulfillment, but it will not be man's fulfillment; man is only a false dream that will be left behind. For one who is willing to relinquish his identity as a finite and distinct self related to a world, such a prospect might seem at least not unattractive, but it would hardly offer an opportunity for rejoicing, since when the culmination of the process arrived, there would be no human self left to rejoice.

There have been writers who have been able to speak affirmatively about this prospect, but to do so has always involved a heroic self-conquest of the merely human. This is why Wallace Stevens in his poem on the approach to ultimate reality speaks of the bird in the palm at the end of the mind as singing "without human meaning, / Without human feeling, a foreign song."[3] In Stevens'

3. "Of Mere Being," *The Palm at the End of the Mind: Selected Poems and a Play,* ed. Holly Stevens (New York: Alfred A. Knopf, 1971), p. 404. See above, p. 34.

poem the context — the position of the tree "Beyond the last thought," the effect of the song on the listener, the shining of the bird's "fire-fangled feathers" as the wind moves in the branches — makes it clear that the song is a call to transcend the human and to participate, in so far as it is possible to a finite subject, in the life of "Mere Being." To put it in terms of our own discussion, it is a call from the sacred, a challenge to stop clinging to our humanity and to open ourselves to the *mysterium tremendum et fascinans* that presents itself to us in the wind, the song, and the fire.

The challenge, however, has its own ambiguity. At first it might seem that this tradition would identify the sacred with the One in such a way that all multiplicity and particularity would simply stand opposed to it as forms of the profane. To a certain extent this is the case; for both Yeats and Rilke, for example, who stand in the direct line of the idealist tradition,[4] the highest goal to which man is called is unity of being and this is a sacred calling. As Yeats put it in his essay on "The Symbolism of Poetry," "beauty is an accusation"; beauty, he meant, is both a call from sacred value at the heart of being and a foreshadowing of the coming vision of true being in its unity and wholeness in "the new sacred book, of which all the arts . . . are beginning to dream." To fulfill its purpose, Yeats said, poetry must deliver this imperative to man in order to awaken him to his highest possibilities, and to do so effectively it must communicate the sacred character of its demand: "How can the arts overcome the

4. It is difficult to determine how extensive was the influence of the German philosophers on Yeats in his younger years — he may have learned their pattern of thought more through English sources, such as Coleridge, than through direct readings — but by 1931 he was able to say, in an introduction to a book on Bishop Berkeley, "Two or three generations hence . . . no educated man will doubt that the movement of philosophy from Spinoza to Hegel is the greatest of all works of intellect." *Essays and Introductions* (New York: Macmillan, 1961), p. 396.

slow dying of men's hearts that we call the progress of the world, and lay their hands upon men's heartstrings again, without becoming the garment of religion as in old times?"[5] For both poets fragmentedness and the divided mind that goes with the vision of fragmentedness were the chief obstacles preventing man from responding adequately to this calling. Rilke described the problem in the third of his *Sonnets to Orpheus:*

> A god can do it. But how, tell me shall
> a man follow him through the narrow lyre?
> His mind is cleavage. At the crossing of two
> heartways stands no temple for Apollo.
>
> [En Gott vermags. Wie aber, sag mir, soll
> ein Mann ihm folgen durch die schmale Leier?
> Sein Sinn ist Zwiespalt. An der Kreuzung zweier
> Herzwege steht kein Tempel für Apoll.][6]

True being, as Rilke goes on to say, is not to be found in this profane condition of duality in which the subject always stands opposite an object and reaches toward it as one fragment of being toward another. Even the desire to overcome the opposition only perpetuates it. The resolution is to be found only in transcending the divided vision altogether, a relinquishing of the self and of the self's strivings. True song, he says, the true poem of being, is not desire:

> Real singing is a different breath.
> A breath for nothing. A wafting in the god. A wind.
>
> [In Wahrheit singen, ist ein andrer Hauch.
> Ein Hauch um nichts. Ein Wehn im Gott. Ein Wind.]

5. "The Symbolism of Poetry," ibid., pp. 153, 162-63.

6. *Sonnets to Orpheus,* trans. M. D. Herter Norton (New York: Norton, 1962), pp. 20-21. Subsequent references to this volume will identify the sonnets by number rather than by page. This, for example refers to *Sonnets,* I, 3, i.e., the third sonnet in Part I.

As Rilke put it earlier in *The Notebook of Malte Laurids Brigge*, even God, by which Rilke always meant the One, the Absolute — even God "is only a direction given to love, not its object."[7] Perfect union with God, from this point of view, would not be the self's attainment of a goal, but rather an evaporation into the One.

But this conception of the challenge of the sacred is only one side of what is actually, for the tradition deriving from the idealists, an unavoidable paradox: true being is to be found only in the Absolute, and to give onself to that is a sacred calling, but at the same time there is a similarly powerful calling, which in its own way is also sacred, either to carry the world with one into the ultimate union, or else to transform it even in its secularity from a condition of fragmentedness to one of organic wholeness — to unite the One and the many, the sacred and the world.

Both Yeats and Rilke felt fully the paradoxical character of this challenge, and both attempted, each in his own way, to fulfill its demands through a simultaneous affirmation of both horns of the dilemma it presented. As Yeats invoked the rose of eternal beauty to enter into the world and deliver him from total subjection to temporality, he also affirmed his loyalty to the world, warning the rose not to overwhelm it completely:

> Come near, come near, come near — Ah, leave me still
> A little space for the rose-breath to fill.
> Lest I no more hear common things that crave. . . .[8]

So too, Rilke, invoking the angel that in the *Duino Elegies* is a symbol of supra-temporal and supra-personal being, fends the angel off even as he beckons to him:

7. Trans. John Linton (London: Hogarth Press, 1950), p. 234.

8. "To the Rose upon the Rood of Time," *The Collected Poems of W. B. Yeats: Definitive Edition, with the Author's Final Revisions* (New York: Macmillan, 1957), p. 31.

Don't think that I'm wooing!
Angel, even if I were, you'd never come. For my call
is always full of "Away!" Against such a powerful
current you cannot advance. Like an outstretched
arm is my call. And its clutching, upwardly
open hand is always before you
as open for warding and warning,
aloft there, Inapprehensible.

[Glaub *nicht,* dass ich werbe.
Engel, und würb ich dich auch! Du kommst nicht. Denn mein
Anruf ist immer voll Hinweg; wider so starke
Strömung kannst du nicht schreiten. Wie ein gestreckter
Arm is mein Rufen. Und seine zum Greifen
oben offene Hand bleibt vor dir
offen, wie Abwehr und Warnung,
Unfasslicher, weitauf.][9]

Both also shared a common conception of the responsibility of the poet as a mediator between the world and the One. As Yeats put it, alluding once again to Nicholas of Cusa, "If it be true that God is a circle whose centre is everywhere, the saint goes to the centre, the poet and artist to the ring where everything comes round again."[10] The saint, in other words, may seek the eternal directly, but the poet must "find his pleasure in all that is ever passing away that it may come again, in the beauty of woman, in the fragile flowers of spring, in momentary passion, in whatever is most fleeting. . . ." To do so, however, is to seek the same ultimate goal as the saint, for in Cusanus' infinite circle the center and the circumference are one; the poet, immersing himself in and celebrating the cycles of time, makes his art a means by

9. *Duino Elegies,* the German text, with an English translation, introduction, and commentary by J. B. Leishman and Stephen Spender (New York: Norton, 1963), pp. 62-65. Page references for subsequent passages will be cited parenthetically in the text.

10. "Discoveries" (1906), *Essays*, p. 287.

which time and the eternal become united. Rilke had a similar calling in mind when he said in the First Elegy:

> Yes, the Springs had need of you. Many a star
> was waiting for you to espy it. Many a wave
> would rise on the past towards you; or, else, perhaps,
> as you went by an open window, a violin
> would be giving itself to someone. All this was a trust.
> But were you equal to it?
>
> [Ja, die Frühlinge brauchten dich wohl. Es muteten manche
> Sterne dir zu, dass du sie spürtest. Es hob
> sich eine Woge heran im Vergangenen, oder
> da du vorüberkamst am geöffneten Fenster.
> gab eine Geige sich hin. Das alles war Auftrag.
> Aber bewältigtest du's?]
>
> [*Elegies,* pp. 22-23]

According to Rilke, to fulfill this trust man must accomplish certain tasks, overcome certain obstacles, and make some important but very difficult affirmations. The source of the obstacles is the condition of duality that is intrinsic to the human mode of being: "That's what Destiny means: being opposite, / and nothing else, and always opposite" ("Dieses heisst Schicksal: gegenüber sein / und nichts als das und immer gegenüber"; *Elegies,* pp. 63-69). This cleavage of conscious being into subject and object prevents us from realizing the true unity of being that underlies the phenomenal world: we can conceive of that unity, perhaps even to some extent imagine it, but we can never fully enter into it in experience: ". . . spectators always, everywhere, / looking at, never out of, everything!" (". . . Zuschauer, immer, überall, dem allen zugewandt und nie hinaus!" *Elegies,* pp. 70-71). And not only does duality cut us off from conscious experience of the unity of being, it also gives rise to tendencies in the subject that accentuate the sharpness of the cleavage — especially fear, the instinct to preserve one's separate identity. As Rilke describes it, fear is present at the very birth of consciousness and contributes to the energy with which consciousness breaks up being's unity into fragments:

> And how dismayed is any womb-born thing
> that has to fly! As though it were afraid
> of its own self, it zigzags through the air
> like crack through cup. The way the track of a bat
> goes rending through the evening's porcelain.
>
> [Und wie bestürzt ist eins, das fliegen muss
> und stammt aus einem Schoos. Wie vor sich selbst
> erschreckt, durchzuckts die Luft, wie wenn ein Sprung
> durch eine Tasse geht. So reisst die Spur
> der Fledermaus durchs Porzellan des Abends.]
>
> [*Elegies,* pp. 70-71]

This fear drives us in flight from our own condition of mortality, and it incites us to grasp at objects that we hope can serve as defenses. The result is never a successful defense, but only distraction of mind, the inability to attend to the true task before us. In the Tenth Elegy Rilke speaks of how superficial pleasure-seekers are enticed to the false promise of immortality:

> . . . "Deathless,"
> that bitter beer tastes quite sweet to its drinkers
> so long as they chew with it plenty of fresh distractions. . . .
>
> [. . . "Todlos,"
> jenes bitteren Biers, das den Trinkenden süss scheint,
> wenn sie immer dazu frische Zerstreuungen kaun . . .]
>
> [*Elegies,* pp. 80-81]

And in the First Elegy when Rilke spoke of the "trust" that is our responsibility to the world and asked if we were equal to it, he went on to speak of distraction as the principal danger to be on guard against:

> Were you not always
> distracted by expectation, as though all this
> were announcing someone to love?
>
> [Warst du nicht immer
> noch von Erwartung zerstreut, als kündigte alles
> eine Geliebte dir an?]
>
> [*Elegies,* pp. 22-23]

The answer to this is to transcend the posture of opposition and defense by learning the love that seeks no object but is a simple gift of oneself to being:

> Is it not time that, in loving,
> we freed ourselves from the loved one, and quivering,
> endured:
> as the arrow endures the string, to become, in the
> gathering out-leap,
> something more than itself? For staying is nowhere.
>
> [Ist es nicht Zeit, dass wir liebend
> uns vom Geliebten befrein und es bebend bestehn:
> wie der Pfeil die Sehne besteht, um gesammelt im
> Absprung
> *mehr* zu sein als er selbst. Denn Bleiben ist nirgends.]

To do this is to win the freedom to go on to the real task that calls to man, the transformation of the world from an evanescent stream of external images to an inner spiritual vision:

> Earth, isn't this what you want: an invisible
> re-arising in us? Is it not your dream
> to be one day invisible? Earth! invisible!
> What is your urgent command, if not transformation?
>
> [Erde, ist is nicht dies, was du willst: unsichtbar
> in uns erstehn? — Ist es dein Traum nicht,
> einmal unsichtbar zu sein? — Erde! unsichtbar!
> Was, wenn Verwandlung nicht, ist den drängender
> Auftrag?]
>
> [*Elegies,* pp. 76-77]

Poetry is the principal means to this transformation. We are here to say words — House, Bridge, Fountain, Gate, Jug, Olive Tree, Window — and in saying them, to praise the world to the Angel, so that in his gaze it may stand "redeemed at last, in a final uprightness" ("Gerettet zuletzt, nun endlich aufrecht"; *Elegies,* pp. 62-63). These things depend on us for their fulfillment: ". . . fleeting, they look for / rescue through something in us, the most fleeting of all" (". . . vergänglich, / traun sie ein Rettendes uns, den Vergänglichsten, zu"; *Elegies,* pp. 76-77). And if we can live up to this trust, then we may say,

> So, after all, we have *not*
> failed to make use of the spaces, these generous spaces,
> these,
> *our* spaces.
>
> [So haben wir dennoch
> nicht die Räume versäumt, diese gewährenden, diese
> *unseren* Räume.]
>
> [*Elegies,* pp. 62-63]

The *Elegies* did not begin with much confidence that this task could be accomplished or even that, if it were accomplished, it would be of much value. The gulf separating the world of time and duality from that mode of being symbolized by the angel seemed at first to be too wide to be bridged in any way that would not mean the destruction of the temporal. The First Elegy opened with what was virtually a cry of despair:

> Who, if I cried, would hear me among the angelic
> orders? And even if one of them suddenly
> pressed me against his heart, I should fade in the
> strength of his
> stronger existence. For Beauty's nothing
> but beginning of Terror we're still just able to
> bear,
> and why we adore it so is because it serenely
> disdains to destroy us.

[Wer, wenn ich schriee, hörte mich denn aus der Engel
Ordnungen? und gesetzt selbst, es nähme
einer mich plötzlich ans Herz: ich verginge von seinem
stärkeren Dasein. Denn das Schöne ist nichts
als des Schrecklichen Anfang, den wir noch grade
ertragen,
und wir bewundern es so, weil es gelassen verschmäht,
uns zu zerstören.][23]

[*Elegies,* pp. 20-21]

And to the Second Elegy it was questionable whether our existence participates at all in real being and whether the angels could ever have any awareness of us or our world:

Does the cosmic space
we dissolve into taste of us, then? Do the angels really
only catch up what is theirs, what has streamed from
them, or at times,
as though through an oversight, is a little of our
existence in it as well?

[Schmeckt denn der Weltraum,
in den wir uns lösen, nach uns? Fangen die Engel
wirklich nur Ihriges auf, ihnen Entströmtes,
oder ist manchmal, wie aus Versehen, ein wenig
unseres Wesens dabei?]

[*Elegies,* pp. 30-31]

The Fifth Elegy opens with a picture of men's world as utterly debased, like a threadbare carpet

forlornly
lost in the cosmos.
Laid on there like a plaster . . .

[diesem verlorenen
Teppich im Weltall.
Aufgelegt wie ein Pflaster . . .]

[*Elegies,* pp. 46-47]

But the problem is precisely that this is *men's* world, the product of a superficial vision celebrated in superficial art,

a sham-fruit of boredom, their own
never-realised boredom, gleaming with thinnest
lightly sham-smiling surface.

[zur Scheinfrucht
wieder der Unlust befruchteten, ihrer
niemals bewussten, — glänzend mit dünnster
Oberfläche leicht scheinlächelnden Unlust.]

Again, the energy behind this false art is the fear of death:

. . . the modiste Madame Lamort
winds and binds the restless ways of the world,
those endless ribbons, to ever-new
creations of bow, frill, flower, cockade and fruit,
all falsely-coloured, to deck
the cheap winter-hats of Fate.

[. . . die Modistin, Madame Lamort,
die ruhlosen Wege der Erde, endlose Bänder,
schlingt und windet und neue aus ihnen
Schleifen erfindet, Rüschen, Blumen, Kokarden,
    künstliche Früchte —, alle
unwahr gefärbt, — für die billigen
Winterhüte des Schicksals.]
[*Elegies,* pp. 52-53]

The poem ends with an expression of at least tentative hope that out of the mass of people who crowd the city squares to witness and participate in the spectacles of sham art, some few may finally transcend the common duality of mind to stand "truthfully smiling" ("wahrhaft lächelnden") before the true "rose of onlooking" ("Rose des Zuschauns"), "the spectators ringed round, the countless unmurmuring dead" ("den Zuschauern rings, unzähligen lautlosen Toten").[11]

11. The phrase, "Rose des Zuschauns," is from the beginning of the elegy (p. 46); the ending takes up the image again and shows it in its true fulfillment.

This last image recalls Dante's rose of the blessed in the *Paradiso,* but with the important difference that here it symbolizes the vision that is accessible to those who can step beyond the opposition between life and death and give themselves with undivided hearts to what the *First Elegy* calls the "eternal torrent" that "whirls all the ages through either realm forever" ("Die ewige Strömung / reisst durch beide Bereiche alle Alter / immer mit sich . . ."; *Elegies,* pp. 24-25), or, as the Tenth Elegy puts it, who can follow the Laments ("die Klagen") to "the mountains of Primal Pain" ("die Berge des Urleids") and there find "the source of Joy" ("die Quelle der Freude"), which among men becomes "a carrying stream" ("ein tragender Strom") (*Elegies,* pp. 84-85).

The *Duino Elegies* as a whole are a record of the transition from the near despair of the beginning to a simultaneous affirmation of life and death, joy and sorrow, at the end. As the poet moves through the change of attitude that this transition requires, his vision of the world also changes so that he can say, in the Sixth Elegy, "Life here's glorious" ("Hiersein ist herrlich"; *Elegies,* pp. 60-61), and in the Ninth Elegy can dedicate himself to the world's redemption through song:

> *Here* is the time for the Tellable, *here* is its home.
> Speak and proclaim. More than ever
> the things we can live with are falling away, and their
> place
> being oustingly taken up by an imageless act. . . .
> Between the hammers lives on
> our heart, as between the teeth
> the tongue, which, nevertheless,
> remains the bestower of praise.
>
> [*Hier* ist des *Säglichen* Zeit,
> *hier* seine Heimat.
> Sprich und bekenn. Mehr als je

fallen die Dinge dahin, die erlebbaren, denn,
was sie verdrängend ersetzt, ist ein Tun ohne Bild. . . .
Zwischen den Hämmern besteht
unser Herz, wie die Zunge
zwischen den Zähnen, die doch,
dennoch die preisende bleibt.]

[*Elegies*, pp. 74-75]

The *Sonnets to Orpheus*, which were all composed in February 1922, the same month in which Rilke completed the *Duino Elegies*, rounded out the affirmative vision he had won his way to. In the *Sonnets* the figure of the angel is replaced by that of Orpheus, a significant difference. Whereas the angel was a terrifying figure — "Every Angel is terrible" ("Jeder Engel is schrecklich"; *Elegies*, pp. 28-29) — less a mediating link between the human world and the One than a symbol of the distance separating them, Orpheus represents not just the possibility but the actuality of continuity and communion between levels of being. To the question of Sonnet I, 6, "Ist er ein Hiesiger?", is he one who originates in our world and who is limited to our mode of being, the answer is, "No, out of both / realms his wide nature grew" ("Nein, aus beiden / Reichen erwuchs seine weite Natur"). Orpheus embodies knowledge of both life and death and is therefore able to give expression to praise of the "dual realm" ("Doppelbereich") that is actually one beneath its duality (*Sonnets*, I, 9). And what is more, Orpheus is himself both the One and the many; Rilke uses the myth of Orpheus's dismemberment by the Maenads to describe the birth of beings out of Being:

O you lost god! You unending trace!
Only because at last enmity rent and scattered you
are we now the hearers and a mouth of Nature.

[O du verlorener Gott! Du unendliche Spur!
Nur weil dich reissend zuletzt die Feindschaft

verteilte,
sind wir die Hörenden jetzt und ein Mund der Natur.]
[*Sonnets,* I, 26]

The too limited vision that would cling to one or another form that Being takes fails to see that there is only one life beneath all the forms; this is Orpheus, transformed continually into this one and that one:

Set up no stone to his memory.
Just let the rose bloom each year for his sake.
For it is Orpheus. His metamorphosis
in this one and in this. We should not trouble

about other names. Once and for all
it's Orpheus when there's singing.

[Errichtet keinen Denkstein. Lasst die Rose
nur jedes Jahr zu seinen Gunsten blühn.
Denn Orpheus ists. Seine Metamorphose
in dem und dem. Wir sollen uns nicht mühn

um andre Namen. Ein für alle Male
ists Orpheus, wenn es singt.]
[*Sonnets,* I, 5]

Orpheus is everywhere, in everything, but he rises from fragmentation into wholeness through song, and his reintegration is also the world's. The first sonnet in the sequence describes how when Orpheus sings, the animals come forth from their separate lairs and gather to listen as he builds "temples for them in their hearing" ("ihnen Tempel im Gehör"), and later sonnets go on to tell how Orpheus orders all creatures, animals and humans, through his singing, converting the stream of beings into a single, conscious dance:

Array the criers,
singing god! that they waken resounding,
a current bearing the head and the lyre.

[Ordne die Schreier,
singender Gott! dass sie rauschend erwachen,
tragend als Strömung das Haupt und die Leier.]
[*Sonnets,* II, 26]

The effect is to transpose "all transience into stepping" ("alles Vergehens in Gang") (*Sonnets,* II, 18), to unite time and "the unheard-of centre" ("die unerhörte Mitte") in a dance "in which we fleetingly transcend / dumbly ordering Nature" ("darin wir die dumpf ordnende Natur / vergänglich übertreffen") and through which we aspire to the ultimate "perfect celebration" ("heil[e] Feier") (*Sonnets,* II, 28).

Yeats held a similar ideal of poetry as the means through which time is redeemed from mere flux and fragmentation and given at least a momentary form and wholeness. Like Rilke imagining earth's possible redemption in the form of words told to the angel, Yeats speculates:

The wandering earth herself may be
Only a sudden flaming word,
In clanging space a moment heard,
Troubling the endless reverie.[12]

Also like Rilke, he thinks of the effect of poetry as consisting in a transformation of the self, a union of life and art. In "Byzantium," for example, he describes the change that earthly souls undergo as they become themselves the dance that is one with the fire of eternity:

At midnight on the Emperor's pavement flit
Flames that no faggot feeds . . .
Where blood-begotten spirits come
And all complexities of fury leave,
Dying into a dance,
An agony of trance,
An agony of flame that cannot singe a sleeve.[13]

12. "The Song of the Happy Shepherd," *Collected Poems,* p. 7.
13. In ibid., p. 244.

At times, as in this case, it may appear that the transformation Yeats is speaking of must involve the total destruction of the merely human and finite, but in fact he never gives up his loyalty to the ideal of a transfiguring union in which the earthly retains its identity and value. "We must find some place upon the Tree of Life for the phoenix' nest. . . ," he said in 1906,[14] and the whole body of his work may be said to have been an effort to find and define that place. Man runs his course between extremities, and his limited mode of vision inevitably divides the one tree into opposites — ". . . half all glittering flame and half all green / Abounding foliage" — but the tree is always a single life: ". . . And half is half and yet is all the scene. . . ."[15] We always wander among antinomies — the aged body that has a heart still capable of being "driven wild" by the memory of a Ledean body, the irreconcilable metaphysical views of Plato, Aristotle, and Pythagoras — but always behind these conflicts "Labour is blossoming or dancing where / The body is not bruised to pleasure soul . . ."; the tree is undivided into blossom, leaf, or bole, nor is the dancer distinguishable from the dance.[16]

To human consciousness, however, a clear understanding of this always remains beyond reach. In *A Vision,* speaking of the higher wisdom he attributed to spiritual voices, Yeats said, "My instructors identify consciousness with conflict, not with knowledge . . . ," and he went on to say that they substituted "for subject and object and their attendant logic a struggle towards harmony, towards Unity of Being."[17] True being, of course, always has its unity and has no need to struggle toward it, but man needs

14. "Discoveries," *Essays,* p. 272.
15. "Vacillation," *Collected Poems,* p. 245.
16. "Among School Children," ibid., pp. 212-14.
17. *A Vision: A Reissue with the Author's Final Revisions* (New York: Macmillan, 1961), p. 214.

to work hard to achieve the inner integrity that is a participation in the unity of the One. This participation is itself a kind of living wisdom that surpasses the fragmented vision of consciousness to attain an intuitive grasp of true being in its immediacy; at the very end of his life Yeats said in a letter, "Man can embody truth but he cannot know it."[18] This was more than just the statement of a final insight; it was a summation of the main thrust of his career. He had said much earlier, in 1907, something that pointed in the same direction: "A poet is by the very nature of things a man who lives with entire sincerity, or rather, the better his poetry the more sincere his life. His life is an experiment in living. . . ."[19]

One of the ways in which Yeats pursued that goal was through the practice of poetry in the spirit of a religious vocation, a complete dedication of his personal powers to the sacred calling through his work. In 1906 he said that there were only two paths open to literature in the modern period, one lay "upward into ever-growing subtlety, with Verhaeren, with Mallarmé, with Maeterlinck, until at last, it may be, a new agreement among refined and studious men gives birth to a new passion, and what seems literature becomes religion . . .";[20] the other lay downward with the naturalists. This did not mean that Yeats wished to write a form of specifically religious poetry. On the contrary, he wrote in his *Autobiography* around 1915, "Should not religion hide within the work of art as God is within His world, and how can the interpreter do more than whisper?"[21] Rather, what it

18. Letter to Lady Elizabeth Pelham (1939), The *Letters of W. B. Yeats,* ed. Allan Wade (New York: Macmillan, 1955), p. 922.

19. Unpublished speech of Lionel Johnson, quoted in Richard Ellmann, *Yeats: The Man and the Masks* (New York: Oxford University Press, 1948), pp. 5-6.

20. "Discoveries," *Essays,* pp. 266-67.

21. *Memoirs: Autobiography — First Draft; Journal,* ed. Denis Donoghue (New York: Macmillan, 1973), p. 124.

did mean was making his poetry the vehicle of his quest for unity of being.

He accomplished this through two efforts. One was the use of poetry to construct a balanced view of the universe and of man's life in time in terms of the conflicting forces that shape that life. The other was the use of what he called the "mask," a complementary poetic personality and voice, as a device with which to bring his own self into balance and wholeness.

Probably the most prominent feature of Yeats's effort to construct a balanced vision of the universe is his theory of history as outlined in *A Vision* and as represented in various ways in a large number of his poems. This consisted mainly in the idea that time develops cyclically in complementary patterns that Yeats called "gyres." Any given historical moment is composed of opposing tendencies — subjective and objective, rational and mystical, temporal and spatial, spiritual and fleshly, and so on — and any given historical period is a movement in the direction of one set of opposites or the other.[22] Basically these historical gyres move in two-thousand-year cycles, beginning with the dominance of one pole, say the subjective, moving toward the dominance of the opposite, the objective, after one thousand years, and then returning to the dominance of the original pole again at the end of an additional thousand years. This can also be imagined, Yeats said, in terms of phases of the moon, beginning with the full, the subjective pole, and moving through the dark, the objective pole, and back around again, through a complete cycle of twenty-eight phases. Seen from this point of view, history is always deviating from balance into imbalance and seeking balance again. This is why, in "The Magi" for example, the "pale unsatisfied ones" who once sought the Christ of Bethlehem

22. See *A Vision*, pp. 67-89, and 267-300.

return again, and eternally, "Being by Calvary's turbulence unsatisfied," to seek "The uncontrollable mystery on the bestial floor."[23]

The individual goes through similar patterns of development. Various people in a given period may have personality types corresponding to the various phases of the moon.[24] These may agree or conflict with the dominant tendencies of the historical period they live in. To achieve personal balance and completeness, the individual must incorporate into his total self as much as he can of the qualities of his opposite, his "mask." "Ego Dominus Tuus" outlines this concept through a dialogue between opposing points of view, represented by "Hic" and "Ille." Hic urges the standard conception of sincere being — ". . . I would find myself and not an image" — but Ille, who has a deeper understanding of selfhood, uses an image, the mask, to call to his own opposite, his double, who is both like him and most unlike, in order that this figure may disclose to him the mystery of wholeness. In his poetic practice Yeats implemented precisely this plan; his early poetry tended to be a fairly direct expression of his own personality, but the poetry of his maturity spoke with a voice that was markedly different: cooler, more self-controlled, more objective, and through these qualities, more intense.[25]

Yeats's poetic use of the mask did not, to counter the objections of "Hic," render his self-expression less sincere. Rather it helped his poetry toward a more nearly complete presentation of the true wholeness of his being, and it helped Yeats personally to become aware of and to

23. *Collected Poems,* p. 124.

24. *A Vision,* pp. 105-84, provides analyses of the personality types associated with the twenty eight phases.

25. Yeats probably associated himself with the personality represented by phase seventeen, as examples of which he listed Dante, Shelley, and Landor. The proper mask of this phase is supposed to be "Simplification through intensity." See ibid., pp. 140-45.

live in the complementary qualities that he needed for his true self-realization.

For true being is always whole, simple, fulfilled. It is only in phenomenal experience that it seems torn into opposites. This is true both for the self and for the universe. When Yeats spoke in *A Vision* of the perfection of the "Thirteenth Cone," so called because Christ was the thirteenth after the twelve apostles,[26] he also called it a sphere, because of its completeness, and went on to say that in fact all of the cones are simply distorted reflections of a single ultimate reality:

> I only speak of the *Thirteenth Cone* as a sphere and yet I might say that the gyre or cone of the *Principles* is in reality a sphere, though to Man, bound to birth and death, it can never seem so, and that it is the antinomies that force us to find it a cone. Only one symbol exists, though the reflecting mirrors make many appear and all different.[27]

Like so many modern writers who have formulated new conceptions of the sacred, both Yeats and Rilke had to draw on traditional images while at the same time adapting them for use as vehicles of a new vision. The figure of Orpheus served this purpose for Rilke, that of Christ for Yeats. In his essay, "A General Introduction for my Work," written in 1937, Yeats said:

> . . . my Christ, a legitimate deduction from the Creed of St. Patrick as I think, is that Unity of Being Dante compared to a perfectly proportioned human body, Blake's "Imagination," what the Upanishads have named "Self": nor is this unity distant and therefore intellectually understandable, but imminent [*sic?*], differing from man to man and age to age, taking upon itself pain and ugliness, "eye of newt, and toe of frog."

This is Christ as *conjunctio oppositorum*, a "Unity of Being" that is simultaneously the perfect and eternal

26. See Richard Ellmann, *The Identity of Yeats* (New York: Oxford University Press, 1954), p. 159.

27. *A Vision*, p. 240.

Thirteenth Cone or Sphere and also the immanent life of the temporal world. It is the traditional figure of sacred being, reformulated as "a Christ posed against a background not of Judaism but of Druidism," a symbol of perfection and wholeness that is at the same time, "flowing, concrete, phenomenal."[28]

28. *Essays*, p. 518.

CHAPTER V

A Darkness Shining in Brightness: James Joyce and the Obscure Soul of the World

He was alone. He was unheeded, happy and near to the wild heart of life. . . .

A girl stood before him in midstream, alone and still, gazing out to sea. She seemed like one whom magic had changed into the likeness of a strange and beautiful seabird. . . . Her bosom was as a bird's soft and slight, slight and soft as the breast of some darkplumaged dove. But her long fair hair was girlish: and girlish, and touched with the wonder mortal beauty, her face.

She was alone and still, gazing out to sea; and when she felt his presence and the worship of his eyes her eyes turned to him in quiet sufferance of his gaze, without shame or wantonness. . . . The first faint noise of gently moving water broke the silence . . . hither and thither, hither and thither: and a faint flame trembled on her cheek.

— Heavenly God! cried Stephen's soul, in an outburst of profane joy.[1]

This scene is the climax of *A Portrait of the Artist as a Young Man* — the climax in several senses. It is the high point of emotional intensity in the volume and the moment of Stephen Dedalus's greatest insight into the meaning, not only of his life, but also of life as such.

1. James Joyce, *A Portrait of the Artist as a Young Man* (New York: Viking Press, 1964), p. 171. Subsequent references in parentheses.

In terms of the dramatic structure of the work, it is the moment in which his decision to forego the ecclesiastical priesthood that had been set before him by the director of his college is confirmed by his realization of his calling to a different, more valid, and more challenging secular priesthood of the imagination. In terms of the thematic and imagistic structure of the book as a whole, it is a scene that draws together all the key images of the work — woman, sea, bird, darkness, fire, and, in the remainder of the scene, Lucifer, circles and cyclic motion, and flower — pointing symbolically toward a possible harmonious union of the conflicting tensions they have been associated with in the preceeding episodes. They point to it, though they do not embody it — that remains for *Ulysses* to accomplish. Here they only coalesce briefly in one of those moments of vision that Joyce called an epiphany.[2]

As the scene continues, Stephen turns away and walks alone along the beach:

> On and on and on he strode, far out over the sands, singing wildly to the sea, crying to greet the advent of the life that had cried to him.
>
> Her image had passed into his soul for ever. . . . Her eyes had called him and his soul had leaped at the call. To live, to err, to fall, to triumph, to recreate life out of life! A wild angel had appeared to him, the angel of mortal youth and beauty, an envoy from the fair courts of life, to throw open before him in an instant of ecstasy the gates of all the ways of error and glory. [P. 172]

Then he goes up the beach away from the water and finds a sandy nook to lie down in, "that the peace and silence of the evening might still the riot of his blood":

> He felt above him the vast indifferent dome and the calm processes of the heavenly bodies; and the earth beneath him, the earth that had borne him, had taken him to her breast.

2. For Joyce's use of the term see Morris Beja, *Epiphany in the Modern Novel* (Seattle: University of Washington Press, 1971), pp. 71-111.

> He closed his eyes in the languor of sleep. His eyelids trembled as if they felt the vast cyclic movement of the earth and her watchers, trembled as if they felt the strange light of some new world. . . . A world, a glimmer, or a flower? Glimmering and trembling, trembling and unfolding, a breaking light, an opening flower, it spread in endless succession to itself, breaking in full crimson and unfolding and fading to palest rose, leaf by leaf and wave of light by wave of light, flooding all the heavens with its soft flushes, every flush deeper than other.

With this Stephen dozes off for a while, then later gets up and starts for home, feeling quietly joyful. This is the end of Part IV of the book. Part V begins with a sharp drop in tone — watery tea, pawn tickets, domestic squabbling in the kitchen of the Dedalus household, and screeching from a nuns' madhouse. The anticlimax is significant; it is only by a slow rhythm of rise and fall, insight and forgetfulness, integration and disintegration that genuine progress toward wholeness takes place in Joyce's world, and although the movement toward that goal may be more or less steady, the goal itself never is attained — after every climax comes another letdown, and the cycle begins again. This is true in both *Portrait* and *Ulysses*.

Nevertheless, even if it is not final, Stephen's insight in this passage is genuine insight; the meaning it glimpses is the meaning at "the wild heart of life." What is most significant in it is the way in which it brings opposites together in seemingly paradoxical conjunctions: "error and glory," the Holy Spirit and Lucifer, "Heavenly God" and "profane joy." Joyce has reminded us only shortly before this scene of the traditional associations of his central images of dove and fire: ". . . the unseen Paraclete, Whose symbols were a dove and a mighty wind . . . the eternal, mysterious secret Being to Whom, as God, the priests offered up mass once a year, robed in the scarlet of the tongues of fire" (p. 149). In the present scene, however, the image is transformed: the dove is no longer white, as it traditionally is in the iconography of the Church, nor is it a symbol of an unseen spiritual being. In the form of the "strange and beautiful seabird" Stephen sees wading along the strand, it is fully physical and visible, and its dark color associates it with the flesh and even with what, from the point of view of the Church, would be called sin. It is not superhuman and sexless, but a girl with "long fair hair"; and it is not eternal, but has "mortal beauty" as part of its wonder. Changed as it is, however, this dark-plumaged dove still brings with it an inspiriting, transfiguring fire, the "faint flame" that trembles on her cheeks and sets Stephen's cheeks also aflame and his body aglow and gives rise to his soul's shout of joy.

It is no accident that Stephen should express his joy in the words, "Heavenly God!" — he has been steeped, after all, in a religious tradition — but what the words mean in this new context of "profane joy" is a question of some subtlety.

The key word here is "profane." As Joyce uses it, it has several meanings, but in none of them is it the opposite of "sacred" as I have been using the term in this book. On the contrary, the phrase "Heavenly God!" expresses precisely that sense of the numinous described by Rudolf Otto, the sense of a mystery both awesome and fascinating, charged with intrinsic value. One of Joyce's meanings for profane is related directly to its Latin root, "*pro fanum,*" outside the temple. Stephen had shortly before this scene chosen a secular vocation, though he did not at the time know exactly what that would be, and he was in the process of leaving not only the Church, but also the Christian religion. Stephen, like Joyce, had several reasons for rejecting his ancestral religion. One was that in the form the religion had taken in the Irish

Catholic Church it seemed a system of external authority designed to suppress any original, or even individual, thought; to become, as he later formulated it, "a priest of eternal imagination, transmuting the daily bread of experience into the radiant body of everliving life" (p. 221), he would have to break free from all such constrictions. One of the symbols of the Church's suppressive authority during the earlier part of the book was a negative form of bird imagery: the eagles, for example, that his staunchly Catholic aunt, Dante, had said would come and "pull out his eyes" if he did not "apologise" (p. 8) for some childhood offense; and later, in his school years, his friend and rival, Heron, who "had a bird's face as well as a bird's name" (p. 76) and who once beat him with a cane in an attempt to make him "admit" that Byron, whom Stephen preferred over the more acceptable Tennyson, was "a heretic and immoral too" (p. 81). And then, of course, there was the dove as symbol of the transcendent Godhead, whose authority, to conventional thinking, was immanent only in the hierarchy of the Church, not at all a principle of inner authority for the individual. The transformation of the bird image into the "darkplumaged dove" of Stephen's vision, representing the intrinsic value of the secular, marks an important step in his developing freedom to do his own thinking and pursue his own values.

Another implication of the word "profane," in Joyce's use of it, is that it is opposed to any form of supernaturalism. One of Joyce's greatest concerns throughout his life was the idea of unity of being, and he saw the Church's way of dividing being into natural and supernatural as inherently opposed to this. From his point of view, the Church had an unbalanced vision; it failed to value nature and the flesh, and in fact reduced them to near worthlessness in comparison with the transcendence of God and with spiritual values. It is significant that, as the book describes it, "the figure of woman as she appears in the liturgy of the Church" is "a white-robed figure, small and slender as a boy . . ." (p. 244) — white, the color of spirit and of innocence conceived as the opposite of carnal experience, and sexless. The dark plumage of Stephen's dove signifies the break with this system of values, as do also the crimson and rose of the flower he sees subsequently in his revery. In fact, both images, the dove and the flower, an adaptation of Dante's heavenly rose, are symbols of the unity of being — true unity, not just a union of flesh and spirit as heterogeneous elements yoked together, but the two conceived as merely different aspects of a single reality.

It is no accident that this idea of flesh and spirit as aspects of a single reality should be reminiscent of the thought of Giordano Bruno. "His gods were Ibsen, Giordano Bruno and Julian the Apostate," Joyce's friend Louis Gillet wrote of him, and in fact both Ibsen and Bruno were sources for Joyce's attempt to work out a unitary vision.[3] Bruno, whose thought was briefly sketched in the second chapter, offered the attractive hypothesis of a monistic conception of nature as an organic whole animated from within, an incarnate world-soul that is matter considered from outside, spirit considered from inside. He also offered what was perhaps an equally attractive ambiguity: the universe is a single whole, but at the same time it is composed of a vast number of monads, each of which contains implicitly a reflection of all others and of the whole. Nature, seen in this light, could be both a pantheistic, fully immanent version of the "heavenly God" of Stephen's exclamation,

3. Quoted in Frances M. Bolderef, *Hermes to his Son Thoth: Being Joyce's Use of Giordano Bruno in Finnegans Wake* (Woodward, Pennsylvania: Classic Non-fiction Library, 1968), p. 39.

"the obscure soul of the world, a darkness shining in brightness," as *Ulysses* calls it,[4] and a network of fully individual consciousnesses. Stephen's famous aesthetic theory, if it is read in connection with these complementary aspects of Bruno's thought, appears in some respects more closely related to Bruno's way of conceiving the structure of being than to that of Aquinas, from whom it takes its terminology: *integritas,* the wholeness of the aesthetic image, which serves as an epiphany or microcosm of the wholeness of being; *consonantia,* its aspect as "complex, multiple, divisible, separable, made up of its parts, the result of its parts and their sum, harmonious" (p. 212); and *claritas,* the "radiance" of understanding in which this simultaneous wholeness and harmony are apprehended in "the luminous silent stasis of esthetic pleasure" (p. 213).

Ibsen, the "Christianier . . . sage," as Joyce called him in *Finnegans Wake,*[5] had an interest in the reconciliation of opposites even more closely parallel to Joyce's than was Bruno's, chiefly because it was more tentative and expressed a greater sense of the tension between spiritual and fleshly values. Although Joyce's thought had strong pantheistic tendencies, it also tended strongly toward philosophical skepticism, and Joyce consequently tended to feel more at home with tension than with resolution. Joyce learned Norwegian to be able to read Ibsen in the original and in 1901 even wrote him a letter in Norwegian.[6] In Joyce's conception of drama as outlined in his

4. New York: Vintage Books, 1961, p. 28. Subsequent references in parentheses.

5. New York: Viking Press, 1958, p. 53.

6. Letter to Ibsen, March, 1901, *Letters of James Joyce,* ed. Stuart Gilbert (New York: Viking Press, 1957), p. 51. See also Richard Ellmann, *James Joyce* (New York: Oxford University Press, 1965), pp. 89-91. The most extensive study of the influence of Ibsen on Joyce is Bjørn J. Tysdahl, *Joyce and Ibsen: A Study in Literary Influence* (Oslo: Norwegian Universities Press, 1968).

early critical writings, he considered the essential subject matter of drama to be "strife, evolution, movement,"[7] a conception that applied well to Ibsen's portrayal of the conflicting forces of energy and control, pagan and Christian, in all of his plays after *Emperor and Galilean,* alluded to in *Finnegans Wake* as "quaysirs and galleyliers"[8] (*Kejser og Galilæer,* in Norwegian). Joyce probably found Ibsen's basic conflict closely parallel to that which he knew in his own life, and it is not surprising that he found Julian the Apostate a sympathetic figure; Joyce, too, was in search of a Third Kingdom that would unite those opposing forces as Ibsen's Julian wished to.

To speak of these opposing forces in Ibsen's terms as pagan and Christian would not, however, be adequate to the special shape their relationship took in Joyce's thought. Like that of his Stephen as Cranly describes him near the end of *Portrait* (p. 240), Joyce's mind was "super-saturated" with the religion in which he disbelieved, and his idea of the opposing forces that made up human life was given a special character by his persisting Catholic sensibility; in particular, he tended to associate flesh with sin in his imagination and to present the problem of the union of spirit and nature in imagery that made it a union of spirit and sin. It is significant that in the wading girl scene Stephen thinks of the call of "the life that had cried to him" as a call "to live, to err, to fall" (p. 172). Meditating earlier on his decision not to go into the priesthood he thought in similar terms of a necessary "fall" into the world:

> The wisdom of the priest's appeal did not touch him to the quick. He was destined to learn his own wisdom apart from

7. *The Critical Writings,* ed. Ellsworth Mason and Richard Ellmann (London: Faber and Faber, 1959), p. 40.

8. *Finnegans Wake,* p. 540.

others or to learn the wisdom of others himself wandering among the snares of the world.

The snares of the world were its ways of sin. He would fall. He had not yet fallen but he would fall silently, in an instant. [P. 162]

This recalls the earlier image of the fall of Lucifer used by the preacher during the school retreat:

Lucifer . . . was a son of the morning, a radiant and mighty angel; yet he fell. . . . What his sin was we cannot say. Theologians consider that it was the sin of pride, the sinful thought conceived in an instant: *non serviam, I will not serve.* [P. 117]

For Stephen to take on the wings of Lucifer and to will his own fall is to declare his individuality and his acceptance of his worldly vocation. The "wild angel" that appears to Stephen in the wading girl scene "to throw open before him in an instant of ecstasy the gates of all the ways of error and glory" (p. 172) is a compendium of several winged figures: Lucifer; Daedalus, the "fabulous artificer. . . . a hawklike man flying sunward above the sea" (p. 169), Stephen's namesake and model; the dark-plumaged dove, the incarnate soul of the world; and Stephen himself in his new life as rebel and artist.

The moment of his acceptance of this calling is Stephen's silent fall into life, the world, and the flesh, his rebirth as what *Finnegans Wake* calls a "foenix culprit."[9] That the fire of this new Pentecost that sets aglow the cheeks of the girl and Stephen is the fire of sin as well as of inspiration is suggested by its foreshadowing in the earlier scene in which Stephen, after being moved to repentance by the retreat, perceives his sinfulness in terms of imagery that, although he probably had no appreciation of it at the time, is definitely pentecostal:

9. Ibid., p. 23.

> His blood began to murmur in his veins, murmuring like a sinful city summoned from its sleep to hear its doom. Little flakes of fire fell and powdery ashes fell softly, alighting on the houses of men. . . . Little fiery flakes fell and touched him at all points, shameful thoughts, shameful words, shameful acts. Shame covered him wholly like fine glowing ashes falling continually. [P. 142]

At the moment of his confession and resubmission to the Church the vivifying fire is nearly smothered in the ashes of shame, but it does not become extinguished altogether, even after he goes on to a routine of super-piety. In fact it is this very fire that maintains the necessary balance in his life between spiritual aspiration and his rootedness in nature and eventually makes possible his fortunate fall. His spirituality following the confession rapidly becomes a kind of egoistic parody of itself as, driving his soul daily "through an increasing circle of works of supererogation" (p. 147), he feels "his soul in devotion pressing like fingers the keyboard of a great cash register" and sees "the amount of his purchase start forth immediately in heaven"(p. 148). During this period his mind is loveless, lucid, and indifferent except for moments when he feels "a subtle, dark and murmurous presence penetrate his being and fire him with a brief iniquitous lust" (p. 149). This, it seemed to him at the time, "was the only love . . . his soul would harbour." His problem there, however, was only that his attempt at total sublimation was stifling the fire of life, but when he finally accepts his calling into "the ways of error and glory" it flames forth to transfigure both Stephen and his vision of the world. As Joyce later put it in *Finnegans Wake,* "felixed is who culpas does."[10]

The difficulty with the interpretation of life that divides it into distinct realms of spirit and flesh is that the result-

10. Ibid., p. 246.

ing conflict between them leads to an inner, psychological split between cold lucidity in the life of the mind and dark fire in the life of the body. This division affected the entire character of Stephen's relation to women prior to the vision of the wading girl. During his adolescence, the figure of woman split for him into prostitutes on the one hand and the sublimated figures of mother and Virgin on the other. As his body followed its "devious course" through the streets in pursuit of its fleshly satisfaction, "circling always nearer and nearer in a tremor of fear and joy" (p. 102), he felt "the vast cycle of starry life" (p. 103) carrying his mind along in another circle like that of "the barren shell of the moon" (p. 96). And even in the midst of this carnality "the glories of Mary held his soul captive" (p. 104). In the scene with the wading girl, however, he catches a glimpse of the possibility of a love of woman that would not force her into this kind of false division, but would see her accept "the worship of his eyes . . . without shame or wantonness" (p. 171). The image of this girl's foot stirring the water transforms the sea from something cold and "infrahuman" that "his flesh dreaded" (p. 167) into a symbol of the vital union of flesh and spirit, and it transforms the image of the circle from negative to positive, from the inhuman cycles of moon and stars into a "vast cyclic movement of the earth" and into the crimson and rose flower.

And yet, this is only a vision. It is a turning point in Stephen's life, but a turning point primarily in terms of intention. Stephen sees what he is called to live for, and he chooses to dedicate himself to it, but he has not yet become the life he envisions. He sees it in its sacred immanence, but as a glimmer and a potentiality, a goal seen from afar. It is an epiphany in the sense of a revelation of meaning, but not yet in the other important sense in which the term is used in tradition, that of an incarnation, the embodiment of that meaning in a living person. Although the boys Stephen sees swimming on his way to the revelation banteringly greet him as "Stephanos Dedalos! Bous Stephanoumenos!" (p. 168) ("bullock crowned with a wreath"), he is neither the wearer of a crown, nor exactly a Daedalus. Rather he is more of an Icarus, as their cries, "One! Two! . . . Look out! O, Cripes, I'm drownded!", punctuating his revery of the hawklike man flying sunward obliquely suggest, and as his later reflections in *Ulysses* on the Pyrrhic victory of his sojourn in Paris (pp. 42, 210) confirm. Joyce's true king and hero, the incarnation of the "darkness shining in brightness," is not Stephen, but Leopold Bloom.

The advent of Bloom in *Ulysses* is foreshadowed at the very end of *Portrait* as Stephen's friend Cranly warns him of the loneliness that will be Stephen's destiny in the exile from Church and home he has chosen: "Not only to be separate from all others but to have not even one friend. . . . And not to have any one person . . . who would be more than a friend, more even than the noblest and truest friend a man ever had" (p. 247). Stephen interprets these words as a reference to the desire of Cranly himself for such a friend in Stephen, and of course he is correct, but in the light of the book's sequel they also foreshadow something more; neither Stephen nor Cranly could at that point have any suspicion that not long afterward, on June 16, 1904, Stephen was to meet just such a person.

But Joyce could. Even as he was finishing *Portrait of the Artist* in 1914, Joyce was already at work on its sequel, *Ulysses*.[11] The story seems to have been based on an actual meeting with such a man in Joyce's life on the night of June 22, 1904. Joyce was hurt in a street brawl,

11. Richard Ellmann, *Ulysses on the Liffey* (New York: Oxford University Press, 1972), pp. xv-xvi.

and according to Richard Ellmann, "it was probably on this occasion that he was dusted off and taken home by a man named Alfred Hunter," who was rumored to be Jewish and to have an unfaithful wife.[12] Joyce was deeply moved by this kindness from a man he hardly knew and who seemed to be quite different from him in background and temperament. In September 1906 he wrote his brother, Stanislaus, that he was planning a story about Hunter, but in February 1907 wrote again that he had never got any further with it than the title, "Ulysses."

When the story became the novel it was about a day in the life of a man like Hunter, Leopold Bloom, who helps Stephen Dedalus in just this manner. Bloom is by ancestry a Jew, though he has been baptized a Christian and practices no religion at all, and he has an unfaithful wife, Molly, whose lover is her concert agent, Blazes Boylan. The story is both simple and impossible to summarize; the dramatic incidents are few, but the detail, including significant detail, of the day is enormous. Basically what happens is that both Stephen and Bloom, separately, get up around eight o'clock, eat breakfast, and in a rather desultory way go about their respective businesses — Stephen as a schoolteacher, and Bloom as an advertising canvasser. During the day their paths cross several times — as Bloom is on his way to the funeral of a friend, Paddy Dignam, at the newspaper office, and in the National Library — until finally they converge in the interns' lounge of the maternity hospital. From there the two proceed to the red light district, where Bloom picks up Stephen after he is knocked down in a fight, then takes him to a cabman's shelter for a cup of coffee, and finally home to Bloom's for a cup of cocoa, after which Stephen leaves and Bloom goes up to bed.

12. *Letters of James Joyce,* vol. 2, ed. Richard Ellmann (New York: Viking Press, 1966), pp. 168, 209.

As the parallel and ultimately converging paths of Stephen and Bloom indicate, the over-all pattern of the book is the gradual evolution of contrary qualities toward a *coincidentia oppositorum.* This idea Joyce derived from Giordano Bruno, who in turn adapted it from Nicholas Cusanus, but with the added idea, that was entirely Bruno's, that *coincidentia oppositorum* was not only an ontological principle, but an ethical one as well.[13] By this Bruno meant that the attraction of opposites was the basis of all social and political relationships. Joyce applied Bruno's ethical adaptation of this idea to an interpretation of human life on both interpersonal and personal levels. On the interpersonal level, for example, Bloom and Stephen represent a variety of contrary qualities: Hebraic and Hellenic, practical and theoretical, scientific and artistic, and so on — even stocky and lean. Bloom may seem an ambiguous figure to a one-sided world — Mulligan, in the Circe episode, for examples, calls him "bisexually abnormal" (p. 493) and says that "ambidexterity is also latent." On the personal level, however, the "cultured allroundman" (p. 235) is actually, even if in the imperfect manner characteristic of all natural reality as Joyce conceives it, an incarnate *coincidentia oppositorum,* as is evidenced by "the surety of the sense of touch in his firm full masculine feminine passive active hand" (p. 674).

According to Bruno, because nature is always striving toward balance and completeness, there is a greater attraction between two contraries than between like and like. The operation of this principle is evident in Stephen's life. Various people try to draw Stephen into relationships — one might even call them collusions — designed to

13. Arthur D. Imerti, introduction to Bruno, *The Expulsion of the Triumphant Beast* (New Brunswick, N.J.: Rutgers University Press, 1964), pp. 35-36.

lead to one kind of fulfillment or another, but Stephen instinctively evades them all. He was doing this even in *Portrait,* where he refused to be drawn into political and cultural nationalism, the world peace movement, and the outward conformism to the Catholic religion that Cranly urged on him. The first chapter of *Ulysses* shows Stephen's roommate in the Martello tower they share, "stately, plump Buck Mulligan" (pp. 2-3), urging a similar outward conformism on Stephen as well as trying to draw him into a project to revive a "new paganism": ". . . if you and I could only work together we might do something for the island. Hellenise it" (p. 7). Mulligan later relates this to the thought of Nietzsche: "I'm the *Uebermensch.* Toothless Kinch [his nickname for Stephen] and I, the supermen" (p. 22). Stephen is not attracted to this, however, any more than Joyce was. Although Joyce had once signed his name "James Overman" to a card and had lived in a similar tower with the original of Mulligan, Oliver St. John Gogarty, who advocated a new paganism with Nietzsche as its principal prophet, he no longer found Nietzsche of much interest by the time he was working on *Ulysses:* in 1913 he tried to divert one of his pupils in Trieste from Nietzsche to Aquinas, whom Joyce said he read in Latin, a page a day, for the sharpness of his reasoning.[14]

Stephen does not need Hellenizing; he already tends to be overbalanced in the direction of the qualities one associates with Greek culture, as his name suggests — "Your absurd name, an ancient Greek," says Mulligan (p. 3). His Aristotelianism and Thomism are both in the Hellenic tradition of analytical reason. Mulligan also calls Stephen "Kinch, the knifeblade" (p. 4), and in the form in which it has taken shape Stephen's mind does

14. Ellmann, *James Joyce,* pp. 168, 178, 352-53.

tend to be more an instrument for dissection than for synthesis. To bring the elements of life together would require qualities of mind different from those Mulligan either preaches or exemplifies. Mulligan would reconcile reason with religion, for example, by fakery: "You wouldn't kneel down to pray for your mother on her deathbed when she asked you. Why? Because you have the cursed jesuit strain in you, only it's injected the wrong way. To me it's all a mockery and beastly" (p. 8). Mulligan solves the problem by an irreverent, superficial conformism; Stephen, in contrast, is bound by his temperament to live profoundly and honestly, and in spite of his rejection of traditional religion, reverently. When Haines, their English guest in the tower, says he supposes Stephen is not "a believer in the narrow sense of the word," Stephen answers, "There's only one sense of the word, it seems to me" (p. 19); Stephen is not any longer a believer, but he knows the word means something, and he is not one to smooth over differences by treating it as if it did not. Stephen has all the Hellenic intellect he needs, and Mulligan's Hellenism, like everything else that comes from him, is mostly hot air.

The intellectual clarity associated with the Hellenic tradition has a definite value in this work — the issues that matter must be sharply defined and not blurred, as people like Mulligan and Haines would blur them — but it also has its limitations. The "obscure soul of the world" is "a darkness shining in brightness which brightness [cannot] comprehend" (p. 28), and the brightness that cannot comprehed it is precisely the analytic intellect. What the darkness is waits to be revealed in the dark figure of Bloom, and when it is known, it is known in a non-discursive, intuitive way — in Stephen's grateful, if diffident recognition of an act of love.

The real significance of what Mulligan says in the first chapter is completely unknown to him, and also to Stephen, but to the attentive reader — at least to one who has read the book before — there is a great deal of meaning in what at first might seem only joking and horseplay. Mulligan says, for example, that he thinks his name "has a Hellenic ring": ". . . Malachi Mulligan, two dactyls" (p. 4); he chooses to ignore the fact that Malachi was a Hebrew prophet, and perhaps does not know that it was Malachi who, in the last lines of the Hebrew Bible, predicted the return of Elijah: "Look, I will send you the prophet Elijah before the great and terrible day of the Lord comes. He will reconcile fathers to sons and sons to fathers, lest I come and put the land under a ban to destroy it" (Mal. 4:5-6). Although he has no idea of the implications of what he is doing, it is just such a prophecy Malachi Mulligan is making in the mock mass with which he opens the book: *"Introibo ad altare Dei. . . .* For this, O dearly beloved, is the genuine Christine: body and soul and blood and ouns. Slow music, please. Shut your eyes, gents. One moment. A little trouble about those white corpuscles" (p. 3).

In Catholic tradition the mass is, among other things, a kind of drama moving toward an epiphany, the manifestation of and assimilation to a *coincidentia oppositorum* — God and nature, spirit and flesh — in the Eucharist. *Ulysses* as a whole is a similar drama moving toward a similar epiphany and communion. Joyce himself probably had this in mind when he began the book this way; he once told his brother — speaking specifically of his poems, though the observation would apply to his art generally:

> Don't you think . . . there is a certain resemblance between the mystery of the Mass and what I am trying to do? I mean

> that I am trying . . . to give people some kind of intellectual pleasure or spiritual enjoyment by converting the bread of everyday life into something that has a permanent artistic life of its own . . . for their mental, moral, and spiritual uplift. . . .[15]

In the case of *Ulysses* the Host of the mass will be Bloom, who is associated throughout with eucharistic imagery. Mulligan's reference to his difficulty with the white corpuscles indicates the central miracle has not yet taken place. He is speaking, evidently, of the soap in the shaving bowl. Soap is a cleansing agent, as are the white corpuscles in the blood, which fight disease; it is an appropriate parallel to the "Lamb of God, which takes away the sins of the world," but Mulligan's is not the right soap. The right soap is Bloom, who is addressed as "Flower of the Bath" and "Wandering Soap" in the litany of the Daughters of Erin in the Circe episode (p. 498). When the "masculine feminine passive active" Bloom becomes manifest, he will be "the genuine Christine," incarnate in all his fleshly imperfection as "body and soul and blood and ouns." But Mulligan is no true priest to this Host, only his harbinger, and an unwitting one at that.

That Mulligan is unwitting of the deeper pattern of meaning embedded in the events of this day is not, however, a deficiency peculiar to him; it is a quality he shares with all of the other characters in the book, including Bloom himself. At one point in Bloom's day, while he is eating lunch, he thinks of the word "parallax" and asks himself what it means (p. 154). He has no idea, except that it may be related in meaning to "parallel," but he continues to wonder about it occasionally as the day goes on. Parallax is one of the important informing principles of the book, and that Bloom does not know what it means

15. Stanislaus Joyce, *My Brother's Keeper: James Joyce's Early Years* (New York, 1958), pp. 103-4, quoted in Beja, *Epiphany*, p. 71.

is an example of the pervasiveness of the problem the word refers to, the inability of an observer to see accurately something parallel to his line of sight, especially if, as in photography, he is too close to it, or if, as in astronomy, his own position is moving in relation to it. Stephen, Bloom, Mulligan, and the rest of the people of Dublin are lost most of the time in a universe of relativity in which it is difficult to see anything straight, and even when a person embodies, as Bloom does, something as close to an absolute value as the universe of this book has to offer, it is difficult for him to see it because he is too close to it. Bloom is a living parallel to Ulysses, as the title of the book indicates, and also to other important mythic figures or images, such as Moses, Elijah, Christ, and the Eucharist, but he is never aware of it, nor is anyone else, except for Stephen in a brief moment of vision the following night. As the words of a song from the pantomime of Turko the Terrible, another parallel and foreshadowing of Bloom, say: "I am the boy / That can enjoy / Invisibility" (p. 10). It is not always exactly enjoyable, but most of the time it is true invisibility.

One reason it is not always pleasant for Bloom is that it often proceeds from a blindness that is distinctly hostile. An example is the anti-Semitism of many of the characters in the novel. Haines, whose dream of a black panther the night before is another prefiguration of Bloom, hates Jews; he wanted to shoot the panther in his sleep, and if he knew the other "dark . . . pard," Bloom (p. 218), he would probably feel similarly hostile to him. One of the more violent scenes of the book occurs in the Cyclops episode when Bloom reminds "the citizen," who is both anti-Semitic and staunchly Catholic in a debased, nationalistic way, that Christ was a Jew like Bloom; "the citizen" shouts, "By Jesus, I'll crucify him so I will" (p. 342), and chases him out of the pub. Even a relatively more serious Christian, such as Mr. Deasy, the headmaster of the school Stephen teaches at, says, "They sinned against the light. . . . And you can see the darkness in their eyes" (p. 34).

The scene with Mr. Deasy is an especially interesting one for the complexity of its irony and for the way in which, without either Stephen or Mr. Deasy understanding the implications of their words, it points toward the central meaning of the book.

> — History, Stephen said, is a nightmare from which I am trying to awake.
>
> From the playfield the boys raised a shout. A whirring whistle: goal. What if the nightmare gave you a back kick?
>
> — The ways of the Creator are not our ways, Mr. Deasy said. All history moves toward one great goal, the manifestation of God.
>
> Stephen jerked his thumb towards the window, saying:
>
> — That is God.
>
> Hooray! Ay! Whrrwhee!
>
> — What? Mr. Deasy asked.
>
> — A shout in the street, Stephen answered, shrugging his shoulders. [P. 34]

Ironically both are correct, though neither understands in what way. Mr. Deasy is thinking of the Augustinian idea of history as guided by the primarily transcendent God of Christianity toward a definite terminus of time. Stephen no longer believes in that God and implies that if the word God had actual reference at all it would have to be to the natural life around them, since that is the only reality there is. Stephen is wrong, however, in thinking that history is simply a chaos; it *is* moving toward the manifestation of God, but not Mr. Deasy's God — rather the book's immanent God, "the obscure soul of the world." And the vehicle of this manifestation is already wandering the streets, as they talk, on his way to a bath house. Even the reference to "a shout in the street" is obliquely prophetic when read in the light of a later incident that makes Bloom into, if not exactly a shout, then a noise in the street: about 1:00 A.M. that night when Bloom and Stephen are sitting in the cabman's shelter, Bloom notices that his name has been incorrectly recorded by the newspaper, in a list of mourners at Paddy Dignam's funeral, as "L. Boom" (p. 647).

After Stephen leaves the school he goes for a walk along Sandymount strand in the direction of the Pigeonhouse, Dublin's light and power station. But whereas his walk along the beach in *Portrait* — a different beach, about a mile away — had led to an epiphany of meaning that had seemed to make his life take shape, his rumination on this walk courses through a Protean wilderness of fragments from his readings and of random present reflections and feelings. For Stephen none of it adds up to anything at all, but for the reader the chapter offers foreshadowings of developments to come and some insights into the conflicting elements that make up Stephen's mind. Stephen begins the chapter thinking about Aristotle, the master of those who know — *"maestro di color che sanno"* (p. 37) — which reflects his concern with rational knowledge of objective reality, the "ineluctable modality of the visible" his opening words refer to, but as his meditation moves on it tends increasingly to touch on the subjective and nonrational. Stephen is very distrustful of mysticism, as his opposition to AE and the theosophical circle in the ninth chapter, the Scylla and Charybdis episode, indicates, but a balanced vision of life requires the ability to thread one's way, as Bloom does symbolically in that episode, between the rock of rationalism and the whirlpool of mysticism. In public controversy, Stephen tends to veer toward Scylla, even to the point of virtually becoming himself the monster on the rock, a Thomistic "bulldog of Aquin" (p. 208), but his rumination in the third chapter shows that his interests have actually been more varied and that his mind contains at least the elements necessary for wholeness. He has read, for example, the Kabbalah and remembers its "Adam Kadmon" (p. 38), the primordial complete man, a version of *coincidentia oppositorum,* and he has read the mystical writings of Traherne — an anachronism of Joyce's, by the way, since Traherne's *Centuries of Meditation,* to which Stephen's "corn, orient and immortal" (p. 38) is an allusion, was not published until 1908.

He has also read what he calls "the fading prophecies of Joachim Abbas" (p. 39). This would be an allusion to the *Vaticinia de summis pontificibus,* a collection of prophecies concerning the supreme pontiffs compiled about 1304 and attributed to Joachim of Fiore[16] — a book that Joyce spent October 22 and 23, 1902, reading in the library Stephen refers to, Marsh's Library, near St. Patrick's Cathedral.[17] Joyce evidently found Joachimite thought of some interest since he copied out passages from the book and a few years later wrote his brother, Stanislaus, from Rome asking him to send him "the Latin quotations from the prophecies of Abbot Joachim of Flora."[18] That Joyce spoke of the author as Joachim himself, suggests he did not realize it was a spurious work, but that is hardly surprising, since scholars of Joachim, even at the present time, have not yet completely established a canon of his authentic writings.[19] Nor is it especially important, since the main significance of the allusion has to do with the general Joachimite expectation of the new age of the Spirit, rather than with any particular details of prophecy. From Stephen's point of view

16. See Reeves, *Prophecy in the Later Middle Ages,* pp. 96, 523.

17. Robert M. Adams, *Surface and Symbol: The Consistency of James Joyce's* Ulysses (New York: Oxford University Press, 1962), p. 125.

18. Letter of ca. August 12, 1906, *Letters* 2:148.

19. See Reeves, *Prophecy,* p. 511.

Joachimism was a false hope, now fading. The immanent God never arrived and never will; instead of the fire of true inspiration, all that came was the misguided enthusiasm that "laid fire" to the "brains" of "the hundred-headed rabble of the cathedral close" (pp. 39-40). Stephen is correct that Joachim's prophecies have faded; few people in the Dublin of Ulysses would even remember them, and what mysticism there is tends to be the Charybdian kind of the theosophists. He does not realize, however, that for him that day, though in a considerably changed form — secularized, and on an individual rather than a worldwide level — the prophecy of the advent of immanent Godhead is to be fulfilled in his meeting with one who will be both *dux* to Stephen and himself the embodiment of the Kingdom, and even a new Fiore or Flora: Leopold Bloom, known also as Henry Flower (p. 72), Senhor Enrique Flor (p. 321), and Don Poldo de la Flora (p. 78).

Various other thoughts Stephen has on his walk also foreshadow this meeting. He thinks, for example, of death — "the man that was drowned nine days ago off Maiden's rock" (p. 45), and "Full fathom five thy father lies" (p. 50) — and of transfiguration — "a seachange this, brown eyes saltblue" (p. 50) . He thinks of Moses, "tucked . . . safe among the bulrushes" (p. 45), and of Haines' dream of "a pard, a panther" (p. 47). And more importantly, he remembers his own dream: "Open hallway. Street of harlots. . . . Haroun al Raschid. . . . That man led me, spoke. I was not afraid. The melon he had he held against my face. Smiled: creamfruit smell. That was the rule, said. In. Come. Red carpet spread. You will see who" (p. 47). Haroun al Raschid, Caliph of Baghdad in the *Arabian Nights,* is supposed to have wandered incognito in the streets of his city. Bloom, too, is a kind of priest-king, as his association with the figure of the Messiah indicates, but he is incognito even to himself as he wanders through the streets of Dublin. He is also, like Moses, a potential prophet and leader, and, by association with Christ, one capable of raising Stephen from the dead, "Sunk though he be beneath the watery floor" (p. 50).

When we finally meet Bloom, in the fourth chapter, we find him dressed in black to go to Dignam's funeral, making him, like the Moorish and Jewish philosophers, Averroes and Moses Maimonides, whom Stephen thinks of at Mr. Deasy's, a man "dark . . . in mien and movement" (p. 29).

Balancing Stephen's Hellenic and intellectual tendencies, Bloom's stream of thought tends to run along lines more sensual and oriental: "Wander through awned streets. Turbaned faces going by. Dark caves of carpet shops, big man, Turko the terrible, seated crosslegged smoking a coiled pipe. Cries of sellers in the streets. Drink water scented with fennel, sherbet" (p. 57). Practically oriented and realistic, however, unlike the Charybdian "hermetic crowd" (p. 140), Bloom maintains a clear distinction in his mind between reality and fantasy: "Probably not a bit like it really. Kind of stuff you read . . ." (p. 57).

Later when he looks at the Zionist leaflet he picks up at Dlugacz's butchershop about Agendath Netaim, a redevelopment project in Palestine, with headquarters in Bleibtreustrasse ("Remain Faithful Street"), Berlin, he lets his mind run lovingly over images of "orangegroves and immense melon-fields," but manages to keep his balance, tempering the nostalgia of the displaced Israelite with practicality and tempering practicality with fidelity to the beauty of the ideal: "Nothing doing. Still an idea behind it. He looked at the cattle, blurred in the silver heat. Silvered powdered olivetrees. Quiet long days: pruning ripening" (p. 60). He also realizes that if such an idea were ever to become flesh, it could not happen through a return to the past — "No, not like that. A barren land, bare waste. . . . Sodom, Gomorrah, Edom. All dead names. A dead sea in a dead land, grey and old" (p. 61)[20] — and knows that renewal would have to begin at home, even humbly and realistically, as he later imagines, in his own backyard: "Make a summerhouse here. Scarlet runners. Virginia creepers. Want to manure the whole place over. . . . Reclaim the whole place" (p. 68). Balanced as always, he also remembers that real gardens "have their drawbacks," such as bees and flies.

A garden with drawbacks is the perfect metaphor for the universe Joyce constructs in this book: life is a garden of fruit and flowers, in which even the finest flowers, such as Bloom, have their plagues, such as Bloom's sexual weaknesses and his lack of a son, and such as the bees and flies, like Blazes Boylan, that the other flower, his wife, Molly, entices into the garden. And also like a garden, it is perpetually fading and perpetually renewing. As it is put in the Oxen of the Sun episode, "Agendath is a waste land" and "Netaim, the golden, is no more," but still "parallax stalks behind and goads" the beasts of the valley "onward to the dead sea . . . to drink, unslaked and with horrible gulpings, the salt somnolent inexhaustible flood" (p. 414). Above their heads as they drink, the starlike flower of the transfiguring ideal, even in this desert of profane secularity, is reborn: ". . . the equine portent grows again, magnified in the deserted heavens, nay to heaven's own magnitude till it looms, vast, over the house of Virgo. And, lo, wonder of metempsychosis, it is she, the everlasting bride, harbinger of the daystar, the bride, ever virgin."[21]

20. Edom is a mistake on Bloom's part, what Richard Ellmann calls a "Bloomism." See Ellmann, *Ulysses on the Liffey*, p. 36.

21. "Equine," which seems rather odd in this context, may be an allusion to Bruno's discussion of metempsychosis, in which he speaks of "equine" and "porcine" modes of existence; see Imerti in Bruno, *Expulsion*, p. 35.

The reborn ideal takes on many incarnations as it goes through its metempsychoses. In the passage just mentioned it is "Martha, thou lost one" and "Millicent, the young, the dear, the radiant" — Martha Clifford, the woman with whom he is carrying on a clandestine correspondence under the name of Henry Flower, and Milly, his daughter. It also takes on the forms of Molly, and of Bloom's son, Rudy, who, if he had lived, would now be eleven years old, and eventually also the form of Stephen.

That Rudy would now be eleven is significant, since the book makes the number eleven, two parallel ones, into a symbol of the rebirth of the lost son in a new parallel. Later in the day, Bloom notices an advertisement for Kino's 11 / — trousers (p. 153), and subsequently K 11 becomes a recurrent motif in Bloom's stream of thought; K is the eleventh letter of the alphabet, and K 11, therefore, suggests emphatic paralellism. Of course, the meaning of this would be rather dark even to Bloom, but the intuition he does have of its meaningfulness helps him to get through to the discovery of a new son in Stephen. It is significant that that night, during the Circe episode, in the midst of a "festivity" that Bloom calls "a sacrament," when he is asked a question about parallax, his answer is K 11 (pp. 488-89).

The theme of metempsychosis is connected with this. It is first introduced when Molly, who has run across the word in a book, asks Bloom what metempsychosis means (p. 64). Her mispronunciation of it as "met him pike hoses" (p. 154) reminds us of the K 11 trousers and connects both that and metempsychosis with another motif of rebirth from death and the restoration of a son, Reuben J. Dodd's recovery of his son, who after trying to drown himself in the Liffey — recalling Stephen's broodings on "Elsinore's tempting flood" (p. 44) — is pulled out by a boatman's pike "by the slack of the breeches" (p. 94).

Besides referring to transmigration of souls in the sense of parallels between one person and another, metempsychosis, in this book, also serves as a principle of the psychology of the individual. The rebirth of Rudy in Stephen will also be a spiritual rebirth for Stephen when he recognizes the quality of Bloom's kindness to him and affirms it as a sacred value. The idea of such rebirth is touched on in a thought that crosses Stephen's mind in the first chapter: "I am another now and yet the same" (p. 11). He is a different person, he says, from the boy who carried the incense boat in the school chapel at Clongowes, and yet the same; and that night in the cabman's shelter when he mumbles, "*Christus* or Bloom his name is" (p. 643), he will be still another, and yet the same.

Metempsychosis was a doctrine of the Pythagoreans that was revived in the renaissance by Giordano Bruno. Connecting it with the idea of *coincidentia oppositorum,* Bruno made it a principle of evolution: all beings would pass through a succession of incarnations, gradually integrating all contrary qualities into a harmony.[22] Something like this happens in *Ulysses,* at least for those who, like Stephen, are evolving — though it happens within an individual life, not in a literal transmigration of souls in successive lifetimes. Joyce derived a lot of ideas from Bruno, but he used them as devices for the construction of his books, not as articles of belief. In fact it is difficult to determine that Joyce actually "believed" anything in the sense of affirmation as a fact. His affirmations tend, rather, to be of values. Stephen makes progress toward a clearer understanding of values, and this is the kind of evolution that matters to Joyce.

To see how the supreme value takes shape, and how the various transformations or metempsychoses about to happen are prepared, let us return to Bloom and follow

22. Ibid., pp. 35-36.

him through his day. At 10:00 A.M. he sets out from home for the bath. On his way he passes by a church, All Hallows, where a mass is taking place. Although he has been outwardly Christianized, Bloom considers religion a kind of narcotic and does not understand very well what is going on as the priest distributes the communion wafers: ". . . are they in water," he asks (p. 80), when he sees the priest making the sign of the cross with the Host over the chalice, a gesture that looks to Bloom as if he is shaking water from it. The question prepares us for the moment shortly afterward when Bloom, having arrived at "the mosque of the baths," thinks to himself, "This is my body," as he watches the water in the tub rise around the "languid floating flower" of his penis (p. 86). The reference, which is an allusion — certainly on Joyce's part, perhaps on Bloom's — to the *"Hoc est enim corpus meum"* of the mass, might seem at first glance, as it did to many early readers of the book, simply to degrade the image of the Eucharist, but in fact, like most such allusions in Joyce, it works several ways. It does treat the traditional imagery of the sacred ironically, but it does so in part in order to purify it of the false solemnity associated with worship of the transcendent God Joyce had rejected and to render it serviceable in communicating a sense of the true sacred embodied in secular flesh, even all too human flesh like Bloom's. Far from attempting to expunge the sense of the sacred, Joyce was trying to revise both the concept of the sacred and the sensibility associated with it to make them adequate to what he considered its true form: incarnate immanence.

This becomes clearer when we consider another motif that associates Bloom with Christ. As Bloom is on his way to the bathhouse, he is accosted by an acquaintance, Bantam Lyons, who asks to see the racing news in Bloom's paper and mutters something about "Ascot. Gold cup"

(p. 85). Bloom tells him he can have the paper, as he was about to throw it away. Lyons thinks Bloom is giving him a tip on a horse named Throwaway, a long shot for the race that afternoon, and goes off to place a bet on it. As the motif of the throwaway develops it becomes associated with Christ as "the stone which the builders rejected" (Mark 12:10, an allusion to Ps. 118:22), the Messiah rejected by the conventional because he was not recognizable in terms of the religion of his time. Later, as Bloom is on his way to lunch, a young man on the street places another kind of "throwaway" (p. 151), a handbill, in Bloom's hand. When he looks at it he sees the first four letters and thinks that perhaps the sheet has his name on it: "Bloo . . . Me? No. Blood of the lamb. . . . Elijah is coming." The sheet is an advertisement for a revival. Bloom crumples it up a few moments later and drops it into the river. The prophecy of the future coming of Elijah, of course, was connected for the ancient Hebrews with the expectation of the Messiah, and Bloom and the throwaway sheet are linked by it. Bloom gives the subject no special further thought, but during the Wandering Rocks episode as various Dubliners meander through the city, the throwaway Elijah is mentioned several times (pp. 227, 240, 249) as drifting down the river and out into the bay "amid an archipelago of corks," like Bloom, "the new Messiah for Ireland" (p. 337), wandering unrecognized through the city.

The throwaway theme culminates in the Cyclops episode, when Bloom, not understanding what is going on, has a run in with a group of Dubliners in a pub who have heard about the supposed tip on Throwaway, who won the race at twenty to one odds, and think that Bloom is too stingy to treat them to a drink with his winnings. The amosphere of the entire scene is hostile, even before they start thinking about the money he is supposed to have made on the race. For one thing, in a manner typical of the average Dubliner in this book, they are anti-Semitic. Earlier in the day Bloom had had to endure the anti-Semitism of his fellow mourners at the funeral (pp. 92-93, for example), and in this scene he has to pretend not to hear when "the citizen" says of the Jews, "Those are nice things . . . coming over here to Ireland filling the country with bugs" (p. 323). Also they distrust him because of his sense of balance in discussion, his awareness that there are two sides to a question: the narrator of the episode, one of the members of the group, speaks contemptuously of "Bloom with his *but don't you see?* and *but on the other hand*" (p. 306).

The narrator also refers to him as "old cod's eye" (p. 315), linking him with the image of the fish, a traditional iconographic emblem of Christ. This was prepared for in the preceding chapter when Bloom was associated with a fish sandwich under a glass bell: ". . . on a bier of bread one last, one lonely, last sardine of summer. Bloom alone" (p. 289).

In the midst of all of this, Bloom has the temerity, and also the courage, to speak against persecution and hatred, and to say that the supreme value in life is love:

> That's not life for men and women, insult and hatred. And everybody knows that it's the very opposite of that that is really life.
>
> — What? says Alf.
>
> — Love, says Bloom. I mean the opposite of hatred. [P. 333]

In a book in which even the few who live and think deeply, like Stephen, tend to be cagey and "noncommital" (p. 643) about what matters most, this is a dramatic affirmation.

As one might expect, it does nothing to increase Bloom's standing with the group. When he steps outside for a minute, they think "he's gone to gather in the shekels" on Throwaway, and one says, "He's a bloody dark horse himself" (p. 335). Then when he fails to stand them drinks on his return and continues defending the Jews, an argument that culminates with his "Christ was a Jew like me" (p. 342), the citizen chases him out of the pub, a living throwaway and Elijah as well:

And there came a voice out of heaven, calling: *Elijah! Elijah!* and he answered with a main cry: Abba! Adonai! And they beheld Him even Him, ben Bloom Elijah, amid clouds of angels ascend to the glory of the brightness at an angle of fortyfive degrees over Donohoe's in Little Green Street like a shot off a shovel. [P. 345]

In a characteristically Joycean way, this apotheosis of Bloom is followed by an anticlimax that places him very solidly on the earth: in the next chapter we find him masturbating by the sea as he flirts from a distance with a girl on the beach, Gerty MacDowell. Even here, though, the irony works two ways. Masturbating Bloom seems, in Nietzsche's phrase, "human, all too human," but as Bloom puts it himself, "Still you have to get rid of it someway" (p. 370), and his attitude afterward toward his, for lack of any other word, partner in the act is kindly: "Poor girl!", he thinks when he discovers she walks with a limp (p. 367). The flowerlike burst of the roman candle at Bloom's sexual climax — ". . . it was like a sigh of O! and everyone cried O! O! in raptures and it gushed out of it a stream of rain gold hairs threads . . ." (pp. 366-67) — may be a satirical parody of the prayers of the men on retreat in the nearby church, the Star of the Sea, to the Virgin as "mystical rose" (p. 356), but it is also a genuine transformation, or metempsychosis, of that image as well as of Dante's rose of the Mystical Body and of the crimson and rose flower of Stephen's vision by the sea in *Portrait*. So, too, does the Benediction hymn,

Tantum ergo sacramentum, sung by the choir point to Bloom, even if it is heard in meaningless fragments as *"Tantumer gosa cramen tum"* (p. 360).

The next chapter, the Oxen of the Sun episode, shows Bloom on an errand of compassion, asking after Mrs. Purefoy at the maternity hospital, "woman's woe with wonder pondering" (p. 388). The corresponding episode in Homer is about the destruction of Odysseus's crew for the sacrilege of killing and eating the cattle of the Sun god; Odysseus alone shunned the feast, and he was therefore spared. Joyce's chapter begins with incantations praying for "quickening and wombfruit" (p. 383), a phrase that points both to the literal childbirth taking place in the hospital and to the quickening and rebirth of Stephen to come. Stephen is there visting Mulligan, who is an intern at the hospital. Bloom, "that man mildhearted" (p. 385), enters, with characteristic moderation, into the festivity of the interns, but his mind is on the suffering of Mrs. Purefoy, who has been in labor three days. "Young Malachi" and the other interns make jokes about fertility in general, while Bloom and Stephen alone remain outside their laughter. This is the first important meeting of Bloom's and Stephen's paths; not only are they in the same room, but also both stand apart from the general shallowness and irreverence of a group of ordinary, Mulligan-minded Dubliners. Bloom, recognizing Stephen as the son of his friend, Simon Dedalus, remembers the loss of his own son and feels concern for Stephen, "for that he lived riotously with those wastrels and murdered his goods with whores" (p. 391). When the group decides to set out for some pub-crawling, Bloom goes along to discreetly keep a fatherly eye on him. The chapter, which began with the most primitive form of language and followed English prose style through all its developments, ends in the style of a revivalist handbill: "Elijah is coming. Washed in the Blood of the Lamb. . . . Shout salvation in king Jesus" (p. 428).

The Circe episode, which is written in the form of a Strindbergian dream play, is probably the most complex in the book, and nearly impossible to summarize. In terms of action, Stephen gets into difficulty, first in a whorehouse and later in a street fight, and Bloom, after overcoming some difficulties of his own, gets him out of trouble both times. What makes the chapter so complicated is that during all of this both Bloom and Stephen, on the level of the unconscious, are going through dream encounters with their respective demons.

Bloom's task is to live the love that he preached in the Cyclops episode, and he first has to deal with a number of inner obstacles. One of the earliest is the appearance of the ghost of his own father, Rudolph Virag, who appears to warn him against wasting his money in the company of *goyim*. The way Rudolph feels Bloom's face "with feeble vulture talons" (p. 437) is reminiscent of the negative bird imagery in *Portrait* that represented the external authority of convention. Another obstacle is his own feelings of guilt about his various transgressions against traditional sexual morality; these feelings are personified in a large number of accusing voices that denounce him at various times throughout the episode. Another is the danger of psychological inflation resulting from his awareness of the high value of the ideal he serves. There are scenes, for example, in which he imagines himself as "His Most Catholic Majesty" (p. 487), King Leopold, bearing "the orb and sceptre with the dove" (p. 481) and as the Messiah, both "ben Joseph" and "ben David" (p. 495), whose name is *"Emmanuel"* (p. 496, "God with us" in Hebrew). In a characteristic double irony, however, this royal and Messianic imagery that builds him up for a letdown also tells the truth about him; in order to embody that truth adequately, he has to do it in a modest and realistic way, recognizing his own human weaknesses while at the same time not letting these deter him from fulfilling his vocation.

His greatest weakness is the necessary correlative of one of his great strengths, his ability to enter sympathetically into the feelings of women. At the maternity hospital we saw him wondering at woman's woe, and in the last chapter of the book Molly says that the reason she was first drawn to him, which is probably also the reason she still prefers him to Blazes Boylan, is that "he understood or felt what a woman is" (p. 782). This ability to combine in himself both masculine and feminine feelings is what makes him "the new womanly man" (p. 493), and it is also what makes him susceptible to being unmanned, as in fact happens, by the whoremistress, Bella Cohen (pp. 526 ff.). She gives him a woman's name and makes him dress, like Hercules in the service of Omphale, in women's clothes, and generally abuses him. However, although she tells him, "You are down and out and don't you forget it" (p. 543), nevertheless, as Bloom said on entering the establishment, "The just man falls seven times" (p. 501), and he rises again too. In this case the popping of his trouser button breaks the spell and recalls him to his manhood, whereupon he takes charge of Stephen's money and begins his job as pastor to the wayward lamb.

Stephen in the meantime has become royally drunk and has been fighting his own demons. One takes the form of his cap, evidently a symbol of his razorlike rationalism, which speaks contemptuously of the idea of a possible reconciliation of the rational and mystical sides of life, dismissing "with saturnine spleen" precisely the balancing elements Stephen will need for his eventual growth: "Bah! It is because it is. Woman's reason. Jewgreek is greekjew. Extremes meet. Death is the highest form of life. Bah!" (p. 504). It bodes well for Stephen that here he is arguing against his cap, and especially that the argument he uses involves the idea of a cyclical development in which "the fundamental and the dominant," although they are separate, are separated by an "Interval which. Is the greatest possible ellipse. Consistent with. The ultimate return". It is significant that when the cap challenges Stephen to proceed with the explanation of this paradoxical idea, Stephen bursts out, "What went forth to the ends of the world to traverse not itself. God, the sun, Shakespeare, a commercial traveller, having itself traversed in reality itself, becomes that self. . . . Self which it itself was ineluctably preconditioned to become" (p. 505). This is an echo of a passage on the thought of Giovanni Battista Vico in Benedetto Croce's *Estetica:* "Man creates the human world, creates it by transforming himself into the facts of society: by thinking it he re-creates his own creations, traverses over again the paths he has already traversed, reconstructs the whole ideally, and thus knows it with full and true knowledge."[23] It is significant that Stephen should draw on, or at least parallel, Vichian thought in his attempt to understand life, because Vico was an important influence on Joyce's thinking and the passage points to the important Vichian element in the book's central meaning.

To state briefly the main argument of Vico as he presented it in *The New Science,* man is a cultural entity and must be understood in terms of his cultural creations — language, history, and religion.[24] All cultures develop

23. Quoted in Ellmann, *James Joyce,* p. 351.

24. *The New Science of Giovanni Battista Vico* (1744), trans. Thomas Goddard (Ithaca, N.Y.: Cornell University Press, 1948).

according to a cycle of three stages — an age of the gods, an age of heroes, and an age of men — each with its characteristic forms of government and religion. The process is governed by Divine Providence, but this is conceived of as a rational principle immanent in the world, rather than as a will transcendent over it. At the end of each complete cycle occurs a *ricorso*, or "reflux," which culminates it in a period of reflection and then begins a new cycle all over again. The similarity to Joachim's idea of the three stages of history is obvious, but there are two important new elements. One is that the pattern is cyclical and the work of a completely immanent principle. The other is that the moment of reflection in Vico's cycle offers to a person with Joyce's interests the possibility of a unified vision embracing all three of the phases of the cycle. This is one of the functions of the messianic imagery Joyce uses with regard to Bloom. The figure of the Messiah in tradition unites precisely Vico's three categories — divine, heroic, and human — as incarnate Emmanuel, priest, king, and Son of Man.

While Stephen is tracing the cycle from God through the sun, Shakespeare, and commercial traveler, he is annoyed by what he calls "a noise in the street," "The Holy City" played on a gramophone. The phrase, of course, recalls Stephen's dismissal of God as "a shout in the street" at Mr. Deasy's, and this dismissal is similarly ironic. Stephen still cannot see clearly the true Emmanuel in the street, but his progress toward that vision is reflected in the fact that he carries the course of his evolving God not only through the artist, Shakespeare, but also through the figure of the "commercial traveller," which is what Bloom, in fact, is. It is significant also that after ending that speech with the exclamation *"Ecco!"* ("Behold!"), he hears newsboys shouting of the "safe arrival of Antichrist" and then "turns and sees Bloom," who appears as "Reuben J. Antichrist, wandering jew" carrying over his shoulder "a long boatpole from the hook of which the sodden huddled mass of his only son, saved from Liffey waters, hangs from the slack of its breeches" (p. 506). Stephen could not have any idea at this point of what this apparition means, but it foreshadows what is coming, as does also his later *non sequitur* reply to somebody's remark that it is long after eleven: "What, eleven? A riddle" (p. 557).

Even as his salvation approaches, however, Stephen distrusts it and tries to defend himself against it. He remembers, dimly, his dream of the night before and recognizes this as the dream's locale — "It was here. Street of harlots. . . . Where's the red carpet spread?" (p. 571) — but still preoccupied with rebellion, when he hears Bloom saying, "Look. . . . I say, look," he cries, "Break my spirit, will he?", and starts to sharpen "his vulture talons" (p. 572). As Stephen's father in the form of a buzzard appears to take up the challenge, the scene transforms into a horse race, in which "a dark horse riderless, bolts like a phantom past the winningpost" (p. 573). Before Stephen can recognize the true identity of the dark horse or the Haroun al Raschid of his dream, however, he still has to break free from or at least loosen the hold of the various demons that keep him captive.

His father is one of these, but even more powerful, and potentially much more destructive is his mother. When she appears it is as an "emaciated" figure "in leper grey with a wreath of faded orange blossoms and a torn bridal veil, her face worn and noseless, green with grave mould" (p. 579). The Freudian symbolism of the Oedipus complex is evident here, but a still more important aspect of the temptation she represents is symbolized by the grave mould. If it is true that "death is the highest form of life," it is nevertheless also true that there are different kinds of death: some lead to rebirth, but some lead only to a dead end. His mother's message to him is, "Repent! O, the fire of hell! . . . Beware! God's hand!" (pp. 581-82). The kind of dying to self she calls him to would lead to the destruction of his individual intelligence, not its fruition in a higher form. To defend himself against this threat, he renews his cry of "Non serviam," and then, thrashing about with his stick, he breaks the light and runs out of the whorehouse and into the street. Bloom, at this point, recovers Stephen's stick, which he has abandoned in his flight, settles Stephen's account with the prostitutes, and runs after him to give him back the stick.

In the scene on the street, Stephen gets into a squabble with some soldiers over what is supposed to have been an insult to a girl, Cissey Caffrey. Actually what seems to be the main cause of offense is an ecstatic outburst — "White thy fambles, red thy gan / And thy quarrons dainty is" (p. 598) — which is really a sort of compliment and a sign of Stephen's rapprochement with the figure of woman. During the scene, Edward VII appears "with the halo of Joking Jesus" to say, "My methods are new and are causing surprise / To make the blind see I throw dust in their eyes" (p. 591), an announcement of Stephen's impending deliverance from the strictures of rationalism. When Bloom enlists the help of a passing friend, Corny Kelleher, in explaining things to a constable, Kelleher says that Stephen "won a bit on the races. Gold cup. Throwaway. . . . Twenty to one" (p. 604). Stephen has, of course, but in a different way.

When all the rest withdraw, Bloom is left standing over Stephen, who is lying on the ground, perhaps with some literal dust in his eyes. At first Bloom "stands irresolute," but then tries to rouse Stephen by calling his name: "Eh! Ho! Mr. Dedalus! . . . Stephen! . . . Stephen!" (p. 608). Stephen, hearing his name, wonders, "Who?", and then mutters something about a "black panther." He is not at the moment in a condition to rise. As Bloom stands watch over him, he sees appear slowly "against the dark wall . . . a fairy boy of eleven, a changeling" (p. 609), and, "wonderstruck," whispers, "Rudy!"

Eventually Bloom is able to brush Stephen off and help him to his feet "generally in orthodox Samaritan fashion" (p. 613) and lead him to the cabman's shelter, where he persuades him, after some coaxing, to take a sip of coffee. It is only very gradually that Stephen comes to see and appreciate Bloom's kindness, but the sip of coffee is the beginning of a communion that slowly unfolds during the next hour or so. As they converse over the coffee, Bloom tells Stephen, with some improvements, the story of his altercation with the citizen and of his statement that "Christ was a jew too, and all his family, like me" (p. 643), and directs to Stephen "a glance . . . of entreaty." Stephen responds to this by mumbling, "*Christus* or Bloom his name is, or after all, any other, *secundum carnem*." That he mumbles this "in a noncommital accent" shows how cautious he is about entering fully into the communion to which Bloom invites him, but it expresses his recognition of this metempsychosis, according to the flesh, of the figure of the Messiah, and with it he sets one foot, at least, across the threshold of "the new Bloomusalem" (p. 484).

Stephen's communion is completed in the next chapter after he goes home with Bloom, following a "parallel course" (p. 666), and accepts with full appreciation his host's offer of cocoa:

> Was the guest conscious of and did he acknowledge these marks of hospitality?
>
> His attention was directed to them by his host jocosely and he accepted them seriously as they drank in jocoserious silence Epps's massproduct, the creature cocoa. [P. 677]

And yet, although they are momentarily united in this communion as "Stoom" and "Blephen" (p. 682), they are still separate individuals, and Stephen still has to go on to pursue his own path in life. Consequently Stephen declines "promptly, inexplicably, with amicability, gratefully" (p. 695) Bloom's offer of a bed for the night and his implicit, by intention, offer of "a prolongation of such extemporisation."

Bloom subsequently lights Stephen's way out to the garden where they are confronted by the spectacle of "the heaventree of stars hung with humid nightblue fruit" (p. 698). There he completes the revelation of life's meaning to Stephen, and his own role as prophet and priest, by pointing out his wife's luminous window, "with indirect and direct verbal allusions or affirmations: with subdued affection and admiration: with description: with impediment: with suggestion" elucidating "the mystery of an invisible person, his wife Marion (Molly) Bloom, denoted by a visible splendid sign, a lamp" (p. 702). Bloom is one aspect of the "who" predicted in the "You will see who" of Stephen's dream (p. 47), and she is the other. Bloom is the flower of life, but by his own testimony and hers, so is she, as she says in her monologue in the next chapter: ". . . he said I was a flower of the mountain yes so we are flowers all a womans body yes" (p. 782). Bloom unites the masculine and feminine poles of humanity in himself, but he would not be complete without his "affection and admiration" for the embodiment of the feminine in his female counterpart as well.

By pointing her out to Stephen and disclosing his love for her he points the way for Stephen to pay similar homage someday to a woman "without shame or wantonness" (*Portrait,* p. 171) and thereby to fulfill in incarnate life the hope that had been presented to him in the vision of the wading girl. The association of Molly with the "inconstant series of concentric circles of varying gradations of light and shadow" (p. 736) made by the reflection of her lamp on the ceiling also links the revelation of Molly with the image of the crimson and rose flower that had culminated the earlier vision.[25] Stephen may not at this point make any conscious connection between this vision and the earlier one, but that he understands and shares Bloom's appreciation of the mystery he points to is revealed by the look they exchange: "Silent, each contemplating the other in both mirrors of the reciprocal flesh of theirhisnothis fellowfaces" (p. 702).

Then, after a joint micturition, the "centripetal remainer" opens the garden gate for Stephen, the "centrifugal departer," who leaves and is no more heard from.

This leaves the reader wondering what will happen in the days that follow: will Stephen come to give Italian lessons to Molly or to engage in the "series of static, semistatic and peripatetic intellectual dialogues" he and Bloom had discussed (p. 696), or will he go his separate way to write books like *Ulysses*?[26] To try to answer questions like these, however, would simply be to pretend that Joyce had not terminated the novel on the last page, and to take such questions very seriously would be to miss the point of the novel he wrote. What has happened that is important is that Bloom has brought "light to the gentiles"

25. It is perhaps worth noting that Molly's birthday, September 8 (p. 720), is also the day of the Feast of the Blessed Virgin Mary.

26. Ellmann, *Ulysses on the Liffey,* pp. 159-62, discusses various approaches to the ending of *Ulysses.*

(p. 676) and that Stephen has caught a glimpse of a paradoxical glory; the only important question is what will this particular gentile do with the dark illumination he carries away with him. Since the book is over at the end, there can be no detailed answer to the question of what will happen next, but on the basis of the rhythms of life as the book has disclosed them, we can make the general prediction that, to borrow for a moment the language of the chapter in which Stephen departs, it will be regrettably, though forgivably, ineluctably — an anticlimax. But the just man falls seven times, or perhaps seventy times seven, and each times rises again, and Stephen may turn out to be a just man. He carries away with him, at any rate, a more than merely intellectual understanding of what one such man is and of what and how he loves.

It is clear from all of this that *Ulysses* expresses a strong sense of the sacred. Admittedly there are other patterns of imagery in the book which we have had to pass over, but the prominence of the traditional images of the sacred that we have traced is unquestionable; they run throughout the book and appear with particular frequency in climactic passages, and they consequently make an important contribution to the tone in which the values that are supreme to the book are represented.[27] But having established this we are still left with a number of questions. Does this mean, for example, that Joyce was working out

27. It is perhaps worth mentioning that one of the mythic parallels I have not discussed in this chapter is that of Stephen to Christ. There are numerous links between Stephen and Christ, such as the Palm Sunday imagery in the Aeolus episode and references to the passion in the Circe episode. The reason I have not discussed them in connection with my theme is that whereas the parallels between Bloom and Christ have a positive significance, the parallels between Stephen and Christ tend to be negatively ironic: Stephen likes to compare himself to various heroic figures, but the comparison usually ends up deflating him, as in the episode in *Portrait* referred to earlier in which Stephen imagined himself as Daedalus, but was really more like Icarus.

in this book an alternative religious vision to the Christian one he rejected? If so, what kind of vision is it? Does it have a clear conceptual structure, or is it primarily affective? If, as seems the case from the preceding discussion, Joyce's concept of divinity in so far as he had one was exclusively immanentist, then what about the element of transcendence that is always necessary to any sense of the sacred? In order to clarify these issues and approach, at least, some answers, it will be necessary to take them up one by one.

First let us consider the conceptual problem: what idea or ideas of the structure of being are implied in Joyce's works? It would not, of course, be necessary that an author have any clear ideas on this subject in order to write a book, even books like *Portrait of the Artist* and *Ulysses,* but Joyce was more learned than the average author in the areas of theology and philosophy, and even if he may not have had any definite answers of which he was convinced, he seems at least to have had a clear understanding of the shape of the problem. As I mentioned earlier, he said that he read his Aquinas, a page a day, and he also read Bruno and Vico as well as a good many others who thought about such questions. He also cared strongly about the problem. In a letter of November 1902 he wrote, "All things are inconstant except the faith of the soul, which changes all things and fills their inconstancy with light. And though I seem to have been driven out of my country here as a misbeliever I have found no man yet with a faith like mine."[28] The faith he speaks of here is obviously not that of the traditional Christianity in which he was "a misbeliever," nor may it necessarily have involved a firm belief in an alternative, but the tone expresses concern, a desire at least for something worth

28. *Letters,* 1:53.

believing in. This letter is from the beginning of Joyce's career; it is interesting that his friend, Louis Gillet, has described him as having a continuing interest in questions of belief and divinity even at the end:

In the last few years he showed himself very much occupied with a certain Jesuit priest. . . . Joyce had heard him . . . in a very curious lecture on comparative phonetics and linguistics, and these new ideas . . . seemed to him most daring. According to this clergyman, all languages constitute a system of the Revelation, and their history in the world is the history of the Logos, the history of the Holy Spirit. . . . One feels . . . that such a speech offered Joyce material for long reveries.[29]

The "daring" point of view the priest was presenting seems pantheistic or at least easily assimilable to a pantheistic vision, and if Joyce had a definite belief, or wanted one — as seems more likely the case — it would seem to have been belief in a pantheistic vision like Bruno's, the universe seen as a revelation or unfolding from within of an immanent Logos or Holy Spirit. Traditionally the Logos is associated with the Son rather than with the Holy Spirit, but a pantheistic point of view, in so far as it drew on the traditional terms and imagery, would assimilate all of the persons of the traditional Trinity into the third.

It is also worth keeping in mind, however, in connection with the question of Joyce's beliefs that he read and was much impressed by the skeptical philosophy of David Hume.[30] If Aristotle was the "master of those who know," then, in Richard Ellmann's phrase, Hume was for Joyce the master of those who do not know.[31] Joyce may have found the pantheist alternative attractive, but he knew and respected both sides of the question. Robert Scholes

29. Louis Gillet, *Claybook for James Joyce,* trans. Georges Markow-Totevy (London: Abelard-Schuman, 1958), p. 113.
30. Ellmann, *Ulysses on the Liffey,* pp. 93-96.
31. Ibid., p. 95.

and Richard M. Kain in *The Workshop of Daedalus* contrast Joyce's "tolerant skepticism" with the "militant atheism" of his brother, Stanislaus;[32] it would have to be contrasted also to any form of belief that could be definite enough to be militant, including pantheism. Ellmann has suggested that the randomness and mazelike quality of the Wandering Rocks episode in *Ulysses* was Joyce's attempt to give chaos its due by building an "uncertainty principle" into the structure of the book.[33] If this is the case, it is probably a reflection of the presence of the same principle as one of the deeply ingrained elements in his own mind.

But what can we say of the book? If both points of view are represented in it — Bruno's and Hume's — are they perfectly in balance, or does the book lean toward one or the other? On the whole, the way the book is constructed makes it seem to lean more toward Bruno's; its intricate symbolism and elaborate mythic parallels — not only to Odysseus, but also to Moses, Elijah, and Christ, among others — set up patterns of correspondences that knit together what might otherwise seem an incoherent universe, making it into a quasi-organic whole that would seem to justify a phrase like "the obscure soul of the world."

Yet, if the world does seem to have in it the kind of principle of unity that could be called a soul, this soul is nevertheless obscure. Since all the characters, including those who best represent that soul's life, suffer from parallax, it is never very clearly visible. And also, since so few adequately represent it, it seems not to be very substantial.

32. Robert M. Scholes and Richard M. Kain, *The Workshop of Daedalus: James Joyce and the Raw Materials for* A Portrait of the Artist as a Young Man (Evanston, Illinois: Northwestern University Press, 1965), p. 75.

33. Ellmann, *Ulysses on the Liffey*, p. 92.

It almost seems as if that soul is real only in the moments when someone like Bloom is living its life. The rest of the time perhaps there is only flux and reflux within chaos.

Whatever may be the answer to that question, however — the question that *Portrait* phrased in connection with Stephen's epiphany by the sea as "a world, a glimmer, or a flower?" — the world of Joyce's books does now and then reach up toward an ideal that would be a soul for it and even attains it occasionally in an incarnate flower like Leopold Bloom.

This, at least, is definitely true within the framework of the book, and it can serve as the basis for an answer to the question of the structure of the sense of the sacred that the book so effectively communicates. Love, as lived in the flesh by a man like Bloom, is presented to us as a supreme value, and Joyce marshals a vast array of the traditional imagery of the sacred to clothe it in splendor and thereby impress it on our minds and hearts as a glory that, in all the fleshliness and frailness of its secularity, is nevertheless a *mysterium tremendum et fascinans*. Its being may be entirely immanent in secularity, but its very ephemeralness and fragility give it a transcendent quality from the point of view of our experience of it. It manifests itself to us as a call to our consciences, an ideal to live up to, and as such it at least transcends our ordinary capacities. The philosopher Martin Heidegger, whose point of view with regard to ontology, like Joyce's, also emphasized the immanence of being, has said of the call of conscience that, although it can be adequately understood simply as the appeal of our own authentic selfhood, it is experienced as a call from beyond ourselves, because for the most part we live so far from authentic selfhood that nothing could seem stranger to us.[34] Joyce, in *Ulysses,* has made it seem strange in just that way — and beautiful.

34. Martin Heidegger, *Being and Time,* trans. John Macquerrie and E. S. Robinson (Evanston, New York: Harper and Row, 1962; London: SCM Press, 1962), pp. 319 ff.

CHAPTER VI

The Perilous Journey to Wholeness in Thomas Mann

The Magic Mountain is, according to its author's own description, "a novel of initiation."[1] Initiation is a process of spiritual maturing consisting of a series of experiences in which a person gains knowledge of the fundamental mysteries of life. The story of the novel is outwardly uneventful — the seven year sojourn of a young citizen of Hamburg in a Swiss tuberculosis sanatorium — but during the course of it its protagonist, Hans Castorp, penetrates into areas of inward experience rarely glimpsed by those who live in what the novel calls "the flatland" down below. According to Mircea Eliade, the process of initiation "usually comprises a threefold revelation: revelation of the sacred, of death, and of sexuality."[2] In his seven years of "stocktaking" at the International Sanatorium Berghof, Hans comes to know intimately all three of these and learns how to meet the challenges each of them offers.

The starting point of Hans's spiritual journey is the

1. "The Making of *The Magic Mountain*," in Thomas Mann, *The Magic Mountain*, trans. H. T. Lowe-Porter (New York: Alfred A. Knopf, 1944), p. 727.
2. *The Sacred and the Profane*, p. 188.

desacralized world of the late nineteenth century, a world materially prosperous but spiritually starved. Hans is a typical, even archetypal member of this world, and the inner weakness that occasions his retirement to meditation is actually a sort of saving grave visited by life upon one who is not in any way special, but representative even to the point of mediocrity:

> A man lives not only his personal life, as an individual, but also, consciously or unconsciously, the life of his epoch and his contemporaries. . . . Now, if the life about him, if his own time seem, however outwardly stimulating, to be at bottom empty of . . . food for his aspirations; if he privately recognize it to be hopeless, viewless, helpless, opposing only a hollow silence to all the questions man puts . . . as to the final, absolute, and abstract meaning in all his efforts and activities; then . . . a certain laming of the personality is bound to occur . . . a sort of palsy, as it were, which may even extend from his spiritual and moral over into his physical and organic part. In an age that affords no satisfying answer to the eternal question of "Why?" "To what end?" a man who is capable of achievement over and above the average and expected modicum must be equipped either with a moral remoteness and singlemindedness which is rare indeed and of heroic mould, or else with an exceptionally robust vitality. Hans Castorp had neither the one nor the other of these; and thus he must be considered mediocre, though in an entirely honourable sense. [P. 32][3]

The world the novel describes is one that has lost its roots in the religious tradition that had once offered at least partial answers to the larger questions about the meaning of man's life. The remaining vestiges of that tradition are for the most part either completely secularized or spiritually moribund. When Hans sits down to a meal, for example, he rubs his hands together, "a habit

3. Page references are to the edition of *The Magic Mountain* cited above in note 1.

of his when he sat down to table, perhaps because his ancestors had said grace before meat" (p. 13), and although both the guests and the management of the sanatorium take pains "to observe Sunday and distinguish it from the rest of the week" (p. 110), it is only by special dishes, band concerts, and other purely secular forms of festivity that they do so: ". . . the Hofrat [Dr. Behrens, the head of the establishment] honoured the sabbath by performing a 'stunt' with his bootlaces before the gentlemen's eyes" (p. 112). Even where the religious tradition is still active, it seems for the most part either withered — as in the case of the nurse who "had the look of a Protestant sister — that is to say, one working without a real vocation and burdened with restlessness and ennui" (p. 10) — or perverse, as in the case of the terroristic Jesuit, Herr Naphta, or the woesome Herr Wehsal, with his lugubrious pietism and his fascination with instruments of torture.

It is significant that the one element of the ancient tradition that still spoke to Hans in his youth was his family's christening basin and plate, the instruments of initiation, and also that the interpreter of what they represented was Hans's grandfather, a man who seemed out of place in the modern world, "a typical Christian gentleman, of the Reformed faith" (p. 23), distrustful of "godless" economic progress (p. 24), who seemed his true self to Hans only when dressed in the ceremonial garb of his office as town-councillor, "the sober, even godly, civilian habit of a bygone century" (p. 25) — black cloak, lace cuffs, starched ruff, and "old-fashioned, broad-brimmed hat." The basin and plate no longer serve their function effectively, and Hans's true initiation eventually has to be carried out in a different manner which would seem highly questionable to his pious grandfather. To cling to a religious tradition that no longer serves its purpose would be a mistake that would prevent authentic and valid religious experience in the present — the kind of mistake made by the parents of Potiphar in Mann's later work, *Joseph and His Brothers*[4] — and Hans has to leave these elements of his past behind in the flatland along with the rest of his earlier life, but his childhood fascination with what they represented was at least a sign of his suitability for a genuine initiation, and perhaps even an influence on his later receptivity to it. They spoke to him of a tradition that linked him with religious mysteries and an alternative vision to that of bourgeois materialism. As he listened to his grandfather tell him of his great-, and great-great-, and so on, grandfathers, the sound seemed to him to reverbebrate in the depths of time, an effect of sound that is unfortunately lost in the English translation — the German is "Ur-Ur-Ur-Ur":[5] "what a hollow sound it had, how it spoke of the falling away of time, yet how it seemed the expression of a piously cherished link between the present, his own life, and the depth of the past" (p. 22). It may have been for the sake of hearing that sound, the narrator says, that Hans so often asked to see the basin, and when he heard it, "religious feeling mingled in his mind with thoughts of death and a sense of history."

Since this tradition no longer functions effectively and in its absence there is no other to take its place, Hans has to undergo his seven-year initiation without the guidance and protection that a religious tradition normally affords. This makes his adventure more than ordinarily perilous.

4. See *Joseph and His Brothers,* trans. H. T. Lowe-Porter (New York: Alfred A. Knopf, 1948), pp. 582 ff. Mann said in his "Einführung in den Zauberberg für Studenten der Universität Princeton," *Der Zauberberg* (Berlin: S. Fischer Verlag, 1954), p. xv, that *The Magic Mountain* can be best understood when read in relation to, among other works by Mann, the Joseph novels.

5. *Der Zauberberg,* p. 33.

The dangers an initiate has to face are never *merely* symbolic, if the experience is to be vital, but a religious tradition of initiation has as one of its functions to control these and to replace them to some extent with symbolic perils so that the initiate may be protected from actual physical death or complete psychological disintegration; left to himself, he would have to stumble through them more or less in the dark, and the successful outcome of the process would be pretty much a matter of chance. Hans himself says at one point late in the book that it is "chance — call it chance" that has led him through his path of "alchemistic-hermetic pedagogy, transubstantiation, from lower to higher, ascending degrees" (p. 596); though perhaps one could also say that he has had the over-all guidance of the *genius loci,* the spirit of the magic mountain, the guidance of life itself which sends him a variety of pitfalls, epiphanies, and pedagogues: he is referred to often as a *"Sorgenkind des Lebens,"* a phrase that implies not only that he *needs* care — the meaning of the translation's version of it, "the delicate child of life" — but also that life does indeed nurture him and nurse him through the illness that is the process of his rebirth.

In his essay on "The Making of *The Magic Mountain,*" Mann spoke favorably of a critical interpretation of the work as a modern parallel to the traditional quest of the Holy Grail, and he linked the "frightful and mysterious ordeals" of the Chapel Perilous with those of rites of initiation.[6] In the Grail legend, a "guileless fool" stumbles by a series of providential accidents, including sins, into the recovery of the symbol of health, wholeness, and holi-

6. Mann was referring to the unpublished doctoral dissertation of Howard Nemerov, "The Quester Hero: Myth as Universal Symbol in the Works of Thomas Mann" (Harvard, 1940). All of the following quotations from "The Making of *The Magic Mountain*" appear in *The Magic Mountain,* pp. 728-29.

ness — three terms that are etymologically and conceptually related — that can restore the waste land and the community of Grail knights from the sickness, physical and spiritual, in which they languish. Mann said that although he did not have this parallel consciously in mind while he was writing the book — ". . . it was both more and less than thinking" — he himself was "a guileless fool . . . guided by a mysterious tradition" and that "not only the foolish hero but the book itself" was seeking what the Grail represents: ". . . the idea of the human being, the conception of a future humanity that has passed through and survived the profoundest knowledge of disease and death." Mann did not define the goal of the quest further than this in his essay, but the book makes clear, in ways that will require some exploration, that the complete man who results from this quest or initiation is a conscious *coincidentia oppositorum,* uniting in himself in a harmonious balance all the contraries of which life is composed and raising human life thereby to a sacred level commensurate with the "reverence before the mystery that is man" upon which, Mann says, all humanity depends.

There are also a number of other mythic parallels in *The Magic Mountain* besides that of the Grail quest — Odysseus, for example, and Aeneas, and Dante. One that has not ben discussed as far as I know by any of Mann's critics, but which I think is particularly illuminating, is that of Oedipus. Since Freud's development of the theory of the Oedipus complex, critics seem to have been so interested in the psychoanalytic aspect of the story of Oedipus that they have tended not to give much thought to other aspects of the legend, but there is a good deal more to it than that alone, and its larger pattern applies to Hans Castorp's story in a number of interesting ways.

In the same speech in which Hans tells Clavdia

Chauchat, the woman with whom he has been in love during most of his stay on the mountain, that it is "chance" *("Zufall")* that has brought him "to these heights of the spirit," he tells her also that there are two paths to life (significantly not *in* life, but *to* life [*"zum Leben"*]: ". . . one is the regular one, direct, honest. The other is bad, it leads through death — that is the *spirituel* way" (p. 596). Mann, in "The Making of *The Magic Mountain,"* cited this passage and identified the second path with that of the initiation Hans goes through. The original German for the last phrase is *"der geniale Weg."*[7] Mann's own translation of this in the essay is "the way of genius,"[8] a translation that probably makes it a little clearer than Mrs. Lowe-Porter's that this is a path of inspiration in which one is subject to superhuman forces, perhaps divine, perhaps demonic.

In the *Oedipus at Colonus* of Sophocles, Oedipus also speaks of two ways. One is that of "kingliness," the upright path of reason, self-control, and honesty, represented in that play by Theseus, whom Oedipus describes as "a man who has no stain of evil in him,"[9] and whom Oedipus, polluted as he is, feels unfit to touch; the other is that of Oedipus himself in which "suffering and time, / Vast time"[10] are the instructors and which leads through evil to eventual apotheosis. In connection with what Hans says about his own career, it is also interesting that Oedipus, too, speaks at one point (in *Oedipus the King*) of chance (Τύχη) as the guiding force in his life: " . . . I account myself a child of Fortune, beneficent fortune. . . . She's the mother from whom I spring;

7. *Zauberberg,* p. 849.

8. *Magic Mountain,* p. 727.

9. Sophocles, *Oedipus at Colonus,* trans. Robert Fitzgerald, in *Sophocles I* (Chicago: University of Chicago Press, 1954), ll. 8, 1134-35.

10. Ibid., ll. 6-7.

the months, my brothers, marked me, now as small, and now again as mighty."[11] In fact, Oedipus' destiny has several sources, each of which could be termed his mother in a different way — Tyche, Jocasta, and the Sphinx.

Like Parsifal and Hans Castorp, Oedipus, too, is a sort of "guileless fool" who stumbles into his destiny through a well-meaning, but foolish temerity. At one point he taunts Tiresias the prophet with having been unable to answer the riddle of the Sphinx and boasts, "I solved the riddle by my wit alone,"[12] but, since Tiresias is clearly represented in the play as a true seer, it is more likely his silence with regard to the riddle was the fruit of prudence than of ignorance. The riddle Oedipus answered is traditionally supposed to have been, "What walks on four legs in the morning, two legs at noon, and three legs in the evening?" This is a description of the cycle of human life with a rise to the full stature of manhood followed by a fall. When Oedipus answered the riddle, the Sphinx, by her suicide, gave him the life the riddle described and thus became, in a sense, the spiritual mother of his life as king, as violator of his physical mother, and as outcast. Through what might be called his "folly" in answering the riddle, Oedipus came to experience human life in its fullness, rising to heights beyond those attained by other men, and falling to depths similarly beyond the ordinary.

What the Sphinx represents in the legend is a matter of some complexity. Sophocles does not describe her or the encounter Oedipus has with her, but only alludes to what would have been common knowledge to his audience. In

11. *Oedipus the King,* trans. David Grene, in *Sophocles I,* ll. 1080-84. Cf. Jocasta's speech in lines 977-78: "Why should man fear since chance [Τύχη] is all in all/for him, and he can clearly foreknow nothing?"
12. Ibid., l. 398.

origin, the Sphinx was a figure from Egyptian mythology with a human head and the body of a lion, probably representing the king. It was adapted into Greek mythology at a very early time as a female figure. Her mother was supposed to have been Echidna (the Greek for "snake"), who was half woman and half serpent. There are different versions of the lineage of Echidna, but one that is especially interesting in relation to Mann's use of the Sphinx symbol in *The Magic Mountain* represents her as the daughter of Gaea and Tartarus, which is to say, of the earth and the underworld. Echidna is supposed to have mated with her brother, Typhoeus, to give birth to Orthrus and with Orthrus to give birth to the Sphinx.[13] This lineage would clearly make the Sphinx a symbol of autochthony, of the origin of life from the depths of nature. Part animal and part human, she would represent that side of man that is still linked with its subrational source, and in her menacing aspect she would represent the danger of man's being swallowed up once again by the darkness from which he has perhaps only partially

13. Carl Jung has employed a similar genealogy in his own interpretation of the Sphinx symbol in mythology. Cf. Jung, *Symbols of Transformation: An Analysis of the Prelude to a Case of Schizophrenia,* trans. R. F. C. Hull (New York: Pantheon Books, 1956), p. 182: "The genealogy of the Sphinx has manifold connections with the problem touched upon here: she was a daughter of Echidna, a monster with the top half of a beautiful maiden, and a hideous serpent below. This double being corresponds to the mother-imago: above, the lovely and attractive human half; below the horrible animal half, changed into a fear-animal by the incest prohibition. Echidna was born of the All-Mother, Mother Earth, Gaia, who conceived her with Tartarus, the personification of the underworld. Echidna herself was the mother of all terrors, of the Chimera, Scylla, the Gorgon. . . . One of her sons was Orthrus, the dog of the monster Geryon, who was slain by Heracles. With this dog, her own son, Echidna incestuously begat the Sphinx. This would be sufficient to characterize the complex whose symbol is the Sphinx. It is evident that a factor of such magnitude cannot be disposed of by solving a childish riddle. The riddle was, in fact, the trap which the Sphinx laid for the unwary wanderer. . . . The riddle of the Sphinx was herself — the terrible mother-imago, which Oedipus would not take as a warning."

emerged. Claude Lévi-Strauss has recently interpreted the entire Oedipus myth in a similar way as "the attempt to escape autochthony" and "the impossibility to succeed in it."[14] Oedipus' lameness, from which he takes his name (Swollen-foot), is, according to Lévi-Strauss, a symbol of this: his being exposed on Mount Cithaeron with his feet staked to the ground represents his, and man's imperfect separation from his origin in the earth.

To carry this line of interpretation a little further, in a direction that may throw some light on Mann's recurrent use of an incest motif in many of his works,[15] the incestuous union of Oedipus with his physical mother, Jocasta, would be a parallel or microcosm of his relationship with the other sources of his life, the Sphinx and the earth, as would the similar origin of the Sphinx in the incestuous unions of Echidna with Orthrus and Typhoeus, and ultimately of the earth with its own depths.

Mann did not have an elaborately developed metaphysics or cosmogony, but those he did have tended toward an autochthonous monism of the kind that this reading of the Oedipus myth would imply, and interpreted in the light of such a theory the relationship of man's spiritual consciousness with the nature from which he springs is one that could aptly be termed an incestuous union of life with itself. Something of this way of thinking can be seen in Mann's description of the relationship between man and nature in an essay he wrote on his

14. *Structural Anthropology,* trans. Claire Jacobson and Brooke Grundfest (New York: Basic Books, 1963), p. 216.

15. The motif appears in, for example, the brother-sister union in "Blood of the Walsungs," the union of Huia and Tuia, also brother and sister, in *Joseph in Egypt,* Adrian Leverkühn's incestuous relationship in fantasy with his "little sister," the mermaid, in *Doctor Faustus,* the unions of brother and sister, and mother and son in *The Holy Sinner,* and in Felix Krull's fascination with a brother-sister pair he sees in Frankfurt.

personal philosophy for the volume, *I Believe,* edited by Clifton Fadiman:

> Have I said too much in saying that the human being is a great mystery? Whence does he come? He springs from nature, from animal nature, and behaves unmistakably after his kind. But in him nature becomes conscious of herself. She seems to have brought him forth not alone to make him lord over his own being — that is only a phrase for something with much deeper meaning. In him she lays herself open to the spiritual; she questions, admires and judges herself in him, as in a being who is at once herself and a creature of a higher order. . . . For it was to the end of her own spiritualization that she brought man forth.[16]

Or to put the idea another way, in the words of Hans's friend, spiritual father, and sexual rival, the "kingly" Mynheer Peeperkorn, who is himself, as an embodiment of "riddling royalty' '(p. 590), a combination of Oedipus, Laius, and Sphinx, man "is the feeling of God. God created him in order to feel through him. Man is nothing but the organ through which God consummates his marriage with roused and intoxicated life" (p. 603). Man's contemplation of life is life's contemplation of itself, and his love of life is the spirit's love of its own dark depths, the abyss from which it springs.

This union of life as spirit with life as nature is an activity that is, in a phrase that recurs several times in *The Magic Mountain,* "highly questionable." It is a narcissistic self-intoxication that can entice one away from the world of work and of political organization — in general, the life of reason and service to the community. It is no wonder Hans's pedagogical guide, the rationalistic

16. *I Believe: The Personal Philosophies of Certain Eminent Men and Women of Our Time* (New York: Simon and Schuster, 1939), p. 192. Mann's contribution to the volume was translated by H. T. Lowe-Porter.

Settembrini, considers the German taste for music "politically suspect" and is repelled by the Catholic Naphta's reference to St. Bernard of Clairvaux's third stage of mystical contemplation as "the bed of repose. . . . the place of intercourse between the wooing and the wooed" (p. 376).

The Sphinx is alluded to several times in *The Magic Mountain.* One instance has just been mentioned, that of Mynheer Peeperkorn, but since he is the book's principal *coincidentia oppositorum,* it is to be expected that he would unite in himself this figure along with many others, and it is not his most important aspect. The person who is most closely associated with the figure of the Sphinx is the catlike Clavdia Chauchat. Like the Sphinx, she is of oriental origin (Russian in her case), and in this book everything eastern is symbolic of the irrational and the chaotic and poses a temptation to moral and psychological disintegration, while at the same time, by the infatuation it elicits, it tends to draw what might otherwise be an arid, uprooted intellect into a vivifying union with the darker side of life, the emotional and the mystical. One day while Hans and his cousin, Joachim Ziemssen, are visiting the private apartment of Dr. Behrens and discussing the Asiatic features of Frau Chauchat, her high cheekbones and oriental eyes, Behrens says, "Yes, there's something about her. . . . Riddle of the sphinx" (p. 257). Then Behrens makes the young men some coffee, with an "Indian or Persian" coffee mill given him by an Egyptian princess and decorated with obscene pictures, and offers them some of his special cigarettes, another gift from the same princess: "Hans Castorp helped himself to his; it was unusually large and thick, and had a gilt sphinx on it. He began to smoke — it was wonderful, as Behrens had said" (p. 262).

Tobacco, coffee, and various other drugs are used in the book as symbols of the enticing and dangerous side of nature. Behrens, at the beginning of this conversation, spoke of the delights of cigar smoking and also of the potentially lethal melancholia to which overindulgence in tobacco can give rise. It is significant that near the end of the book, when Hans has completely succumbed to the dissolving influence of the atmosphere of the magic mountain, to the point of no longer carrying a watch or using a calendar, he also ceases to send home for his Maria Mancini cigars, a Bremen brand, but takes up a local product, "Light of Asia" (p. 708). The mention of the Sphinx image in connection with the cigarettes of the Egyptian princess during the conversation about Clavdia Chauchat is a signal of the potential danger that is mixed with the allure of this Sphinxlike woman, especially when this passage is read in the light of a later, more extensive description of the princess:

> There was the Egyptian princess who had given the Hofrat the extraodinary coffee-machine and sphinx cigarettes, a sensational person with cropped hair and beringed fingers yellow with nicotine, who went about — except at the main meal of the day, for which she made full Parisian toilet — in a sack coat and well-pressed trousers; and who scorned the world of men, to lay hot and heavy, though fitful seige to an insignificant little Roumanian Jewess named plain Frau Landauer. . . . [P. 548]

As one might say, there are *coincidentiae oppositorum* and *coincidentiae oppositorum*, and some of them are "highly questionable."

Clavdia's manners and general style of life are the very opposite of those Hans has learned to value in his civilized, *bürgerlich* German home. When he first becomes aware of her, it is by the noise she makes letting the door of the sanatorium dining room slam shut behind her, a practice that turns out to be habitual with her and that repels him, as do her general slackness and the way she has of slouching at the table. But the same qualities also attract him; as Fräulein Englehart, with whom he covertly shares his fascination with Clavdia, says, "Russian women all have something free and large about them" (p. 137). In fact, it is his attraction to Clavdia that at a key moment becomes the decisive factor in keeping him at the sanatorium. He had come only to visit his cousin, but then developed a cold and decided to see Dr. Behrens for an examination. Without the examination, which turns up what Behrens calls "a moist spot" (p. 181), Hans would have returned home at the end of his planned three weeks, and just before he is about to go to be examined, he feels better and thinks of canceling the appointment, but then Clavdia, with whom he has never spoken, throws him an expectant look with her narrow eyes, as though she knows about the approaching appointment: "and the eyes said thou, for that is the language of the eyes, even when the tongue uses a more formal address" (p. 176). This look, the narrator tells us, "shook and bewildered Hans Castorp to the depths of his being." As a result of it, his idea of skipping the examination withers and becomes "transmuted into a hideous sense of futility," and he proceeds "inwardly reeling, though outwardly firm in step and bearing" to the consulting room.

The kind of potential danger her influence may lead him into if he abandons himself too completely to it is suggested most clearly by her own words in the conversation she and Hans have at the Mardi Gras party the night before her first departure from the sanatorium. It is their first conversation, and to enter into it Hans has had to take advantage of the general license and abandonment of civilized norms that such an occasion offers — symbolized by his breaking away from Settembrini, who calls after him that what he is doing is madness, and by his conversing with her in a foreign language and his use of the intimate "*tu*" form of address. When he asks her what she thinks about morality, she answers:

> *La morale? . . . il nous semble* [she is referring to conversations with a Russian friend], *qu'il faudrait chercher la morale non dans la vertu, c'est-à-dire dans la raison, la discipline, les bonnes moeurs, l'honnêteté, mais plutot dans le contraire, je veux dire dans le péché, en s'abandonnant au danger, à ce qui est nuisible, à ce qui nous consume. Il nous semble qu'il est plus morale de se perdre et même de se laisser dépérir, que de se conserver.* [P. 340][17]

> [Morality? . . . it seems to us that one must seek the ethical not in virtue, that is to say, in reason, discipline, good morals, honesty, but rather in their opposite, I mean in sin, in giving way to the dangerous, to what is harmful, to what devours us. We think it is more moral to lose oneself and even to let oneself perish than to preserve oneself.]

Here she is echoing, of course, various New Testament sayings about the necessity of self-surrender to spiritual growth, that only what allows itself to die can bear fruit or come to true life; but there are different ways of carrying out the process of metaphoric dying, and some of them lead only to dissolution. The path Clavdia invites him on is both potentially fruitful and potentially destructive; following it, Hans has to find his way through a maze in which it would be easy to become lost for good. He is hardly up to finding his way through it on his own, but fortunately life sends its *Sorgenkind* sufficient help of various kinds to bring him through and to make his exper-

17. This and subsequent French quotations appear both in the original and in Lowe-Porter's translation of *The Magic Mountain*. Translations are mine.

iences, both for Hans and for the reader, a story of growth and illumination.

At the time of this conversation, Hans has already been walking for some months the path Clavdia describes. In the course of the earlier conversation with Behrens, the gentlemen had turned, while smoking their Sphinx cigarettes, to a discussion of the physiology of flesh and of organic life. Behrens told Hans and his cousin that the body is made up mostly of water and that it has a fundamental tendency to dissolve into formlessness. In death this tendency finds its fulfillment — ". . . you flow away, so to speak — remember all that water" — but even during life dissolution is constant: ". . . living consists in dying, no use mincing the matter — *une destruction organique* . . ." (p. 266). Hans was attracted to the subject at that time by what he termed "the plasticity of the female form" (p. 261), of one female form in particular, but this fascination drew him into the study of the organic in general, so that he bought medical books and "read with compelling interest of life, and its sacred, impure mysteries" (p. 274). This was a considerable change from his earlier attitude toward the flesh as exemplified in his reaction one day when Behrens greeted him and his cousin with an inquiry after the functioning of their "sanctified metabolisms": " 'Sanctified metabolism' — what sort of gibberish is that? If I understand what he means by metabolism, it is nothing but physiology, and to talk about its being sanctified — irreverent I call it" (p. 174).[18] Of course Hans had at that time failed to appreciate the ironic tone of Behrens' remark, but it is characteristic of

18. Cf. Eliade, *The Sacred and the Profane,* p. 178: "Just as modern man's habitation has lost its cosmological values, so too his body is without religious or spiritual significance."

Mannian irony that what it at first denies it later reaffirms in a qualified way with a sense of the ambiguity of what is affirmed.[19] Thus, sitting on his balcony dreaming over his medical studies, Hans came to see the mysteries of the flesh as simultaneously "sacred" and "impure." He also extended this observation to life as a whole and to the universe: "And life? Life itself? Was it perhaps only an infection, a sickening of matter? Was that which one might call the original procreation of matter only a disease, a growth produced by morbid stimulation of the immaterial?" (pp. 285-86). And in a dream vision he saw life itself take on the form of a woman's flesh:

> He beheld the image of life in flower, its structure, its flesh-borne loveliness. . . . She leaned above him, she inclined unto him and bent down over him, he was conscious of her organic fragrance and the mild pulsation of her heart. Something warm and tender clasped him round the neck; melted with desire and awe, he laid his hands upon the flesh of her upper arms, where the fine-grained skin over the triceps came to his sense so heavenly cool; and upon his lips he felt the moist clinging of her kiss. [P. 286]

It is because of this preparation that when he finally enters into conversation with Clavdia he is able to understand what she tells him about *"la morale"* and to observe in turn that *"le corps, l'amour, la mort, ces trois ne font qu'un"* (p. 342) ("The body, love, death, the three are but one").

19. It is interesting to compare what Hermann Hesse said (in a letter to Mann, November 8, 1950), as recounted by André von Gronicka, about the complexity of Mann's irony in *The Holy Sinner:* " 'Most readers,' he thought, 'would have sufficient insight to be aware of the irony in this delightful composition,' but he had his serious doubts, that 'all would be able to sense the earnestness and the piety which underlie these ironies and lend them their true, lofty gaiety.' " Von Gronicka, *Thomas Mann: Profile and Perspectives* (New York: Random House, 1970), p. 150.

Since Clavdia leaves the next day, after their only night together, Hans has no immediate opportunity to explore further the particular path intimacy with her would lead him on, but she has served as his introduction to the aspect of the universe that wears her face in his fantasies, and even in her absence he has plenty of opportunity to meditate on that and even to wrestle with its perils. He ponders, for example, the mystery of time: ". . . the motion by which one measures time is circular, is in a closed circle; and might be described as rest, as cessation of movement . . ." (p. 344) — a potentially dangerous line of thought because if one let it tempt one into a vision of time as *only* "rest" and "cessation of movement," this could be *"se laisser dépérir"* in a way that would be fatal. As simply a meditation this might seem too abstract to be really dangerous, but in one of the climactic chapters of the book, the "Snow" chapter, the temptation it contemplates becomes enacted in deadly earnest.

There Hans, who has taken up cross-country skiing, sets out one day into a landscape that seems the very embodiment of death: "No summit, no ridge was visible, it was a haze and a nothing toward which Hans Castorp strove . . ." (p. 478). The "absolutely symmetrical, icily regular" crystals of snow are made from the same water that is "the source of protoplasm, of plant life, of the human body," but in their coldness and precision of form, they are to water as rest and cessation of movement are to time, and they are described as having an "uncanny . . . anti-organic . . . life-denying character" (p. 480). The entire adventure is an example of the real danger Clavdia's influence can lead him into. As he sets forth, leaving behind the spokesman of reason and responsibility, Herr Settembrini, he says to himself, *"Praeterit figura huius mundi*" (p. 478) ("The form of this world passes away"), "quoting Naphta, in a Latin hardly humanistic in spirit." And as he notices the blue light reflected from holes in the snow it makes him think of the lure that draws him: "It reminded him of the colour of certain eyes, whose shape and glance had spelled his destiny; eyes to which Herr Settembrini, from his humanistic height, had referred with contempt as 'Tartar slits' and 'wolf's eyes . . .' " (p. 479). He proceeds on and on into "the wild silence" and the "gathering darkness" until a welling up of actual fear makes him conscious "that he had deliberately set out to lose his way" (p. 481). Even after he realizes this, however, he still feels enticed by a sense of "challenge" and presses imprudently on — ". . . perhaps a blame-worthy, presumptuous attitude, even united to such genuine awe." When he finally does decide to turn back, a storm has come up, cutting out almost all visibility so that he becomes hopelessly lost. He realizes that if he sits down, he will be "buried in six-sided crystalline symmetricality" (p. 484), but the temptation is great. It is only against a powerful inner resistance that he pushes on, and even then his course only carries him back again to where he was, forcing him to realize that he is in imminent danger of being swallowed up by his Sphinx as he wanders "in a circle . . . like the riddling year itself" (p. 487). Finally he takes what shelter he can in the lee of a hay hut, so tired that he passes directly from waking consciousness into a dream.

The dream is of a classical scene, a park of shady trees and sunlit rain, followed by a rainbow that is like music. Everywhere there are people, "children of sun and sea. . . . Beautiful young human creatures, so blithe, so good and gay" (p. 491). Some are at work with horses, some are dancing to the music of a girl playing a shepherd's pipe. Hans is struck by the beauty of the whole scene, but he is especially moved by "the mutual courteous regard" these people show to each other, "a calm reciprocal reverence," and by their combination of dignity and lightness, "a high seriousness without austerity" (p. 492). Their manner toward one another even has "a ceremonial side": as the young men pass a mother suckling her child, they "lightly and formally" cross their arms on their breasts and bow, and the maidens shape "the suggestion of a curtsy, as the worshipper does when he passes the high altar" (p. 493).

Nearby is an ancient temple. When Hans enters it, he sees a statue of two female figures, mother and daughter, the older "right goddesslike and mild, yet with mourning brows," holding the younger in a "protecting embrace" (p. 494). Passing behind the stone figures, he discovers in the sanctuary a scene that grips him with "an icy coldness" — "Two grey old women witchlike. . . . dismembering a child," a symbol of the "*destruction organique*" that is the necessary complement to life's fecundity. With this he awakens, finding himself once again in the snow, the storm having cleared.

At this point in the book, this dream is the most important revelation life has so far bestowed on her *Sorgenkind*. There is more to come as the book moves on, but Hans's assimilation of the meaning here disclosed to him becomes the basis for his later ability to thread his way between the Scylla and Charybdis of Settembrini and Naphta and to understand his subsequent experiences. Reflecting on it, he sees it as a disclosure from within the depths not merely of his own soul but of the world-soul in which he participates: "Now I know that it is not out of our single souls we dream. We dream anonymously and communally, if each after his own fashion. The great soul of which we are a part may dream through us . . . its own secret dreams, of its youth, its hope, its joy and peace — and its blood-sacrifice" (p. 495). From his vision of the necessary relationship between joy and death and his appreciation of the courtesy and reverence of "the children of the sun" that grows out of their "silent recognition of that horror" he draws the conclusion that one must hold in balance in one's mind both the existential reality of death and the beauty of life, with reverence before both, but with one's primary loyalty to life: *"For the sake of goodness and love, man shall let death have no sovereignty over his thoughts"* (pp. 496-97). He realizes that Settembrini, "for ever blowing on his penny pipe of reason," and Naphta, who lumps together God and the Devil in a mere confusion, both miss the properly humane and religious norm: ". . . in the center is the position of the *Homo Dei,* between recklessness and reason, as his state is between mystic community and windy individualism" (p. 496). The secret Hans now understands is that "it is love, not reason, that is stronger than death."

Important as this realization is to Hans, however, it is still mainly a vision and consequently rather abstract. To fully integrate its meaning into his concrete life, he will have to face new challenges and enact the love he now contemplates theoretically. Although he reflects, "Now I have it fast. My dream has given it me, in utter clearness, that I may know it for ever" (p. 497), when he returns to the sanatorium, the arms of habit enfold him, and what he had seen, though it does not vanish completely, goes the way of most dreams: "An hour later the highly civilized atmosphere of the Berghof caressed him. He ate enormously at dinner. What he had dreamed was already falling from his mind. What he had thought — even that selfsame evening it was no longer so clear as it had been at first" (p. 498).

Hans's next important revelation comes to him not in the form of a dream, but incarnate — in the figure of the elderly Dutchman from Java, Mynheer Peeperkorn. Many of Mann's critics have failed to appreciate Peeperkorn's full signficance, but in fact, his role is crucial to the book; he is a living embodiment, the clearest that Hans encounters, of the sacred mystery at the heart of the book's universe, the very incarnation of wholeness and, in the special form that Mann is working out in this book, of holiness.[20]

Peeperkorn's arrival is at first a cause of great embarrassment and chagrin to Hans, because he arrives as the companion of Clavdia Chauchat, whose return Hans had been looking forward to with the expectation that they would continue the relationship they had begun on the night before she left. Now he finds her in the possession of another man, whom he does what he can to despise in the traditional maner of rivals in love. This is not exactly easy for him, however. It is facilitated somewhat by the Dutchman's general incoherence of speech — such as, "Ladies and gentlemen. Very well. Very well indeed. Very. Settled. But you will keep in mind, and — not for one moment — not one moment — lose sight of the fact — but no more" (p. 551) — but the personality behind the words is so sensibly powerful that even Hans has to be impressed by it. An example of what the power of

20. This way of interpreting Peeperkorn was first put forward in a clear and fully adequate form in an article by Oskar Seidlin, "The Lofty Game of Numbers: The Mynheer Peeperkorn Episode in Thomas Mann's *Der Zauberberg,*" PMLA, 86, no. 5 (Oct. 1971): 924-39. For a brief account of previous inadequate interpretations see Seidlin's note 17, p. 937.

Peeperkorn's personality can effect and of the unique qualities he brings to the sanatorium can be seen in an incident that takes place at the beginning of his stay. At breakfast he beckons to one of the waitresses, a dwarf Hans had been rather startled by at his own first meal there and whom no one had ever spoken to except in an impersonal way. Peeperkorn wishes to place an order, but first he addresses her as an individual:

> My child. . . . You are small — what is that to me? On the contrary. I find it a positive good, I thank God that you are as you are; I thank God you are so small and full of character. What I want of you is also small and full of character. But in the first place, what is your name? [P. 552]

"Smiling and stammering," she answers that her name is Emerentia — in Latin, "deserving," a word used especially to refer to one who has fulfilled a term of service. Her role in the book has been an entirely silent one to this point, and Peeperkorn by his question frees her from her silence and brings her into the human community as a recognized person.

What he orders from the dwarf he has disenchanted in this way is itself one of the central symbols of the book: ". . . bread, Renzchen, bread; yet not baker's bread. . . . Not corn that is baked, my angel, but corn that is burnt — in other words, distilled. Bread of God, bread of sunshine. . . . a gin, love, and haste thee." When she brings his "bread" to him, in a glass filled to overflowing, he appears "to chew the liquid somewhat" (p. 553) before swallowing it. The union of liquid and solid in this wet "bread" makes it a symbol of incarnate life as the book has described it, an unstable combination of water and form, and the reference to it as "bread of God" makes it a sacrament — though a sacrament not only of the

Christian God, but also of the god of nature and of wine, Dionysus.[21]

The implications of this symbol are developed in subsequent episodes as Peeperkorn teaches Hans, with whom he has soon become very close, of "the simple — the holy . . . the primeval gifts of God" (p. 564) and explains, in an "oft-repeated phrase," that the holiness of which he is speaking is "holy, holy, my friends. In every sense. Christian and pagan" (p. 572). At the midnight supper at which he and Hans become friends, he likens himself to Christ at Gethsemane, then alternates this pose with that of a pagan priest: "He unclasped his hands and spread them wide and high before him, palms outward — it looked like a heathen prayer. His majestic physiognomy, but now imprinted with Gothic anguish, blossomed once more in pagan jollity" (p. 570). With a "sybaritic dimple" in his cheek he says, "The hour is at hand," and sends for the wine card.

In a conversation with Settembrini, who, rather out of character, has reproached Hans for becoming so friendly with a man who is supposed to be his sexual rival, Hans describes Peeperkorn's magnetism as the effect of a union of physical and spiritual presence:

> So it is not physical. And yet the physical has something to do with it; not in a muscular sense — it's something quite different, mystical; because so soon as the physical has anything to do with it, it becomes mystical, the physical goes

21. For a more extensive analysis of the sacramental symbolism here, see Seidlin, "The Lofty Game of Numbers," pp. 928-29. With regard to the connection of Christ and Dionysus in this image of the liquid "bread," the "Korndestillat," and in the figure of Peeperkorn generally, Seidlin says, "What unites them is the idea of the Incarnation: in Christ the world, the divine spirit becomes flesh, the heavenly descends upon the earth, light shineth in darkness; in Dionysos the seemingly blind forces of nature are transfigured into the divine, the seeds imbedded in the black womb of the earth break through into the brightness above, in the festive appearance of the god the light of torches illuminates the darkness of the night" (p. 928).

over into the spiritual, and the other way on, and you can't tell them apart. . . . But the result is what we see, the dynamic effect — he puts us in his pocket. We've only one word for that — personality. [P. 583]

And he does put them in his pocket, especially Settembrini and Naphta, who with their learning and their eloquence had before his arrival been able to dominate any company they were in. Peeperkorn is a living balance between their extremes, so that when they argue in his presence, their debate fizzles out and their respective positions converge in him: ". . . both seemed to fit him and to neutralize each other when one looked at him — both this and that, the one and the other" (p. 590). Seeing the collapse of their loquacity before this "commanding cipher," Hans comes to realize — quite a realization for a "chatterbox" like Hans, as Peeperkorn calls him at one point (p. 573) — that "either one expresses a mystery in the simplest words, or leaves it unexpressed" (p. 590). As Settembrini and Naphta vainly try to keep their debate alive, Peeperkorn reminds them, "But isn't there a — are there not — sacraments of pleasure," and says of the mountain air they breathe, "we should not breathe it in to breathe it out in — Really. — I must implore you. We must not. It is an insult. We should give it out only in the form of praise" (p. 591).

There are other ways too in which Peeperkorn mediates between extremes and unites the various opposites of life. Even his manner of dress, a "clerical waist-coat" (p. 550) and check tail-coat, suggests the union of the sacred and the secular, and his background as a Dutch planter from the East Indies represents a fruitful union of East and West. At our first introduction to him we are told that he might seem rather colorless in comparison with the lesbian, transvestite Egyptian princess of the Sphinx cigarettes (p. 548), but as it turns out he is all that she is, only in a form that is not perverse. The Egyptian princess unites the characteristics of the two sexes, for example, but at the expense of an inversion of her natural sexual identity. Peeperkorn, in contrast, is both fully masculine in personality and fully appreciative of the feminine side of life. His characteristic hand gesture — ". . . the lifted hand, whose thumb and forefingers were joined in an O, while the other three with their lanceolate nails stood stiffly up" (p. 552) — seems a symbol of the union of male and female, especially when one remembers the sexual associations of the lance and dish in the legend of the Holy Grail, of which Peeperkorn himself is the true embodiment.

The contrast between Peeperkorn and the Egyptian princess is important because it makes clear the perils of the path to wholeness and the necessity of a more than rationalistic wisdom to enable one to pass through them safely in a way that raises life to a sacred level rather than lowering it to the demonic. Settembrini is a rather limited person, and always remains one-sided because of it, but he is warning Hans of genuine dangers when he tells him at one point that the world of the sanatorium is an "island of Circe, whereon you are not Odysseus enough to dwell in safety. You will be going on all fours — already you are inclining toward your forward extremities, and presently you will begin to grunt — have a care!" (p. 247). Hans might be said to have taken his first step into Circe's power when he let Fräulein von Mylendonck, the head nurse, sell him a thermometer, a version of Circe's wand, and another step when he let Clavdia's eyes entice him into going through with the physical examination, and still more steps when he began to call Clavdia "*tu*" and to seek her opinions on "*la morale*" and later to set out deliberately, though unconsciously, to lose himself in the snow. Settembrini does not mention, however, that the encounter with Circe ended for Odysseus in a great success; it brought him pleasure in bed with the goddess as well as important information — about the necessity of visiting the realm of the dead — that furthered his voyage home. Hans may not be, as Settembrini says, much of an Odysseus, but Peeperkorn is, and he is able to teach Hans things that enable him to play that role more adequatley than he probably would if left to his own devices.

Peeperkorn tells Hans, for example, accompanying his remarks with his characteristic gesture, "the little circle and the upright fingertips," that all substances are both potentially dangerous and potentially beneficent: ". . . the truth was, in the world of matter, that all substances were the vehicle of both life and death, all of them were medicinal and all poisonous, in fact therapeutics and toxicology were one and the same, man could be cured by poison, and substances known to be the bearers of life could kill at a thrust . . ." (p. 578). The important thing is to know how to use them. Peeperkorn uses quinine, "one of the medicinal poisons," and alcohol and coffee, but it is significant that, unlike Hans and Clavdia, he does not smoke: ". . . he considered the use of tobacco one of those over-refined enjoyments the cultivation of which robbed of their majesty the simpler pleasures of life — those gifts and claims to which our power of feeling was even at best scarcely equal" (p. 564). In a later conversation he explains his meaning further, that the gifts and claims of life present man with a "sacred duty to feel" and that "if man fails in feeling, it is a blasphemy" (p. 603). It is here that he tells Hans that man is the feeling of God and the organ through which God consummates his marriage with life. The life that is the point of union between spirit and flesh can be a poison or an elixir; to use it properly is to transubstantiate both lover and loved into a sacred mode of being.

That Clavdia still has a potentially dangerous Circe aspect during the Peeperkorn episode is made clear by the way she pouts over Hans's friendship with her new lover. Part of her would like to see him feel hatred for his rival and remain her possession alone. Hans does have feelings of this kind to an extent, but to surrender to them would deprive him of the great benefits that friendship with Peeperkorn offers and it would reduce him to a virtually bestial one-sidedness in sexual passion. It would also make his relationship with Clavdia and Peeperkorn, who calls him "my son" at one point (p. 603), into a version of the Freudian Oedipal triangle. Hans is ready to meet this temptation, however. He learned some important lessons from life during Clavdia's absence, especially in the dream in the snow, and it is significant that in his first conversation with her after her return he repeats the formula she had used in her statement about how it is *"plus morale de se perdre et même de se laisser dépérir, que de se conserver,"* but this time in his own language and with a new meaning that purifies it of its tendency to moral dissoluteness: ". . . it is more moral to lose your life than to save it" (p. 558), a reference this time to his cousin's having risked his life in order to return to the flatland and his regiment.[22]

Because he is now able to encounter his Circe without letting her reduce him to bestiality, Hans is able to gain the benefit of the other side of her role as an embodiment of the passionate side of life: she loves Peeperkorn, and

22. Cf. ibid., pp. 933-34.

in spite of the side of her that would like to see Hans hate him, she invites him to participate with her in her love for him. In fact, after a little pouting, she reveals that it was for this purpose that she brought Peeperkorn back to the Berghof: "Shall we be friends? Shall we make a league — not against but for him? Will you give me your hand on it? . . . *Enfin* — if you care to know — that was why I came back here with him — *chez toi*" (pp. 598-99). She is able to share this love now openly with him because she sees that Hans appreciates both what she is and what Peeperkorn is; as she says, "You understand things" (p. 597). What he understands is probably even more than she realizes. Like Odysseus with Circe, Hans is able to appreciate her and all that she represents and values and at the same time to hold his own against her, maintaining the balance of the humane norm. When he tells her of the two paths in life, the "regular . . . direct, honest" one followed by his cousin, and his own, *"der geniale Weg,"* she tells him that what he says "sounds human [*"mänschlich"*[23] in her pronunciation] and good" p. (596), but it is significant that he adds a few moments later, about the idea of the *"menschlich":*

> You love the word, and I love to hear you say it, in your quaint pronunciation. My cousin Joachim did not like it — on military grounds. He thought it meant general licence and flabbiness; and in that sense, as an unlimited *guazzabuglio* of self-indulgence, I have my own suspicions of it, I confess. But in the sense of freedom, goodness, *esprit* [*"Genialität"*[24]], then it is great, we can freely apply it to our talk about Peeperkorn. . . . [P. 598]

As it turns out, it is not with a handshake that they seal the pact of friendship with each other for the man

23. *Der Zauberberg,* p. 849.
24. Ibid., p. 851.

they both love — "... *mit dir für ihn,*" as Hans puts it ("with you for him")[25], — but rather, by her instigation and his cooperation, with a kiss: "... a Russian kiss, the kind that is exchanged in that spreading soulful land, at high religious feasts, as a seal of love" (p. 599). The narrator goes on to comment on the significant ambiguity of the feelings expressed in such a kiss:

> Is it not well done that our language has but one word for all kinds of love, from the holiest to the most lustfully fleshly? All ambiguity is therein resolved: love cannot but be physical, at its furthest stretch of holiness; it cannot be impious, in its utterest fleshliness. ... In the most raging as in the most reverent passion, there must be *caritas.* [P. 599]

A love that was only self-seeking, as the negative side of Hans's fascination with Clavdia might have tempted him toward, would have led only to hatred, but balanced, as it is here, with self-giving *caritas,* Hans's and Clavdia's love is able to attain its full stature. As both passion and friendship it unites them not in surrender to death — the union of *"le corps, l'amour, la mort"* Hans spoke of at the Mardi Gras party (p. 342) — but in devotion to life. By resisting the dangerous side of his Circe, Hans has not only freed himself from the threat of reduction to brutishness, but he has freed her also from the necessity of being merely a temptress. Instead, she becomes in reality what Settembrini, shortly before her return, had ironically called her (p. 519) — Hans's "Beatrice."

Eventually the league Hans forms with Clavdia for Peeperkorn is capped by a complementary league with him for her. Peeperkorn surmises that Hans has been in love with Clavdia and that he himself has consequently been a cause of pain to Hans, and he asks him if it is true.

25. Ibid., p. 852. My translation.

Hans confirms Peeperkorn's suspicions, but adds that the suffering Peeperkorn has brought him "was indissolubly bound up with" the "enormous privilege" of knowing him (p. 609) and that he has not considered it a personal offense: ". . . so far as I personally am concerned, I have a quarrel after all, not with Clavdia, not with you, Mynheer Peeperkorn, but with my lot in general, my destiny" (p. 610). Peeperkorn, in turn, proposes that, instead of rivals, they become brothers and adopt the "thou": "The satisfaction which age and incapacity prevent me from giving you, I offer in another form, in the form of a brotherly alliance . . . let us swear it to each other in the name of our feeling for somebody" (p. 611). The "somebody" their league is for is Clavdia, but it is also a league, through her, for the life whose symbol she is, the life that makes "the holy, the feminine claims . . . upon manly honour and strength" (p. 565). Peeperkorn had already pointed toward this idea when at his and Hans's first meeting he spoke of the possibility that they might someday enter into brotherhood: "Brother-in-blood — prospective. In the near future — after a proper interval for reflection. — Very Good. Set — tled. — Life, young man, is a female. . . . She challenges us to expend our manhood to its uttermost span, to stand or fall before her" (p. 566). Peeperkorn's one great horror — ". . . the hellish despair, the Judgment Day" — is the possibility, which with his age and illness is becoming so great a danger to him, of no longer being able to respond to that challenge: "To *fall,* young man — do you know what that means? The defeat of the feelings, their overthrow when confronted by life — that is impotence" (p. 566). So, just as Clavdia needs a friend to help her care for Peeperkorn, he himself needs a brother to help him love life and love Clavdia.

It is not long after the forming of this pact that Peeperkorn commits suicide with one of the poisons he knew how to use. Although this might appear to have been a surrender to death, it was in reality a last act of defiance. As Hans tells Clavdia afterwards, "He was built on such a grand scale . . . that he considered it a blasphemy, a cosmic catastrophe, to be found wanting in feeling" (p. 624). Clavdia herself calls it an "*abdication*" — which is to say, not a defeat, but the putting aside of his crown before he should become unable to wear it worthily.

Hans has other experiences from which he learns a certain amount before he is eventually awakened from his seven years' dreaming on the mountain by the outbreak of World War I, but the encounter with Peeperkorn remains both Hans's highest point and the book's. Peeperkorn is the embodiment of the highest ideal man can reach toward in the universe Mann constructs in this book: to become the organ of God's union with life, and to remain loyal to this ideal as long as one can, even though one knows that, since he is a product of nature, like the grain that is distilled into the "bread of God," man's final destiny is to be reabsorbed into the darkness from which he has emerged.

Hans offers what is perhaps the best statement of the paradoxical combination of seriousness and jest with which Mann presented the *Magic Mountain*'s vision of the immanent sacred: ". . . he [Peeperkorn] regarded himself as the instrument of God's marriage. That was a piece of majestic tomfoolery — when one is moved one can say things that sound crass and irreverent, but are after all more solemn than the conventional religious formulas" (p. 624).

The Magic Mountain was published in 1924. The development of its vision continued in Mann's numerous subsequent works, and his concern with the possibility of an understanding of human life that would unite the sacred and the secular remained constant throughout his career. His next major work, the tetralogy *Joseph and His Brothers,* took up the theme with a comic emphasis — comic in both of the word's senses, humorous and optimistic. *Doctor Faustus* took it up with a tragic emphasis, focusing on the "questionable" side of the narcissistic union of man's life with life and on the demonic aspect of the sacred. Even *Doctor Faustus,* however, is not without hope. On the contrary, it represents sin, in a manner reminiscent of Joyce, as necessary to fullness of being; Dr. Schleppfuss, one of Adrian Leverkühn's instructors in theology, presents the concept of virtue in a manner so ambiguous that it seems almost an invitation to sin: "Piety and virtue, then, consisted in making a good use, that is to say no use at all, of the freedom which God had to grant the creature as such — and that, indeed, if you listened to Schleppfuss, was a little as though this non-use of freedom meant a certain existential weakening, a diminution of the intensity of being, in the creature outside of God."[26] When Adrian makes his pact with the devil, he is attempting to complete humanity by carrying it beyond the confines both of conventional religious piety and of rationalistic humanism. In effect, he is pursuing with Hans Castorp *"der geniale Weg,"* and although his end is grimmer than that of Hans, there are indications that his quest may yet be fruitful for man. The devil, who in this work seems truthful enough, even if he is genuinely evil, tells Adrian, "On your madness they will feed in health, and in them you will become healthy"

26. *Doctor Faustus: The Life of the German Composer Adrian Leverkühn as Told by a Friend,* trans. H. T. Lowe-Porter (New York: Alfred A. Knopf, 1948), p. 101. Subsequent references in parentheses.

(p. 243), and the possibility that this will happen is further hinted at in the story about Pope Gregory the Great that Adrian discovers in the *Gesta Romanorum* and sets to music. This story, which Mann subsequently developed into his novel, *The Holy Sinner,* is about the legendary origin of Pope Gregory in the incestuous union of his mother and father, and about his subsequent incest with his mother, his seventeen years of penance, and his eventual miraculous call to the see of Rome. At the end of the story, Gregory tells his mother, who has come to him for confession and absolution, "O my sweet mother, sister, and wife, O my friend! The Devil thought to lead us to hell, but the greater power of God has prevented him" (*Dr. Faustus,* p. 319). *The Holy Sinner* is an expression of the hope that this might come true for mankind, and in Mann's last novel, *The Confessions of Felix Krull, Confidence Man*, the hope is once again extended, as it was in *The Magic Mountain,* to the cosmos as a whole as Professor Kuckuck describes to Felix the ideal of "universal sympathy" and tells him, when he bids him good night, to "dream of Being and of Life":

> Dream of the whirling galaxies which, since they are there, bear with joy the labour of their existence. Dream of the shapely arm with its ancient armature of bones, and of the flowers of the field that are able, aided by the sun, to break up lifeless matter and incorporate it into their living bodies. And don't forget to dream of stone, of a mossy stone in a mountain brook that has lain for thousands upon thousands of years cooled, bathed, and scoured by foam and flood. Look upon its existence with sympathy, Being at its most alert gazing upon Being in its profoundest sleep, and salute it in the name of Creation! All's well when Being and Well-Being are in some measure reconciled.[27]

27. Thomas Mann, *The Confessions of Felix Krull, Confidence Man: The Early Years,* trans. Denver Lindley (New York: Alfred A. Knopf, 1955), p. 277.

It is significant, however, that what Professor Kuckuck is speaking of here is a dream. *Felix Krull* is the story of a confidence man, a professional illusionist, and the novel is an allegory of art, which is also a kind of cultivation of dreams. Such dreams may be noble, as that which Kuckuck describes certainly is, but until they are incarnate in full actuality they must remain only visions of what might be, and whether they will become incarnate or not is a question that from the point of view of Mann's work as a whole is not yet answered. Perhaps the most adequate statements in Mann's fiction of his assessment of what man is and what he might become are not to be found in any assertions the characters of the novels make but in the closing prayer of *Doctor Faustus* — "God be merciful to thy poor soul, my friend, my Fatherland!" — and the closing question of *The Magic Mountain:* "Out of this universal feast of death, out of this extremity of fever, kindling the rain-washed evening sky to a fiery glow, may it be that Love one day shall mount?"

The ideal that Mann sketches is a variant of the idea of the Third Kingdom, as his name for it, the "third humanism," indicates, and his profession of belief in its eventual realization, in his *I Believe* essay — "In fact, I believe in the coming of a new, a third humanism . . ."[28] — is distinctly reminiscent, even if Mann may not have had it in mind, of Ibsen's similar profession at the banquet in Stockholm in 1887.[29] Mann describes his "third humanism" as a combination of the tradition of secular humanism with the Christian religion's reverence and its awareness

28. *I Believe,* p. 193.

29. See above, p. 49. Fritz Kaufmann, *Thomas Mann: The World as Will and Representation* (Boston: Beacon Press, 1957), p. 27, traces Mann's concern with dialectical synthesis to Ibsen's "Third Kingdom" and to Nietzsche's wedding of the Apollonian and the Dionysian. Another source would be Goethe, whom Mann specifically refers to in this connection in his *I Believe* essay, p. 193.

of the reality of sin. "What Christians call 'original sin,' " he says, "is more than just a piece of priestcraft devised to keep men under the Church's thumb. It is a profound awareness in man as a spiritual being of his own natural infirmity and proneness to err, and of his rising in spirit above it."[30] But at the same time as he describes himself as feeling "the strongest antipathy for the half-educated mob that today sets itself up to 'conquer Christianity,' " Mann also makes it clear that what he believes in is an immanentist monism, not what he calls "the Christian dualism of soul and body, spirit and life, truth and 'the world.' "[31]

Mann's attitude toward the orthodox religious tradition of the West was in fact rather ambiguous. On the one hand he valued it highly, and on the other he felt it was in need of radical revision. In his later years he sometimes spoke of his humanistic ideal as a specifically Christian hope. In a letter in 1953, for example, he wrote:

> . . . it would be good if out of all our sufferings a new feeling of solidarity for mankind would emerge, a unifying sympathy for man's precarious position in the universe, between nature and spirit; in short that a new humanistic ethical system might form and enter into the general consciousness and subconsciousness. It might have a salutary influence on the spiritual climate here on earth. . . . But those are pious wishes. Even Christian wishes, if you will. To me "Christian," in spite of Nietzsche, still is not a term of abuse.[32]

And even Nietzsche's criticism of the Christian religion he preferred to see interpreted as "an event *within* the history of Christianity."[33]

30. *I Believe,* p. 192.
31. Ibid., pp. 192-93.
32. *The Letters of Thomas Mann,* selected and translated by Richard and Clara Winston (New York: Alfred A. Knopf, 1971), p. 652.
33. *The Story of a Novel: The Genesis of Doctor Faustus,* trans. Richard and Clara Winston (New York: Alfred A. Knopf, 1961), p. 191.

Mann was trying to probe past the present boundaries of the concepts with which men define their relation to the universe and to the sacred, and consequently it is not surprising that he should have had some difficulty knowing exactly where to place himself in relation to religious traditions and some difficulty defining what he was reaching toward. What is clear, however, is that in all of his work, Mann was trying to rediscover a sacred dimension in human experience and to present a vision of it to his age. Whatever his relation to religions, his attitude was clearly a religious one. As he put it in his 1948 essay on Nietzsche, "Religion is reverence — reverence first of all for the riddle which man is."[34]

34. "Nietzsche's Philosophy in the Light of Recent History," *Last Essays,* trans. Richard and Clara Winston (New York: Alfred A. Knopf, 1959), p. 177.

CHAPTER VII

The Way Up and the Way Down: The Redemption of Time in T. S. Eliot's "Ash Wednesday" and Four Quartets

In the uncertain hour before the morning
Near the ending of interminable night
At the recurrent end of the unending
After the dark dove with the flickering tongue
Had passed below the horizon of his homing . . .

"Little Gidding"

To turn from the preceding writers of this study, all of whom, whether sympathetic to religion or hostile to it, have stood outside the orthodox religious tradition of the West, to an examination of the religious thought and sensibility of two orthodox Christian poets such as T. S. Eliot and W. H. Auden is to step into territory sufficiently different that it is worth pausing for a moment to consider some of the main features distinctive to it. The chief of these, of course, is to be found in the concept of God. The various writers we have discussed up to this point were not, as we have seen, altogether without a concept of divinity, but where they could speak, directly or indirectly, of deity it was always of what would be called *deus sive natura,* a concept of divinity as entirely immanent in the world. The transcendent pole in the sense of the sacred these writers expressed was not the correlative for them of an actual element of transcendence in the structure of being. Rather it was related to a sense of ideal value, something not real in itself but perhaps realizable, not an actual being but a goal to be striven for. Even when, as in the case of Thomas Mann, they could speak seriously of "God," what was meant was not a center of awareness and liberty independent of man, but what some modern theologians would call a "God in process," the universe attaining to consciousness and personality in man.[1] Thus in the prelude to *Joseph and His Brothers,* Mann describes God not as a being, but as a restless becoming: ". . . a God whose nature was not repose and abiding comfort, but a God of designs for the future . . . who . . . was Himself only in process of becoming, and thus was a God of unrest, a God of cares, who must be sought for. . . ."[2] He must be sought for, not just because man needs Him, but because He needs man in order to come into being. Man's need for God is not a radical ontological dependence on Him; rather one needs God the way one needs loyalty to a supreme value — not for one's being as such, but in order that one may become fully human, in the sense of ethically conscious.

The orthodox Christian would share the belief that man needs God in order to be fully human, and in fact this is an important aspect of both Eliot's and Auden's ways of thinking about their religion, but he would not think of man's quest for God as making up for an ontological

1. The principal representative of this idea in theology is Charles Hartshorne. See Hartshorne, *The Divine Relativity: A Social Conception of God* (New Haven, Conn.: Yale University Press, 1948). Hartshorne bases his thought on the metaphysics of Alfred North Whitehead as presented in *Process and Reality: An Essay in Cosmology* (New York: Macmillan, 1929).

2. *Joseph and His Brothers,* p. 31.

deficiency in God Himself. On the contrary, he would think of God as containing in His infinite being all the perfections of being that are to be found in finite entities, but containing them, in the language of the Thomists, both "virtually *(virtualiter)*" and "in formal transcendence *(formaliter eminenter)*."[3] Loyalty to God is loyalty to a supreme value, but a value already fully actual and concrete in the transcendent being of God.

This means that for the Christian the transcendent pole of the sacred is ontological as well as phenomenological, and as a consequence its role in the sense of the sacred is almost inevitably more prominent than it is for one who does not believe in a transcendent reality. It does not necessarily mean that it must overshadow the immanent pole of the experience of the sacred, but it may have a tendency to do so, and this is what makes for some of the distinctive features of the thought of Eliot and Auden. Both of these poets came to the Christian religion from a largely desacralized vision of the universe, and for both their conversions involved a rediscovery of a sense of the transcendence of God, a sense of God as a *majestas* and *mysterium tremendum,* in comparison with which man seems small and unworthy. In Christian terms, it involved the discovery of a sense of sin.

To understand clearly what this means, one must remember that from a theological point of view the word "sin" does not refer primarily to a particular kind of act or misdeed, but to a condition. As one of the quotations Auden selected for his commonplace book puts it, "Men

3. Reginald Garrigou-Legrange, *Reality: A Synthesis of Thomistic Thought,* trans. Patrick Cummins (St. Louis, Missouri: B. Herder, 1950), p. 87. Thomas Aquinas' treatment of this subject is to be found in his *Summa Theologica,* I, qu. 13.

are not punished for their sins, but by them."[4] Eliot was pointing to the same idea when he said, regarding Dante's use of the fictitious figure of Homer's Odysseus in his picture of the Inferno, "It reminds us that Hell is not a place but a *state;* that man is damned or blessed in the creatures of his imagination as well as in men who have actually lived. . . ."[5] Acts of sin are simply particular expressions of a willed condition of ontological deficiency. To approach God in Christian conversion, one must recognize this condition and one's voluntary part in it and look to God for deliverance from it. This places the center of sacred value outside the world and man in the transcendent being of God. The initial effect of conversion is therefore likely to be that while the sense of the sacred as transcendent becomes very strong, the idea of immanent sacredness comes to seem rather problematic. As the second chapter explained, Christian orthodoxy requires both, and ideally in a close balance, but the movement toward that ideal may involve swings out and back; for a convert especially, it is likely to involve a nearly crushing sense of the majesty of the divine transcendence to compensate for a previous tendency to concentrate exclusively on the value of the finite. From what we can see of Eliot's religious sensibility as it is expressed in his poems, this seems to have been very much the case during the early years of his faith. "Ash Wednesday," for example, describes the beauty of the Christian religion

4. W. H. Auden, *A Certain World: A Commonplace Book* (New York: Viking Press, 1970), p. 180. The quotation is from E. G. Hubbard. Auden goes on to criticize in his own words the inappropriateness of the traditional use of the analogy from criminal law in discussions of sin and damnation (pp. 180-81).

5. "Dante" (1929), *Selected Essays,* new ed. (New York: Harcourt, Brace and World, 1964), p. 211.

very movingly, but it leaves the secular world looking almost as desolate as it did in the *Waste Land.* It was not until the *Four Quartets,* approximately a decade after his conversion, that the immanent and transcendent poles of the sacred came fully into balance in his poetry.

The background preceding Eliot's development toward religious faith seems a classic example of the disappearance of the sacred in the modern world. Eliot was brought up in what he called "the most 'liberal' of 'Christian' creeds — Unitarianism."[6] His grandfather, William Greenleaf Eliot, originally from New England, became a prominent Unitarian minister in St. Louis, Missouri, where Eliot grew up in a household that revered his memory.[7] New England Unitarianism was in part the product of a reaction against Calvinism's extreme emphasis on the transcendent majesty of God and in part the product of late eighteenth and early nineteenth century philosophical idealism. Besides being the most "liberal" of Christian creeds, it was also the most immanentist. For Eliot, the immanent, all pervasive divinity of his family's religion simply evaporated into the all that it pervaded, leaving him in a universe of nonsacred secularity.

The agnosticism Eliot took up also had its roots in the tradition of idealist philosophy and expressed itself philosophically as a monistic metaphysic based on the philosophy of F. H. Bradley, the subject of Eliot's doctoral dissertation.[8] In the form this took in Eliot's own thought,

6. Letter to John Middleton Murry (August 29, 1925), quoted in John D. Margolis, *T. S. Eliot's Intellectual Development 1922-1939* (Chicago: University of Chicago Press, 1972), p. 62.

7. See Herbert Howarth, *Notes on Some Figures behind T. S. Eliot* (Boston: Houghton Mifflin, 1964), pp. 1-14.

8. *Knowledge and Experience in the Philosophy of F. H. Bradley* (New York: Farrar, Straus and Company, 1964). The best study of the relation of Eliot's dissertation to the later development of his thought is J. Hillis Miller, *Poets of Reality,* pp. 131-89.

however, it had none of the pantheistic sacred quality that monism often does. On the contrary, it saw individual minds as inevitably imprisoned in their "finite centers," unable to participate in an absolute point of view that could enable them to see the unity of the whole.

All of Eliot's early poetry is pervaded by this vision of human life as condemned to fragmented subjectivism. "The Love Song of J. Alfred Prufrock," for example, is about the desire of the speaker to escape from his isolation, but when he thinks of trying to break through to others, he reflects that if he did squeeze the universe into a ball "To roll it toward some overwhelming question," the response of the woman he addressed would probably be only, "That is not what I meant at all. / That is not it, at all."[9] The dramatic monologue form Eliot uses in these poems fits his subject — a picture of a mind turning on itself. Even when, as in "Portrait of a Lady," a relationship is described, it is a tenuous one at best, and it seems to be fading before our eyes. The physical world, too, seems as fragmented and desolate as the social:

> The winter evening settles down
> With smell of steaks in passageways.
> Six o'clock.
> The burnt-out ends of smoky days.
> And now a gusty shower wraps
> The grimy scraps
> Of withered leaves about your feet
> And newspapers from vacant lots. . . .

When the speaker of this particular poem, "Preludes,"[10] thinks in the last lines about the possibility of something like a personal God as a unifying principle in the exper-

9. *Complete Poems and Plays, 1909-1950* (New York: Harcourt, Brace and World, 1952), p. 6. This will subsequently be abbreviated as *CPP*.
10. *CPP*, pp. 12-13.

ience of the whole, he poses the idea, then turns away to reject it bitterly:

> I am moved by fancies that are curled
> Around these images, and cling:
> The notion of some infinitely gentle
> Infinitely suffering thing.
>
> Wipe your hand across your mouth, and laugh;
> The worlds revolve like ancient women
> Gathering fuel in vacant lots.

These poems were all written from around 1901 to 1911. "Gerontion," written in 1919, was the first of an important series of poems in which Eliot presented a picture of the spiritual condition of the entire cultural milieu of twentieth century Europe. In this poem the speaker is an allegorical "old man" (the Greek meaning of the title) who stands for what Eliot in his essay, "Tradition and the Individual Talent," called "the mind of Europe."[11] As the poem represents it, this is a mind grown old and disillusioned. There are those who cry, "We would see a sign!" and who take up Christianity, but the speaker's comment on this is, "Vacant shuttles / Weave the wind. I have no ghosts."[12] Turning to history, he says it is a labyrinth in which we become lost in following our own vanities and "whispering ambitions" and that it "Gives too late / What's not believed in, or if still believed, / in memory only. . . ." His final reflection on all the contents of his consciousness is "Tenants of the house, / Thoughts of a dry brain in a dry season."

The image of dryness was carried over into *The Waste Land* (1922). In this poem the modern world is imaged as a barren wilderness waiting for regenerating rains that

11. *Selected Essays,* p. 6.
12. The poem appears in *CPP,* pp. 21-23.

never come. The poem is sufficiently well known not to need much comment, but it is interesting to note that even here, several years before his conversion to the Christian religion, Eliot was beginning to depict certain aspects of religious traditions in a favorable light. The Upanishadic injunctions to give, sympathize, and control in "What The Thunder Said" call for asceticism, in the sense of self-discipline, and for spiritual renewal, and there seems to be nothing ironic about them. The values they proclaim seem exactly what is needed in the world the poem describes. The world, on the other hand, is either unable or unwilling to heed them and at the end it still remains barren and fragmented. It is also worth noting that one of the few emotionally positive moments in the poem involves a description of one of London's Anglo-Catholic churches:

> O City city, I can sometimes hear
> Beside a public bar in Lower Thames Street,
> The pleasant whining of a mandoline
> And a clatter and a chatter from within
> Where fishmen lounge at noon: where the walls
> Of Magnus Martyr hold
> Inexplicable splendour of Ionian white and gold.[13]

The Church of St. Magnus the Martyr actually does stand on Lower Thames Street near the Billingsgate Fish Market.[14] The word "fishmen" recalls the apostles and the ancient use of the fish as a secret sign to identify Christians. White and gold, the colors of the church's interior, are the liturgical colors of Easter, "inexplicable" perhaps because the ideas of regeneration and rejoicing

13. Lines 260-65, *CPP,* p. 45.

14. See Robert A. Day, "The 'City Man' in *The Waste Land:* The Geography of Reminiscence," *PMLA,* 80, no. 3 (June 1965): 289-90. Day says St. Magnus the Martyr is very High Church, complete with confessionals, incense, and relics of saints preserved near the altar.

they symbolize are incomprehensible to those who live in the waste land. Even if Eliot was not yet thinking of becoming a Christian in 1922, *The Waste Land* seems to express a genuine respect for religious traditions, both eastern and western, and to contrast them favorably with the spiritual deadness of most of the modern world.

When Eliot eventually did become a Christian in 1927,[15] it involved, as religious conversion often does, a sharp break with much of his past. For one thing, it set him apart from many in his social and literary milieu. By the mid-1920's he had become a prominent figure; he was famous as the author of poems that were regarded as voicing the feelings of a generation, and he had become an influential critic as the author of, for example, *The Sacred Wood,* and as editor of the *Criterion.*[16] He also had widely ranging friendships among the other principal figures of the London literary world. This was a largely secularist milieu, and there were few among either his friends or his readers whom he could have expected to react with anything but disdain when he eventually made known his conversion to Christian belief.[17] As it was, when he finally did make it public in the preface to *For Lancelot Andrewes* in 1928, the reactions were generally hostile.[18] Eliot later spoke in various places of the loneliness of the position of a Christian in the modern world.

15. Eliot was baptized and confirmed in the Church of England in 1927. For details see Margolis, *T. S. Eliot's Intellectual Development,* pp. 104-5, and Robert Sencourt, *T. S. Eliot: A Memoir,* ed. Donald Adamson (New York: Dodd, Mead and Company, 1971), pp. 131-32.

16. For a description of what Eliot represented to his admirers of that period see Stephen Spender, "Remembering Eliot," in *T. S. Eliot: The Man and His Work,* ed. Allen Tate (New York: Delacorte Press, 1966), pp. 38-39, 44-45, 57.

17. When he did reveal it he came in for some not very good-natured teasing even from some of his friends. Spender, "Remembering Eliot," p. 59, describes Virginia Woolf, for example, teasing Eliot about attending church and praying.

18. See Margolis, *T. S. Eliot's Intellectual Development,* pp. 114-15.

In an article on Paul Elmer More in 1937, for example, he spoke of the "solitary road . . . of Anglican orthodoxy,"[19] and in his essay, "Thoughts after Lambeth" (1931), he said that the review *For Lancelot Andrewes* had received in the *Times Literary Supplement* had amounted to an obituary notice: "Somehow I had failed, and had admitted my failure; if not as a lost leader, at least a lost sheep; what is more a kind of traitor. . . ."[20] He also described his sense of isolation indirectly in his poetry—for example, in "The Journey of the Magi" (1927):

> . . . this Birth was
> Hard and bitter agony for us, like Death, our death.
> We returned to our places, these Kingdoms,
> But no longer at ease here, in the old dispensation,
> With an alien people clutching their gods.[21]

Besides the break Eliot's conversion led to with his milieu, there was also the necessary radical change in his inner life. In his essay, "Second Thoughts about Humanism" (1928), he said that intellectual conviction may develop slowly and "without violence to honesty and nature," but "to put the sentiments in order is a later and an immensely difficult task."[22] He was in the process of trying to accomplish that task as he wrote the poems that eventually made up the six sections of "Ash Wednesday."

Although there are always risks in identifying a poet very closely with the speakers of his poems, "Ash Wednesday" seems more than most poems to invite interpretation as a personal expression reflecting Eliot's feelings and the changes in his attitudes as he slowly adapted his

19. "An Anglican Platonist: The Conversion of Elmer More," *Times Literary Supplement,* October 30, 1937, p. 792, quoted in ibid., p. 139.

20. *Selected Essays,* p. 325.

21. *CPP,* p. 69.

22. *Selected Essays,* p. 438.

life to his new faith during the four years, 1927-30, that he was writing it.[23] It presents a picture of repentance and reorientation in which the speaker's relation to the world gradually alters from one of distrust and despair to a new sense of responsibility to "redeem the time."[24] The speaker of the "Journey of the Magi," after describing the agony of rebirth and his isolation among his own people, says, "I should be glad of another death." "Ash Wednesday" begins with the picture of a similar attitude, the desire of the scattered bones in Section II to remain scattered and forgotten, but it ends with recognition of the Christian's vocation to new life and activity in the service of God. One might say that the poem describes the process by which a new psychological and spiritual identity was developing in Eliot as he wrote it.

Section II of "Ash Wednesday," which first appeared under the title, "Salutation," was published in 1927. This was a year before his public profession of belief in *For Lancelot Andrewes,* but he was already breaking the news of his conversion to his closer friends and feeling the isolation this placed him in.[25] "Salutation" gave expression to this sense of having lost his old identity and of being dead to his former world. "Perch'io non spero" (1928), which became Section I of "Ash Wednesday"

23. Cf. Margolis, *Intellectual Development,* p. 137: "Like his prose of the late twenties, Eliot's poetry of those years was intensely personal in its reflections of his movement toward faith. It is difficult not to see something of Eliot in the speaker of his 'Song for Simeon,' who struggles to accommodate himself to the Christian dispensation. So, too, the purgatorial drama and ultimate spiritual achievement of 'Ash Wednesday' could not but suggest the experiences of its author."

24. *CPP,* p. 64. "Ash Wednesday" appears on pages 60-67. Since my discussion of the poem will take it up by sections and none of the sections is much more than a page in length, page references will be provided in parentheses only when the sections quotations appear in are not identified.

25. In "To Criticize the Critic,"' *To Criticize the Critic and Other Writings* (New York: Farrar, Straus and Giroux, 1965), p. 15, Eliot describes his apprehensiveness in telling his former teacher, Irving Babbitt, about it and says he felt nettled by Babbitt's response.

is an explicit farewell to that world, and together with "Al som de l'escalina" (1929), which became Section III, it describes not only his new resolve but also the real pain to himself that this cost him. These were years in which Eliot had to work hard to rethink his whole vision of life and to accept the personal cost of the death required for the rebirth he was seeking. When "Ash Wednesday" was finished and published as a whole with the addition of Sections IV, V, and VI in 1930, it presented his new vision in complete form as well as the new self that was to live it. This is not to say that either the vision or the self had fully attained the form they would in Eliot's later work, but they were sufficiently developed to enable him to take up his life as a Christian in the world, as one who sees his destination truly though partially and pursues it persistently though with a divided heart during what must inevitably be "this time of tension between dying and birth" (p. 66).

Section I is a farewell to the speaker's former life: "Because I do not hope to turn again . . . / Desiring this man's gift and that man's scope. . . ." He renounces "the blessèd face" and "the voice" of a lady who personifies the beauties of the secular world his new life calls him to leave behind.

Section II, which is written in the past tense, seems, if we take the speaker's background as corresponding approximately to Eliot's, a flashback to the speaker's state of mind immediately following his conversion and baptismal death. It presents a state of isolation bordering on pride and of surrender bordering on lassitude. This is not to say that it is a sinful state, but it is close to it, and if it were persisted in, it would become sinful. What it is is incomplete. It is the necessary death preliminary to rebirth, but it has to be completed by the actual rebirth, a painful, demanding process, and one that the speaker at the time found himself understandably reluctant to accept.

The section opens with a description of three white leopards[26] sitting under a juniper tree, having "fed to satiety" on the speaker's legs, heart, liver, and brains. To God's question, "Shall these bones live?", "that which had been contained in the bones" says that because of the goodness and loveliness of the lady to whom the section is addressed and because she honors the Virgin in meditation "We shine with brightness." Then there is a shift to the singular pronoun as the speaker says he would not want to be restored to life:

> And I who am here dissembled
> Proffer my deeds to oblivion, and my love
> To the posterity of the desert. . . .
> As I am forgotten
> And would be forgotten, so I would forget
> Thus devoted, concentrated in purpose.

God then says, "Prophesy to the wind, to the wind only for only / The wind will listen." As though to carry this out, the bones sing a litany to the lady, who seems an allegorical figure standing for the Church:

26. It seems to me that the context — the Christian death preliminary to rebirth — suggests that the leopards are not the entirely negative figures, sin, the world, the flesh, and the devil, and so on, that some critics have thought, but are essentially positive in their significance. One simple and appropriate interpretation of the leopards would be that they correspond to certain aspects of the Holy Trinity, God Himself as creator of the world, redeemer of mankind and founder of the Church, and immanent presence within the Church. This, after all, is the One, and Three in One, who is supposed to devour every Christian. The whiteness of the leopards, a color traditionally symbolic of holiness, supports this identification, as does the association of leopards and panthers with Christ in the medieval bestiaries. Cf. T. H. White, *The Bestiary: A Book of Beasts* (New York: Putnam's, 1960), pp. 13-15. Also compare Eliot's "Christ the tiger" in "Gerontion" (p. 21).

Lady of Silences
Calm and distressed
Torn and most whole
Rose of memory
Rose of forgetfulness
Exhausted and life-giving
Worried reposeful. . . .

The section closes with the bones still scattered, and by their own description, glad to be that way.

This is one of the more complicated sections of the poem and will need some explication. Its principal significance is to be found in its several levels of irony, some of which are directed against the speaker and some against his audiences, both secular and sacred. The irony derives from various allusions to Biblical passages, most of them contained in the Anglican lectionaries for the morning and evening offices of Ash Wednesday and the Lenten season. An example can be seen in the associations of the imagery of the setting, the desert with scattered dry bones, which echoes Ezekiel 37:1-14 and Isaiah 58:1-12, the first lesson for Mattins for Ash Wednesday. Both of these Biblical passages use imagery of deserts and bones, and both are about death and rebirth, the restoration of flesh to bones and of wasteland to fruitfulness. In the Ezekiel passage, the prophet is taken by God to a valley of dry bones and is asked, "Son of man, can these bones live?" When Ezekiel answers that he does not know, God orders him to prophesy to the bones, which represent "the whole house of Israel," telling them to "hear the word of the Lord" that He will restore them to life: "Behold I will cause breath to enter into you, and ye shall live: And I will lay sinews upon you, and will bring up flesh upon you, and cover you with skin, and put breath in you, and ye shall live; and ye shall know that I am the Lord."[27] Ezekiel speaks to the bones, and they come together and new flesh covers them. Then God tells him to "prophesy unto the wind . . . and say to the wind, Thus saith the Lord God; Come from the four winds, O breath, and breathe upon these slain, that they may live." When he does so they come to life and stand up, "an exceeding great army." In the passage from Isaiah, God reproaches the people of Israel for having failed to practice their religion either persistently or in the proper spirit, but promises that if they return to it,

> then shall thy light rise in obscurity, and thy darkness be as the noonday: And the Lord shall guide thee continually, and satisfy thy soul in drought, and make fat thy bones: and thou shalt be likė a watered garden, and like a spring of water, whose waters fail not. And they that shall be of thee shall build the old waste places: thou shalt raise up the foundations of many generations, and thou shalt be called, The repairer of the breach, The restorer of paths to dwell in. [Isa. 58:10-12]

The spiritual state described in these Biblical passages is that of the Hebrews as the people of God, a nation called out of the world to a sacred mission that was not limited to what we would now call ecclesiastical activities but extended to the whole of their national life. In the house of Israel the sacred and the secular were supposed to be united in a single ideal of a religious civilization. It is worth recalling in connection with this that the problem of the union of the sacred and the secular was to become a recurrent theme in Eliot's thought.[28] He dis-

27. In this chapter I will quote Biblical passages from the Authorized Version of the Bible, since this is the version Eliot would most likely have had in mind when writing his poems.

28. See Adrian Cunningham, "Continuity and Coherence in Eliot's Religious Thought," in *Eliot in Perspective: A Symposium,* ed. Graham Martin (New York: Humanities Press, 1970), pp. 213-14 and 220-24. For a more extensive study of this aspect of Eliot's thought see Roger Kojecký, *T. S. Eliot's Social Critcisim* (London: Faber and Faber, 1971).

cussed it at length a decade later in *The Idea of a Christian Society* (1940) and more briefly in 1931 in "Thoughts After Lambeth," and it was present already as an important concern in the essays of *For Lancelot Andrewes* (1928).

The speaker in this section has died to his old life and is now accepting his death with a little too much enthusiasm in a way that would leave the sacred and the secular fragmented. He would rather spend his days singing litanies to the "Lady of silences" as "Speech without word and / Word of no speech" than begin a new life in which he would have to try to become a "repairer of the breach" and "restorer of paths to dwell in" by speaking the sacred message to the world. It is as though Eliot as poet were objectifying in the speaker his own temptation to withdrawal and criticizing it by his irony in order to free himself to answer the call the speaker does not wish to. That the Biblical passages refer to Israel as a whole both in its sacred and its secular aspects extends the reference implicitly to the spiritual state of the universal Church — the new Israel — and of the English branch of this Church, and also to England as a nation. All are in a state of fragmentation because of their failure to live up to what God calls them to.

Although the speaker wants to remain dead to the world and in effect prays for this in response to God's question, "Shall these bones live?",[29] this is not what God has in preparation for him. Another Biblical allusion, to the story of Elijah in 1 Kings, makes this clear. Elijah, fleeing from the witch, Jezebel, "went a day's journey into the wilderness, and came and sat down under a

29. The change from "can" in Ezekiel to "shall" in Eliot's poem is significant: they *can* live by God's grace, but whether they *shall* or not depends on the speaker's acceptance of this gift.

juniper tree: and he requested for himself that he might die" (1 Kings 19:4). Instead of sending death, however, God sends an angel with food and drink — according to Christian tradition a "type" of the Eucharist. Finally, after Elijah's forty-day fast — a "type" of Christ's fast in the wilderness and also of Lent — God provides him with clear directions as to his mission. These allusions hint that the outcome for the present fugitive will be, or at least can be, similar.

If this is to happen, however, he has to learn to listen to God's call and interpret it soundly. As it is, when God commands him to prophesy to the wind, he adapts the command to fit his own inclinations, taking it to mean not, "Call upon the Holy Spirit to bring the people of God to life," but merely, "Speak only to the Church, for only the Church will listen." The litany that he then addresses to the Church expresses his desire for peace ("Terminate torment") and for seclusion in "the Garden / Where all love ends."

What the speaker wants from the Church is an end, whereas what God and the Church call him to is a beginning. It is significant that the imagery he uses places the Church outside himself as something that he can look to as an extrinsic source of solace. In the promised land that God offers him — "This is the land which ye / Shall divide by lot," an allusion to Ezekiel 48:29 — the new life he is called to is that of the Church as a community of mature Christians; that is, he is called not just to entrust himself to the Church, but to become it, to make its life his life and his voice its voice. When he renounced the earthly lady's "blessèd face" in Section I, he also renounced "the voice," which was also his voice, since as a secular poet he participated in the world's voice. In his old life the world was not something apart from him, he was himself an active element in it, and now he is called to live the Church's life in a similarly active way. The speaker in Section II thinks of the Church quietistically as silent and withdrawn, but as the poem progresses the theme of the Church's need for a voice by which to speak the Word gradually emerges and the speaker begins to understand his responsibility to contribute to it.

Section III, the ascent of the stairs, needs little commentary. It too is a memory, this time of the continuing arduousness of the life of *homo viator,* and its presentation of this is straightforward. Various critics have made different guesses as to the origin of the stair image in earlier sacred and secular literature,[30] but the meaning is clear enough without reference to antecedents: it is difficult to die effectively to the world in the correct way, much more difficult than the speaker in Section II had hoped, but it is essential, and the speaker knows this and is determined to persist. It is worth noting that this section, because its vision is less naïve than that of Section II, shows the speaker developing into a more mature, and correlatively more humble, faith, and in this it shows him already being reborn into his new Christian identity. Significantly, Section III ends with the phrase "but speak the word only," a phrase first spoken by the Gentile centurion stating his trust in Christ's healing power and since repeated during the mass as a communion devotion expressing the same kind of trust. The return to the theme of the word and implicity of the need for a voice prepares us for the new emphasis on this theme in the following sections.

Section IV opens with further reflections on the lady

30. For a list of possible sources see Grover Smith, *T. S. Eliot's Poetry and Plays: A Study in Sources and Meanings* (Chicago: University of Chicago Press, 1960), p. 147.

of Section II, the personification of the Church, but now there is an important difference; this time the lady is not simply withdrawn to contemplation, but walks "among the others," those whose vision remains limited to the secular, and restores by her presence the vitality of secular culture:

Who walked between the violet and the violet
Who walked between
The various ranks of varied green
Going in white and blue, in Mary's colour,
Talking of trivial things
In ignorance and in knowledge of eternal dolour
Who moved among the others as they walked,
Who then made strong the fountains and made fresh the springs

Made cool the dry rock and made firm the sand. . . .

Green is a traditional symbol of hope — as a liturgical color — and also of the vitality of nature. Violet is the liturgical color used during Lent, and it symbolizes repentance, the critical rethinking of one's life that prepares one for renewal. Violet and green are not in conflict here, but are complementary, because repentance does not deny the value of the secular but prepares for its redemption and fulfillment. That the lady goes in "Mary's colour" is appropriate both because Mary is the prototype of the Church and because the association with Mary emphasizes her motherly, life-giving and nourishing, role in relation to the world. The lady's simultaneous ignorance and knowledge and her talk of trivial things are aspects of the paradoxical life of the Church, which lives simultaneously in time and in eternity and which, seeing truly, though darkly, has to become like a little child in order to participate in a wisdom that transcends that of the world. Perhaps as Leonard Unger has suggested, the figure of the lady in this passage is based on some real woman Eliot knew,[31] or perhaps on several real men and women who made the Christian life vivid to Eliot as he was becoming intersted in the faith, and perhaps that is why the passage is written in the past tense and ends with the "Sovegna vos" of Dante (*Purgatorio,* XXVI, 150), a request for prayer in heaven. However that may be, what is significant here is that the lady, whether real or figurative, represents the Church as a vitalizing presence in the world. This shows how far the speaker has come from the quietistic attitude depicted in Section II.

Section IV continues with a pageant in which "the years that walk between" bear away "the fiddles and the flutes" and restore a lady "who moves in the time between sleep and waking, wearing / White light folded, sheathed about her, folded," while "new years" restore "With a new verse the ancient rhyme," which may refer to the injunctions that immediately follow it: "Redeem / The time. Redeem / The unread vision in the higher dream. . . ." The "years that walk between" are probably the years that have passed since the speaker's first turning away from the secular lady, the world, to the Church. At first he had to reject the world vigorously in order to keep from being seduced by visions of fiddles and flutes, the "lower dream" of worldly pleasure sought as a self-sufficient end. The power of their enchantment was depicted in the distractions of the third stair in Section III, and he is not yet immune to it, as Section VI will make clear, but he is now sufficiently disentangled from that kind of inadequate love of the world — the garden god's flute is breathless — to be able to contemplate the secular once again,

31. Leonard Unger, *T. S. Eliot: Moments and Patterns* (Minneapolis: University of Minnesota Press, 1966), p. 50.

this time more objectively, and to begin to understand its true value.

This reassessment of the value of the secular is one of the main themes of the poem. The pitfall of a person attempting to meet the Christian challenge of being in the world but not of it is the temptation to reject the world altogether, and thereby to fall into what has come to be known as Manichaeism, the belief that the secular is intrinsically evil and therefore unredeemable. This is a temptation the speaker was very close to succumbing to in Section II and perhaps even in Section I, but there was also a hint in Section I of a more balanced view: he knew that he had to renounce the secular lady, but he also grasped at least dimly that she was nevertheless "blessèd." Now, in Section IV, that lady is restored to him as one sheathed in white light, the transcendent meaning that waits to be deciphered in secular culture, and as one "between sleep and waking," awaiting the full awakening that that deciphering would constitute. The "higher dream" embodied in secular literature contains intimations of the sacred.[32] This is the "unread vision," the token of the unheard, unspoken word, that needs to be read in order that the time may be redeemed.

The sister in white and blue, the symbol of the Church, is silent, as she has been throughout the poem, evidently because she lacks a voice with which to communicate the sacred message to the modern world; there are no longer any Dantes, Donnes, or Herberts, and even Hopkins would hardly seem to have been speaking to the world at large. But the fountain, a symbol of the vitality of nature and of the secular generally, springs up, and a bird repeats

32. See Eliot's essay, "Dante" (1929), in T. S. Eliot, *Selected Essays*, p. 223, for Eliot's use of the terms "high dream" and "low dream" in his criticism during this period.

the injunction to redeem the time by interpreting the unread meaning in the higher dream of secular civilization. The bird is a traditional emblem of the Holy Spirit and here evidently represents the immanent presence of God as the source of natural grace and divine providence in the world.

One of the less obvious symbols of this section, but one that is worth some attention because it recurs in both V and VI, is that of the yew trees that the silent sister stands between. The yew is traditionally associated with cemeteries and with English history, bears poisonous fruit, and grows straight up, as though reaching for the heavens. All of this suggests that the yew is a symbol of the temporal world as bearing in itself both a tendency toward death and an aspiration toward the sacred. The position of the lady between the yews represents the position of the Church in the midst of the temporal world, and although the Church may at present lack a voice with which to speak the word clearly, occasionally the wind, the Holy Spirit again, shakes whispers, intimations of a higher meaning, from the yews.

That the speaker now refers to the lady as a "sister" is important as an indication of his growing maturity in the Christian life and the new role this places him in in relation to the Church. In Section II, where he was an infant in the faith and wished only a passive role, he referred to her as a mother. Now, without losing sight of her maternal qualities, as his expression of gratitude to her in the opening part of Section IV makes clear, he nevertheless is beginning to develop a sense of his personal calling in the life of the Church, especially the calling to redeem the world's dream by becoming a voice of the Church and writing poems like this one. This means that now he must be not only a son in relation to the Church, but also a brother. The concluding prayer of the poem as a whole will address her as both mother and sister, and it is one of the paradoxes of the Christian life that she must be both. The Christian has to be both a mature and responsible individual and a faithful member of the community of faith. The last line of Section IV, a fragment of the traditional prayer, "Salve Regina," acknowledges the speaker's continuing need for maternal care by casting him once again in the role of a son who, as he contemplates his new task in the world, prays to the Virgin for her prayers that he may successfully pass through the perils of this world.

Section IV is the climax of the poem in its presentation of the goal of Christian maturity as an active life redeeming the time. The speaker realizes at this point that he is called to this and that for him it must involve reading the unread vision in the higher dream, that is, interpreting the religious significance of secular literature and perhaps himself contributing as a poet to formulating the vision in that dream. At the same time, however, the speaker also realizes that religious maturity is still a long way ahead of his present state; he has further rethinking and self-emptying to do before he will be able to trust himself to attempt to revive the voice he renounced in Section I lest it tempt him to return to the worldly ambitions he renounced with it. The remaining two sections are concerned less with the goal of maturity than with the tensions that threaten it in this life of "our exile."

Section V opens with a meditation on the power of the "Word" in the world even when it lacks a "word," or a voice, to make it heard:

> If the lost word is lost, if the spent word is spent
> If the unheard, unspoken
> Word is unspoken, unheard;

> Still is the unspoken word, the Word unheard,
> The Word without a word, the Word within
> The world and for the world;
> And the light shone in darkness and
> Against the Word the unstilled world still whirled
> About the centre of the silent Word.

Even, that is, when it is unrecognized, the Word, in theological tradition the divine Logos, is the principle of the world's life. It is both the source of man's being and the goal of his energy. Even when the world pursues illusory, eccentric goals, its motion is composed of forces drawing it toward as well as away from God, and consequently it always hovers about its true center.

With the quotation from the "Improperia" of the liturgy for Good Friday — "O my people, what have I done unto thee" — Christ's reproach to Israel for having rejected him and his message,[33] the speaker turns his attention to the world's failure to respond to God's call, and also to his own failure to respond to it wholeheartedly. When he asks if the lady will pray for those who have chosen God and yet still oppose him, he is probably thinking both of England's present apostasy and of his own difficulty in maintaining fidelity to God. He would seem especially to have his own condition in mind when he speaks of those who are torn between "word and word, power and power," that is, between the word in service of the Word and the word in service of the literary man's personal eminence, the "transitory power" he has tried to renounce. Feeling the pull of the "lower dream" in this way, he identifies with all those who have affirmed the faith before the world — as Eliot did in the preface to *For Lancelot Andrewes* — but are tempted to fall away from it in the

33. This is a Christian liturgical allusion to God's reproach to Israel in Micah 6:3.

interior desert of the ascetic self-emptying necessary for complete spiritual renewal.

The tone at the end of Section V suggests that the speaker is so keenly aware of this temptation that he is close to succumbing to despair. The fact that he asks if the veiled sister *will* pray for those in this condition is an indication of this; he feels so abject that he begins to doubt if he can receive the divine mercy that is mediated through the Church.

Section VI continues the theme of temptation but shows the speaker overcoming despair by turning humbly to what he had almost doubted God and the Church would provide — forgiveness and renewal of strength in the sacrament of penance, of which the penitent's "Bless me father, for I have sinned" is the traditional opening:

> Although I do not hope to turn again . . .
> Wavering between the profit and the loss
> In this brief transit where the dreams cross
> The dreamcrossed twilight between birth and dying
> (Bless me father) though I do not wish to wish these things
> From the wide window towards the granite shore
> The white sails still fly seaward, seaward flying
> Unbroken wings.

The speaker confesses his temptation to return in the wrong way — "wavering between the profit and the loss" — to natural beauties that are essentially good, but that take on the illusory attractiveness of false dreams — "the empty forms between the ivory gates" — when the vision that beholds them is corrupted.

This life between man's physical birth and his physical death and between his spiritual death and his spiritual birth is a "dreamcrossed twilight" because in it he is neither clear-sighted nor wholly blind. And it is a time of tension because the visions, both false and true, in the three dreams, lower, higher, and highest, engendered by this inevitable condition of partial knowledge and partial ignorance pull him both backward and forward, upward and downward at once. In Section IV the speaker had a glimpse of the possibility of a happier relationship with the world and even of a calling to live it by turning from the lower dream to the unread vision in the higher dream symbolized by the whispers shaken from the yew by the breath of the Holy Spirit. His present awareness of the difficulty of living this is not, however, a sign of decline but of genuine spiritual growth that may one day lead to the fulfillment of his calling. This awareness is humility; in it he recognizes both his present condition and his calling to advance beyond it, and he also understands far more clearly than he did at the beginning what caring and not caring and what sitting still really are and what it is he needs to seek now from the Church — the nurture of a mother *in order that* he may find in her also the partnership of a sister and the quickening Spirit that gives their true life to the fountain and the garden and the river and the sea:

> Blessèd sister, holy mother, spirit of the fountain,
>   spirit of the garden,
> Suffer us not to mock ourselves with falsehood
> Teach us to care and not to care
> Teach us to sit still
> Even among these rocks,
> Our peace in His will
> And even among these rocks
> Sister, mother
> And spirit of the river, spirit of the sea,
> Suffer me not to be separated
> And let my cry come unto Thee.

And yet, even if Eliot may be said to have worked out in this poem the problem of the Christian's vocation to communicate the redeeming meaning of his faith to the world, it is hard to see "Ash Wednesday" itself as an example of this communication. It is not exactly a private poem, but to a person not familiar with the Bible and the Catholic liturgy, it must seem rather obscure. The poem as a whole seems more a parallel to the litany of the bones to the Church in Section II than an answer to the question, "Where shall the word be found . . . ?" (p. 65). And then again, one wonders how many there would be, even among members of Eliot's church, who could be counted on to have read the daily offices and thus be supplied with the background to understand his allusions.

In his subsequent poems and in his plays, Eliot was greatly concerned with finding a voice and language with which to speak to the world as a whole, both to those inside the church and to those outside it. The poems of *Four Quartets,* published between 1936 and 1942,[34] besides developing to full maturity his religious vision, were also an important step forward for him in the development of a poetic language with which to communicate his vision to a large audience on the basis of a common culture. Instead of employing allusions to relatively unfamiliar parts of the Bible, the quartets draw on Biblical imagery that would be recognizable to almost any educated reader, such as the tongues of fire (p. 139) and the dove descending (p. 143). Even Eliot's allusions to the English Civil War in the seventeenth century would not seem obscure to his English audience. And when he alludes to relatively less familiar material, such as the *Bhagavad Gita*

34. "Burnt Norton" was published in 1936, "East Coker" in 1940, "The Dry Salvages" in 1941, and 'Little Gidding" in 1942. They appear in *CPP,* pp. 117-45. Page references for quotations will be given in parentheses.

or the writings of Saint John of the Cross, it is not necessary to know his sources because their meaning is made clear in the poem. This is quite the opposite of his method in "Ash Wednesday," where the meaning of certain passages is almost completely opaque until one compares them with his Biblical sources.

The dominant theme of the *Four Quartets* is the problem of the relationship between time and eternity, which, as the poem presents it, is a version of the problem of the relationship between the secular and the sacred. It is worth remembering in this connection that the Latin *saeculum,* the root of the English "secular," means an age or generation and, by extension, the world of time. The problem as the quartets pose it is that from a point of view within time, time seems an endless, cyclical flux, while man's only access to a sacred dimension of experience seems to be in timeless moments that are "isolated, with no before and after" (p. 129). For man to leave the two separate is to be torn in two, since his natural life is rooted in the temporal world while his longing for the sacred is like an "intolerable shirt of flame" (p. 144) that he cannot remove. But to unite them requires "a lifetime's death in love, / Ardour and selflessness and self-surrender" (p. 136), and to accomplish it is beyond the power of unaided human effort. As the poems describe it, this is a problem common to Christian and non-Christian religions alike, and non-Christian religions, such as the Hinduism of the *Bhagavad Gita,* can offer valid insights into how to carry out the necessary self-surrender. The resolution itself comes about through the raising of the secular into the sacred, a movement that is initiated by a divine "Love" and "Calling" (p. 145), and fulfilled through man's cooperation with divine grace.

The first of the quartets, "Burnt Norton," opens with

a consideration of the possibility that time may be a closed system:

> Time present and time past
> Are both perhaps present in time future,
> And time future contained in time past.
> If all time is eternally present
> All time is unredeemable.
>
> [P. 117]

Two possibilities are implied here. One is the view of time held by Parmenides and Zeno the Eleatic, the idea that time is an illusion and that the only reality is the unchanging One. The other is one of the meanings implicit in the opening sentence of "East Coker," "In my beginning is my end" (p. 123) — the Aristotelian notion of entelechy, that whatever has being in the present contains its future within itself as a potentiality tending toward fulfillment. Eliot may have found this idea in the extreme form that the quartets consider in the thought of F. H. Bradley. In his discussion of time in *Appearance and Reality,* Bradley says, "Time, like space, has most evidently proved not to be real, but to be a contradictory appearance,"[35] and uses as one of his arguments for this position the fact that science, in effect, "quite ignores the existence of time": "For it habitually treats past and future as one thing with the present. . . . The character of an existence is determined by what it has been and by what it is (potentially) about to be. But if these attributes, on the other hand, are not present, how can they be real?"[36] Although Eliot definitely believed that time was

35. Francis Herbert Bradley, *Appearance and Reality: A Metaphysical Essay,* 2d ed. (Oxford: At the Clarendon Press, 1930), p. 36. Cf. the early poem by Eliot, written in 1905, which begins "If Time and Space, as Sages say,/Are things which cannot be . . . ," T. S. Eliot, *Poems Written in Early Youth* (London: Faber and Faber, 1967), p. 17.

36. *Appearance and Reality,* pp. 183-84.

redeemable and the poem as a whole leads toward a vision of redemption, the view considered in these opening lines is not meant to be interpreted as merely superficial. On the contrary, as the poem represents it, this is a perfectly sound theory of time from the point of view of an observer limited to a purely natural or secular perspective. To such a person, the timeless moments, "*Erhebung* without motion" (p. 119), with no before or after, would seem glimpses of a static Being, like the One in the thought of Parmenides, while the endless flux of time would also seem changeless in another way, since it would always be unfolding again and again a limited range of possibilities, as though in a perpetual circle.

A life imprisoned in such repetition would long for escape, either into a universe of larger possibilities or into death. This longing is extended metaphorically in the quartets even to the nonhuman universe in a manner that recalls St. Paul's description of how "the whole creation groaneth and travaileth in pain together" waiting for redemption (Rom. 8:22), as in the lines from "The Dry Salvages":

> Where is there an end of it, the soundless wailing,
> The silent withering of autumn flowers
> Dropping their petals and remaining motionless;
> Where is there an end to drifting wreckage,
> The prayer of the bone on the beach, the unprayable
> Prayer at the calamitous annunciation?
>
> [P. 131]

In this case the prayer of the bone is "to Death its God" (p. 132), a prayer only for an end of meaningless flux. As it is, however, within the world of time,

> There is no end, but addition: the trailing
> Consequence of further days and hours. . . .
> We cannot think of a time that is oceanless

> Or of an ocean not littered with wastage
> Or of a future that is not liable
> Like the past, to have no destination.
>
> [Pp. 131-32]

By itself, time only goes on; the only hope for a real liberation is what from the point of view of nature would be "the hardly, barely prayable / Prayer of the one Annunciation" (p. 132), a prayer for supernatural grace that would raise nature up to a higher level. This would give life an end not in the sense of a termination, but in the sense of a goal beyond itself — beyond, that is, a perpetual repetition of the circle of its limited potentialities,

> Where action [is] . . . movement
> Of that which is only moved
> And has in it no source of movement —
> Driven by daemonic, chthonic
> Powers.
>
> [P. 136]

Hints of that "one Annunciation" come to man in the timeless moments that occasionally fall upon him and lift him out of his ordinary state of half-consciousness into a momentary clarity and brightness, "a white light still and moving" (p. 119). It is the occasional experience of such "moments of happiness — not the sense of well-being, / Fruition, fulfillment . . . but the sudden illumination" (pp. 132-33) that make it seem "as one becomes older, / That the past has another pattern, and ceases to be a mere sequence — / Or even development" (p. 132). Accumulated experience in the temporal dimension does not bring this insight and liberation. On the contrary, the poet says that "the wisdom of old men" is "only the knowledge of dead secrets / Useless in the darkness into which they peered / Or from which they turned their eyes" (p.

125) and that "the gifts reserved for age" begin with "bitter tastelessness of shadow fruit" (p. 141). But at the same time, the "sudden illumination" is only momentary, and it has to be that way, because if it were prolonged, its unchanging brightness would snuff out man's temporal life altogether:

> Yet the enchainment of past and future
> Woven in the weakness of the changing body,
> Protects mankind from heaven and damnation
> Which flesh cannot endure.

Man cannot be saved by the extinction of time, but only by the assumption of time into the dimension of the sacred. The individual moments of illumination are themselves a foretaste of this, because each occurs in a particular point of time and place and transfigures it in a way that gives the secular a sacred value, a value that is not to be lost, but extended to time as a whole:

> . . . only in time can the moment in the rose-garden,
> The moment in the arbour where the rain beat,
> The moment in the draughty church at smokefall
> Be remembered; involved with past and future.
> Only through time time is conquered.
>
> [Pp. 119-20]

There is no real danger of man's losing himself in contemplation of eternity and leaving time behind. The moments of illumination are infrequent and fleeting, and even when they come, man is normally little prepared to open himself completely to them. The common pattern is to have "had the experience but missed the meaning" (p. 133), and only "approach to the meaning restores the experience."

The *Four Quartets* as a whole are an approach to that

meaning. They explore some of those moments of transcendent experience and the experience of history that links them. They also explore the reasons for man's tenuous hold on the illumination that he receives.

After the opening meditation on time, which concludes with the observation that "What might have been and what has been / Point to one end, which is always present" (p. 117), "Burnt Norton" goes on to consider an archetypal experience of illumination — archetypal in the sense that it discloses the structure of possibility both in the poet's life and in human life generally. In it a visit to a rose garden at an English country house, the Burnt Norton of the title, becomes a step "into our first world" (p. 118), an analogue to the Garden of Eden, the archetypal point of origin of the venture of human life at which the possibility was open to live in such a way that time and eternity would be united. The moment of origin is in the past, and to forget this would be to succumb to "the deception of the thrush" (p. 118), but the possibility it presented continues to call to men, and the moments of illumination that come in the present always have about them something of the quality of a memory of man's original home. As it is, however, man "cannot bear very much reality" in his present condition, and it is in the present, to which "what might have been and what has been" point, that man has to live.

One of the principal features of man's present condition is the kind of time he experiences. This is what might be called psychological time, since, although it is not completely unrelated to objective duration, it is largely the product of human preoccupations:

> . . . time counted by anxious worried women
> Lying awake, calculating the future,

Trying to unweave, unwind, unravel
And piece together the past and the future. . . .
[P. 131]

Time of this kind is more like a dream than like reality, and it is of this that the poet says, "Time past and time future / Allow but a little consciousness" (p. 119). Section III of "Burnt Norton" uses the state of mind of a crowd in a subway station as an example of this half-consciousness, "Time before and time after / In a dim light":

Only a flicker
Over the strained time-ridden faces
Distracted from distraction by distraction
Filled with fancies and empty of meaning
Tumid apathy with no concentration. . . .
[P. 120]

In a way that recalls the Buddhism Eliot studied in his younger years and alluded to in the "Fire Sermon" of *The Waste Land* as much as it recalls the Christian thought of Saint John of the Cross, this sort of time seems the creation of human desires: ". . . the world moves / In appetency, on its metalled ways / Of time past and time future" (p. 121). The effect of this imprisonment in appetite is to cut men off from the possibility of transcendence — "Men's curiosity searches past and future / And clings to that dimension" (p. 136) — and to reduce the time of human experience to a waste land: "Ridiculous the waste sad time / Stretching before and after" (p. 122).

"[T]o apprehend / The point of intersection of the timeless / With time, is an occupation for the saint" (p. 136), and the human path to it lies through asceticism, the voluntary extinguishing of the dream:

Descend lower, descend only
Into the world of perpetual solitude,
World, not world, but that which is not world.
Internal darkness, deprivation
And destitution of all property,
Desiccation of the world of sense,
Evacuation of the world of fancy,
Inoperancy of the world of spirit. . . .
[Pp. 120-21]

"This is the one way," the poet says, "and the other / Is the same" — the way of darkness and the way of illumination. Both lead away from the "time-ridden" distraction of the world, and both consist "not in movement / But abstention from movement." Because in man's present condition his appetites are habitually aberrant and tend to draw all of his impulses with them, the path of asceticism requires the suppression of all inner movements, even of what would normally be thought of as the virtues of hope and love:

I said to my soul, be still, and wait without hope
For hope would be hope for the wrong thing; wait without love
For love would be love of the wrong thing; there is yet faith
But the faith and the love and the hope are all in the waiting.
[Pp. 126-27]

This is not to say, however, that the path is unloving in the sense of indifferent; rather it is a preparation for a new kind of love, the supernatural love that "is itself unmoving . . . / Timeless, and undesiring" (p. 122). The difference is that between indifference and detachment:

There are three conditions which often look alike
Yet differ completely, flourish in the same hedgerow:
Attachment to self and to things and to persons, detachment
From self and from things and from persons; and, growing
between them, indifference
Which resembles the others as death resembles life,

Being between two lives — unflowering, between
The live and the dead nettle.

[P. 142]

The suppression of the inner movements of appetite also does not mean that one must not participate actively in man's life in time; it means one must act in a spirit that is detached and thereby genuinely free. Far from preventing action, it is this that makes real action possible, liberating it from the domination of "daemonic, chthonic / Powers" so that it may have as its inner source of movement the love that is itself unmoving and undesiring. This is the significance of the reference to Krishna admonishing Arjuna on the field of battle in Section III of "The Dry Salvages." In the *Gita* Arjuna asked Krishna if participation in war would prevent him from arriving at liberation from attachments, and Krishna replied that perfect detachment was to be found only in selfless fulfillment of his vocation as a warrior. The key to liberation, said Krishna, consists not in abstaining from action, but in acting without thought for the fruits of one's actions.

In order to redeem man's life in time, one must not withdraw from it, but live that life in such a way that it may be drawn into love:

This is the use of memory:
For liberation — not less of love but expanding
Of love beyond desire, and so liberation
From the future as well as the past. Thus, love of a country
Begins as attachment to our own field of action
And comes to find that action of little importance
Though never indifferent. History may be servitude,
History may be freedom. See, now they vanish,
The faces and places, with the self which, as it could,
    loved them,
To become renewed, transfigured, in another pattern.

[P. 142]

The new pattern is "a pattern / Of timeless moments" (p. 144) in which the timeless, unmoving, undesiring love that transcends nature takes on "the aspect of time / Caught in the form of limitation / Between un-being and being" (p. 122) in the temporal world and thus assumes time into itself, time as history and even as prehistory: ". . . the past experience revived in the meaning / Is not the experience of one life only / But of many generations" (p. 133), and the lifetime burning in every moment is not that "of one man only / But of old stones that cannot be deciphered" (p. 129). This is what the fleeting moments of illumination point to as "hints and guesses, / Hints followed by guesses" — the redemption of time and all of the natural world by their assumption into that point of intersection of time and the timeless that is God's gift of Himself to His creation: "The hint half guessed, the gift half understod, is Incarnation. / Here the impossible union / Of spheres of existence is actual . . ." (p. 136).[37]

Gradually, as the quartets proceed through an exploration of the poet's memories of his own childhood in Missouri and the historical experience of his family and of England, from the Renaissance and the English Civil War to the present in the darkest days of World War II, the vision of this meaning — Incarnation — is extended to embrace and transfigure all of these and to redeem the flux of time and matter from the darkness into which their natural trajectory, left to itself, would carry them.

The exploration of history begins with the poet's reflections on a visit to East Coker, the place of origin of the Eliot family in the sixteenth century,[38] and on the

37. The period between "union" and "Of spheres of existence" in the original of this passage on page 136 is a misprint in the American edition, and I have therefore deleted it from my quotation.

38. See Grover Smith, *T. S. Eliot's Poetry and Plays,* p. 269.

power of physical decay to swallow up what is merely natural in man's past:

> In succession
> Houses rise and fall, crumble, are extended,
> Are removed, destroyed, restored. . . .
> Old stone to new building, old timber to new fires,
> Old fires to ashes, and ashes to the earth
> Which is already flesh, fur and faeces,
> Bone of man and beast, cornstalk and leaf.
>
> [P. 123]

As he goes back to the scene in memory, he tells how "the light falls / Across the open field" and "is absorbed, not refracted, by grey stone" (p. 123) and how historic memories linger of rustic laughter and of dancing "round and round the fire" (p. 124), festivities described in *The Boke named The Gouvernour* (1531) by Sir Thomas Elyot, who was born in East Coker and may have been a relation of the poet.[39]

The references to fire and to light falling from the air and being absorbed into stone form part of a larger pattern of imagery of the elements that runs through the four poems and represents the processes of nature. The basic conception is Heraclitean, as Eliot's use of two fragments from Heraclitus as epigraphs suggests. The second of these — "ὁδὸς ἄνω κάτω μία καὶ ὡυτή"[40] (p. 117, "The way up and the way down are one and the same") — refers to the circular pattern by which the traditional four elements transform into one another in a cycle that begins with fire, descends to water and earth, and then returns through earth to fire to begin the cycle again. As another fragment from Heraclitus

39. See James John Sweeney, "'East Coker': A Reading," in *T. S. Eliot* Four Quartets: *A Casebook*, ed. Bernard Bergonzi (London: Macmillan, 1969), p. 38.

40. Diels, *Die Fragmente der Vorsokratiker*, fragment 60.

describes it: "Fire lives in the death of earth, air in the death of fire, water in the death of air, and earth in the death of water."[41] This is the cyclical pattern that the flux of time moves through, a perpetually repeated downward trajectory into "dung and death" (p. 124). Historical action, by its very nature as incarnate life, is always involved in this process of dying: ". . . any action/Is a step to the block, to the fire, down to the sea's throat/Or to an illegible stone" (p. 144). But at the same time, history has a spiritual center — "the still point of the turning world" (p. 119) — of which the fire at the center of the rustic dance becomes a symbol as it is taken into the human life that offers itself to that "still point":

> . . . you can hear the music
> Of the weak pipe and the little drum
> And see them dancing round the bonfire
> The association of man and woman
> In daunsinge, signifying matrimonie —
> A dignified and commodious sacrament.
> [Pp. 123-24]

Just as any action is a step to the block and to the fire, the parallel in man's life to what for the cosmos is "that destructive fire / Which burns before the ice-cap reigns" (p. 125), so part of the meaning one must approach in order to recover the illumination in the moments of transcendent experience is the necessity of accepting one's part in the world's agony:

> Now, we come to discover that the moments of agony
> . . . are likewise permanent
> With such permanence as time has
> People change, and smile: but the agony abides.
> [P. 133]

41. The translation is by Philip Wheelwright, *The Presocratics* (New York: Oddyssey Press, 1966), p. 72.

To accept this in a spirit of self-surrender, entrusting oneself to "the sharp compassion of the healer's art" (p. 127), is to participate in the central sacrifice for which "we call this Friday good" (p. 128). And to do so is to see the "destructive fire" that leads only to death transform into the fire of purgation, "that refining fire / Where you must move in measure, like a dancer" (p. 142).

To live in history is to live in fire. This may be a life of meaningless agony in which one sees the works one clings to eaten up by time despite one's efforts — "Water and fire deride / The sacrifice that we denied" (p. 140) — or it may be a life of sacrifice, of giving oneself to "nourish . . . / The life of significant soil" (p. 137).

It is through such sacrifice that the soil becomes significant. A place in which the life of sacrifice is lived — East Coker, Little Gidding, the England of the Civil War or the Battle of Britain — becomes the vehicle of a meaning that has the power to draw into itself the lives of later generations. Describing a visit to Little Gidding, the poet says that however one comes and for whatever purpose, the journey is likely to have effects beyond one's intent:

> . . . what you thought you came for
> Is only a shell, a husk of meaning
> From which the purpose breaks only when it is fulfilled
> If at all. Either you had no purpose
> Or the purpose is beyond the end you figured
> And is altered in fulfillment. . . .
> You are not here to verify,
> Instruct yourself, or inform curiosity
> Or carry report. You are here to kneel
> Where prayer has been valid.
>
> [P. 139]

Little Gidding was an Anglican religious community raided and dispersed in 1646 during the Civil War by the Puritan forces. Those who gave themselves to the life of that community — Nicholas Ferrar and the families of his brother and brother-in-law — made it an "intersection of the timeless moment," and their presence can still be felt by one who kneels there: ". . . the communication / Of the dead is tongued with fire beyond the language of the living."

Having introduced the subject of the Civil War in connection with Little Gidding, the poet goes on to explore the meaning of the kind of historical conflict it represents. Both sides, the Anglican and monarchist, and the Puritan, in so far as they offered themselves to the purposes of God, were "touched by a common genius," the Holy Spirit, and were thereby "united in the strife which divided them" (p. 143).

The first of the epigraphs from Heraclitus has a bearing on this idea of the possibility of a deeper unity within strife: "*τοῦ λόγου δ'ἐόντος ξυνοῦ ζώουσιν οἱ πολλοί ὡς ἰδίαν ἔχοντες φρόνησιν*"[42] (p. 117, "Although the Logos is common to all, most men live as though each had a separate mind of his own"). When men live only for their own ends, history remains, with the flux of the cosmos, simply an ocean littered with "drifting wreckage" (p. 132). But when men give themselves, even if partially and with dim understanding, to the refining fire that is always calling to them in the midst of the fires of human conflict, then history becomes a pattern of timeless moments and a dance around time's still center. Then men are joined in the life of the one Logos, and when they are gone, their lives become symbols through which it continues to call men out of meaningless flux into the union of time and timeless that is Incarnation:

42. Diels, *Die Fragmente der Vorsokratiker,* fragment 2.

Whatever we inherit from the fortunate
We have taken from the defeated
What they had to leave us — a symbol:
A symbol perfected in death.
And all shall be well and
All manner of thing shall be well
By the purification of the motive
In the ground of our beseeching.

[P. 143]

An awareness of this meaning incarnate in the lives of men in the historical past can also aid one to see it in the conflicts of the present — to see, for example, in the German airplane heading homeward after a night raid over London a "dark dove with . . . flickering tongue" (p. 140). Even the destructive fire of incendiary bombs, seen in this perspective, can become a vehicle through which the Holy Spirit speaks to men of what is always their calling: "The dove descending breaks the air / With flame of incandescent terror," reminding men that their only hope "Lies in the choice of pyre or pyre / To be redeemed from fire by fire" (pp. 143-44).

The redemption of human purposes from the fire of destruction by the fire of purgation gives a new and higher meaning to the saying that the way up and the way down are one and the same: transcendent light emerges from within the very depths of darkness, and the ascent of the soul to its true home becomes one movement with the descent of the divine Logos into the world's life in Incarnation.

To live faithfully this vocation, "with the drawing of this Love and the voice of this Calling" (p. 145), will be to spend one's life exploring, "still and still moving / Into another intensity / For a further union, a deeper communion" (p. 129) and eventually, in the final consummation, to arrive at the original garden of possibility "and know the place for the first time" (p. 145). When this happens, then time will be transfigured in the eternal and the *saeculum* will be entirely what it is now only in moments — the sacred Kingdom:

> When the tongues of flame are in-folded
> Into the crowned knot of fire
> And the fire and the rose are one.

CHAPTER VIII

W. H. Auden: The Ambiguity of the Sacred

To turn to W. H. Auden is to find a considerably more complicated and problematic concept of the sacred than has been seen in any of the preceding writers. The reason is that for Auden there was a very powerful false sacred as well as a true one and that the false one is by far the more prominent in most people's experience. To arrive at a vision of the true sacred, one must first free oneself from the power that the false has over one's imagination. "At all times and in all places," he wrote at one point in *The Dyer's Hand,* "certain objects, beings and events arouse in [man's] imagination a feeling of sacred awe, while other objects, beings and events leave his imagination unmoved. But a Christian cannot say, as a polytheist can: 'All before which my imagination feels sacred awe is sacred-in-itself, and all which leaves it unmoved is profane-in-itself.' "[1] Genuine holiness, in fact, is likely to be overlooked if one tries to evaluate it in terms of the rather dramatic qualities one usually associates with the experience of the sacred:

1. *The Dyer's Hand and Other Essays* (New York: Random House, 1962), p. 459.

The Incarnation, the coming of Christ in the form of a servant who cannot be recognized by the eye of flesh and blood, but only by the eye of faith, puts an end to all claims of the imagination to be the faculty which decides what is truly sacred and what is profane. . . . Christ appears looking just like any other man, yet claims that He is the Way, the Truth and the Life. . . . The contradiction between the profane appearance and the sacred assertion is impassible [*sic*] to the imagination. [P. 457]

The plainness and unimposingness of the true sacred is one of its essential qualities, because it is by this that men are left free to make a personal choice with regard to it. If it overpowered them with awesomeness, it would simply sweep them along, and they would be left in what Kierkegaard, a favorite theologian of Auden's, would call the aesthetic mode of existence; making no choices of their own they would have little real selfhood and would be as easily swept away by the false sacred as by the true. "Christ did not enchant men," said Auden, "He demanded that they believe in Him."[2] The faith that can reach through enchantments to grasp and hold on to reality, besides giving a person the objective reality which is its goal, also gives him the subjective reality of his personal freedom consciously lived.

This is, of course, much more strenuous than the aesthetic mode of existence, where the passions do one's living for one, and the false sacred consequently tends to have a stronger and wider appeal than the true. Enchantment is both exciting and effortless, and it even replaces the tension of faith with a pleasant illusion of certainty: "When enchanted, we neither believe nor doubt nor deny: we *know,* even if, as in the case of a false enchantment, our knowledge is self-deception."[3] "When

2. *A Certain World: A Commonplace Book* (New York: Viking Press, 1970), p. 150.

3. Ibid., p. 149.

the pagan gods appeared to men," Auden wrote in *Secondary Worlds*, "they were immediately recognizable as divine by the awe and wonder they aroused in their mortal beholders, and pre-Christian poets were acclaimed as mouthpieces of the gods because their language was the language of magic enchantment."[4]

Enchantment is the very material of art, and it is the reason why art is so attractive. Distinguishing between the primary world of objective reality and the secondary worlds created by the imagination, Auden said that dissatisfaction with the primary world is the principal motive for art. Art can create a world of which man is in effect the God, omnipotent over it and omniscient, and which demands no faith for the discovery of the sacred within it, but presents its illusory enchantment directly: "Too many of our experiences are profane, unimportant, boring. From a secondary world, we can exclude everything except what we find sacred, important, enchanting" (*Secondary Worlds,* p. 52). Art, consequently, has a tendency to draw men away from the truth into inauthenticity, and one concerned, as Auden is, with truth must be on his guard against its temptations. If one recognizes its limits and uses it properly, on the other hand, it may function as a kind of white magic to free one from false enchantments. As he put it in the epigraph to Part II of the volume *Homage to Clio,*

> Although you be as I am, one of those
> Who feel a Christian ought to write in Prose
> For Poetry is Magic — born in sin, you
> May read it to exorcise the Gentile in you.[5]

Any use of magic, however, is a perilous enterprise, to be undertaken only with a realistic recognition of its dangers.

4. *Secondary Worlds* (New York: Random House, 1968), p. 135.

5. *Homage to Clio* (London: Faber and Faber, 1960), p. 53. This was subsequently used also as the epigraph to *Collected Shorter Poems 1927-57* (New York: Random House, 1966).

The sacred may be true or it may be false; art may seek the true sacred or it may succumb to the allure of the false. It is not too surprising that for Auden, as a Christian, the sacred would seem more problematic than for the non-Christian writers we have examined, but there is also a considerable difference between Auden's way of thinking about the sacred and T. S. Eliot's. In the poems he wrote before he became a Christian, Eliot represented the world as primarily a profane waste land with here and there a few images of sacredness pointing beyond themselves to hopes that might seem either true or false depending on the attitude of the observer — false for Eliot's Gerontion and his Hollow Men, true perhaps to some extent from some points of view within *The Waste Land*. In his Christian poetry, the concept of the sacred remained, from the point of view of its relation to secular experience, very similar to what it had been in the earlier poems; the secular world in itself, as the *Four Quartets* describes it, is like an ocean littered with wreckage except where here and there the experience of a timeless moment illumines it briefly or where the voice of a religious tradition comments on the meaning of such moments. The secular world becomes sacred, from this point of view, by its assumption into God's life in what the quartets call "Incarnation." It is significant that the phrase they use is not "*the* Incarnation," but simply "Incarnation"; as the quartets represent it, Incarnation is not something that is actual only in the person of Christ, but a state in which those who seek Christ participate to the extent that they are united with Him in prayer and the sacramental life of the Church. Implicit in this approach to the Christian religion is the idea that there is a sense in which God may be immanent in the world as well as transcendent. He is not immanent in the secular world by nature, as He would be from a pantheistic point of view, but He becomes immanent in it in another way when He draws it into His mode of being; the idea is that expressed in the Athanasian Creed in its description of the union of the divine and human natures in Christ as happening "not by the conversion of the Godhead into flesh, but by the assumption of the manhood into God." From this point of view, the sacred, although its particular expression may be dim or partial, is always grounded in the presence of God, and its function is to show Him forth and thereby draw the beholder into a closer union with Him.

This is obviously very different, at least in emphasis, from Auden's idea that there may be false forms of the sacred as well as true and that the false ones have so strong a power to seduce one away from the true sacred that in order to approach God adequately one must subject every experience of the sacred to a searching criticism. Eliot was not completely unaware of the possibility of such sidetracking — his idea that waiting without hope for hope would be hope of the wrong thing is related to it — but for Eliot it was much less of a problem than for Auden, perhaps because for him there was very little danger of reading a false sacredness into the secular world; from Eliot's point of view the world tended to seem utterly profane except where a flash of illumination from the realm of the true sacred descended into it. For Auden, on the other hand, the world tends all too easily to fill up with false enchantments that must be seen through if one is to know the real world as it is grounded in the only true God.

There are probably several reasons for the differences in Eliot's and Auden's views of the sacred. One may be temperamental — that Eliot simply had little tendency to find the world so enchanting that it could seem of itself to take on a quality of sacredness. Another, which may in its own way be related to temperamental differences, has to do with theology — the difference in their ways of thinking about the Christian doctrine of Original Sin. Although the doctrine of Original Sin is an important element in the thought of both poets in that it describes man's incompleteness apart from God, the two have followed different traditions as to its precise meaning. Whereas Eliot, who never actually defined any of his articles of belief, followed implicitly the general Catholic tradition of theology, Auden has spoken explicitly about this doctrine and has related his own position on it to that of the Protestant tradition. Reviewing Reinhold Niebuhr's *The Nature and Destiny of Man* in 1941, Auden discussed Niebuhr's criticism of the Catholic theory that Original Sin consists in the privation of a superadded gift, as contrasted with the Protestant theory which holds that it consists in a corruption of man's essential nature, and stated his own preference for the Protestant position.[6] For the Catholic tradition, especially as developed by Aquinas and transmitted into Anglicanism by Richard Hooker, man is basically rational even if somewhat disordered by the effects of his estrangement from God, and reason, if followed carefully, is a reliable guide to man's natural happiness and to his preparation for the revelation and supernatural grace that will complete him by God's gift.

The Protestant reformers, on the other hand, leaned toward Augustinianism and the belief that the disordering of man's nature by the Fall left his passions so strong and reason so weakened that by itself it could no longer serve as an adequate guide.

6. "The Means of Grace," *New Republic*, 104 (June 1941): 766. Cf. Herbert Greenberg, *Quest for the Necessary: W. H. Auden and the Dilemma of Divided Consciousness* (Cambridge, Mass.: Harvard University Press, 1968), pp. 139, 200.

Auden did not wish to depreciate reason totally, however, and argue for a subjectivistic irrationalism. Rather he tried to combine the points of view of both the Catholic and the Protestant traditions, and this may be one reason, besides the fact that he was brought up in an Anglo-Catholic family, why he chose like Eliot to become an Anglican. His mind has tended generally to think in terms of duality and balance, as many critics have pointed out,[7] and balance, for him, is one of the paths out of enchantment. *The Enchafèd Flood,* a critical study of the romantic movement, considers various strategies for balancing reason and passion, neither of which can be, as they tend to claim, the whole of man, and in one passage it associates the opposition between the two with that between Catholicism and Protestantism:

> Minds may be similar, but they are not the whole or even the chief element in a human being. "I would rather," says Ishmael, "feel your spine than your skull, whoever you are."
>
> The Deist religion of reason had a catholic myth, that of the Goddess of reason, but no cultus. . . .
>
> The romantic reaction replaced the Goddess by a protestant variety of individual myths; but it, too, lacked a cult in which all men could take part. Instead it substituted imagination for reason, and in place of the man of *esprit* the artist as priest-magician.[8]

Neither approach, Catholic-rational or Protestant-subjectivist, is adequate by itself to lead men back to wholeness, but must be balanced by an appreciation of the other. For Auden, however, as compared with Eliot, it was the overvaluing of reason that seemed the greater threat. The path to balance requires the realization both that passion

7. Justin Replogle, *Auden's Poetry* (Seattle: University of Washington Press, 1969), pp. 50 ff.

8. *The Enchafèd Flood or The Romantic Iconography of the Sea* (New York: Vintage Books, n.d.), p. 55.

may easily lead reason into self-deception and that even if reason were able to defend itself perfectly against this danger, it would still be only one element in the true wholeness of man's existential life and by itself would terminate in abstractions and hypotheses, not in concrete existence.

Mind, as Auden said, is neither the whole nor even the chief element in a human being; it is the spine, not the skull, that grounds one in existential reality. Citing in *Secondary Worlds* Santayana's definition of skepticism as "the chastity of the intellect," Auden commented, "Precisely. But a chastity which is not founded upon a deep reverence for sex is nothing but tight-arsed old maidery" (p. 126). Kierkegaard put the same idea still more forcefully: "Paganism never gets nearer the truth than Pilate: What is truth? And with that crucifies it."[9] For Auden it was the concern with existential concreteness that was the very heart of Christianity. The life of Christian faith is the very opposite of intellectual abstraction; as Auden said in his introduction to *The Living Thoughts of Kierkegaard,* "Christ is not a teacher of truths but the Truth."[10]

The non-Christian, however, may well ask what this means. One meaning is that whereas man, in his fallen condition, is fragmented, Christ, if he is what the Christian religion claims he is, is living wholeness; another is that, living in the condition of inner unity that constitutes this wholeness, he lives with full consciousness in reality. In his Christmas oratorio, "For the Time Being," Auden described how the Fall has divided man's consciousness

9. Kierkegaard, *The Journals,* in *A Kierkegaard Anthology,* ed. Robert Bretall (Princeton, N.J.: Princeton University Press, 1951), p. 9.

10. New York: David McKay, 1952, p. 17.

into four faculties — intuition, feeling, sensation, and thought:

> We who are four were
> Once but one,
> Before his act of
> Rebellion;
> We were himself when
> His life was free,
> His error became our
> Chance to be.[11]

Separately they pursue either empty abstractions or fragmentary and meaningless concreteness,

> Beautiful facts or true
> Generalisations,
> Test cases in Law or
> Market quotations.
> [P. 415]

Thought in particular says that man's "dreaming brain" becomes for thought, a "fairyland"; abstraction is tantamount to idle phantasy. The advent of Christ is the delivery of human nature, in Him, from this state, and the reunion of all four faculties into integrity. Although men other than Christ remain in the fragmentation and dream-like consciousness that is the state of Original Sin, the fact that there is one person who is a living alternative to this state becomes for them the ground of hope that they too may be delivered into unity and concreteness. Thus when Simeon says that "of this Child it is the case that He is in no sense a symbol," the chorus responds, "We have right to believe that we really exist" (p. 452).

Before men can approach this salvation, however,

11. *The Collected Poetry of W. H. Auden* (New York: Random House, 1945), p. 414. This will subsequently be referred to as *Poetry*.

they must recognize how far they are from it, facing their fragmentedness and uprootedness honestly and realizing how helpless they are to escape from it by the paths they usually follow — the paths Kierkegaard calls the aesthetic and the ethical. Kierkegaard's aesthetic path, as Auden described it in his introduction to Kierkegaard, "regards the passions not as belonging to the self, but as divine visitations, powers which it must find the means to attract or repel if the self is to survive."[12] The ethical believes that "man . . . being endowed with reason, can apprehend God directly as Idea and Law, transcend his finite bodily passions, and become like God" (p. 12). Pursuing this path, the ethical man learns eventually that knowledge of what is good does not automatically cause the knower to will it and that he may even violate it deliberately. The aesthetic man, likewise, learns eventually that his passions diminish in time, leaving him to only intermittently relieved boredom. Auden said, "It is probably true that nobody was ever genuinely converted to Christianity who had not lost his 'nerve,' either because he was aesthetically unfortunate or because he was ethically powerless, i.e., unable to do what he knew to be his duty" (p. 18). This "loss of nerve" is the recognition of aesthetic and ethical insufficiency, or, to put it in theological terms, of Original Sin.

A passage from Dag Hammarskjöld's *Markings* that Auden selected for his commonplace book describes Original Sin and its meaning for human life in terms that are probably very close to those Auden himself would use to define it:

We can reach the point where it becomes possible for us to recognise and understand Original Sin, that dark counter-

12. *Living Thoughts*, p. 9.

centre of evil in our nature — that is to say, though it *is* not our nature, it is *of* it — that something within us which rejoices when disaster befalls the very cause we are trying to serve, or misfortune overtakes even those we love.

Life in God is not an escape from this, but a way to gain full insight concerning it. It is not our depravity which forces a fictitious religious explanation upon us, but the experience of religious reality which forces the "Night Side" out into the light.

It is when we stand in the righteous all-seeing light of love that we can dare to look at, admit, and *consciously* suffer under this something in us which wills disaster, misfortune, defeat to everything outside the sphere of our narrowest self-interest. [*A Certain World,* pp. 343-44]

Hammarskjöld's "something in us which wills disaster, misfortune, defeat" is what Auden, in "Ascension Day, 1964," called the "glum Kundry" that remains in each of us during the time between Christ's departure and return:

. . . Absence remains
The factual loss it is:

Here on out as permanent,
Obvious to all,
As the presence in each

Of a glum Kundry,
Impelled to giggle
At any crucifixion.[13]

To face this, to "dare to look at, admit, and *consciously* suffer" it is to turn toward the reality at the heart of one's life, and to flee from it is to flee not only from God, but also from oneself. The flight from oneself is never successful, but results only in nagging anxiety: "No one has yet believed or liked a lie . . . ," as Auden says in "Another

13. *About the House* (New York: Random House, 1965), p. 81.

Time."[14] Still, there are more candidates for despair than for hope: "So many try to say Not Now, / So many have forgotten how / To say I Am. . . ." Or as he puts it in "Our Bias": "When have we not preferred some going round / To going straight to where we are?"[15]

To go straight to where one is is to turn around and go back through anxiety to discover what one lacks. The closing chorus of "For the Time Being" says of Christ, "He is the Truth / Seek Him in the Kingdom of Anxiety; / You will come to a great city that has expected your return for years."[16] It is also to discover one's true self, the self that may have gone unnoticed for so many years that, in the image of "Like a Vocation," it seems like a lost child calling out of one's depths:

> But somewhere always, nowhere particularly unusual,
> Almost anywhere in the landscape of water and houses,
> His crying competing unsuccessfully with the cry
> Of the traffic or the birds, is always standing
> The one who needs you, that terrified
> Imaginative child who only knows you
> As what the uncles call a lie,
> But knows he has to be the future and that only
> The meek inherit the earth, and is neither
> Charming, successful, nor a crowd;
> Alone among the noise and policies of summer,
> His weeping climbs towards your life like a vocation.[17]

Fortunately, in the words of "Kairos and Logos," "we are not lost but only run away."[18] Our lost reality calls to us and our very suffering can be our guide. Alonso, in "The Sea and the Mirror," counsels his son:

14. *Collected Shorter Poems, 1927-1957* (New York: Random House, 1967), p. 170. Subsequently referred to as *Shorter Poems*.
15. Ibid., p. 171.
16. *Poetry*, p. 466.
17. *Shorter Poems*, p. 149.
18. *Poetry*, p. 16.

But should you fail to keep your kingdom
And, like your father before you, come
Where thought accuses and feeling mocks,
Believe your pain: praise the scorching rocks
For their desiccation of your lust,
Thank the bitter treatment of the tide
For its dissolution of your pride,
That the whirlwind may arrange your will
And the deluge release it to find
The spring in the desert, the fruitful
Island in the sea, where flesh and mind
Are delivered from mistrust.[19]

Believe your pain, seek the Truth in the kingdom of anxiety, and your suffering will lead you through a process of purgation and integration toward the ideal union of opposites that would constitute human wholeness. The process as it is described here, and also in *The Enchafèd Flood,* is basically the Jungian process of the integration of the personality. Early criticism of Auden was so much more interested in Freudian psychology that it took some time for the Jungian side of Auden's thought to become appreciated, but recent studies have found it pervasive, and increasingly so as he approached Christianity in the late 1930's and the beginning of the 1940's.[20] The schema of the four faculties of consciousness, for example, in "For the Time Being" is from Jung.[21] The Christianization of the Jungian process for Auden involved the idea that only in Christ did the process attain its goal; seen in this light, the Jungian hypothesis becomes transformed, in the words of a recent critic, "into a religious one, and

19. Ibid., p. 368.

20. The most extensive study of the influence of Jung on Auden is John E. Stoll, *W. H. Auden: A Reading* (Muncie, Indiana: Ball State University, 1970). See also Greenberg, *Quest for the Necessary,* pp. 111 ff.

21. Jolande Jacobi, *The Psychology of C. G. Jung: An Introduction with Illustrations* (New Haven, Conn.: Yale University Press, 1968), p. 27.

faith in God becomes inseparable from hope for man."[22]

The process Alonso describes, therefore, although it does move in the direction of the goal, does not come to completion in this life, but awaits fulfillment in the life to come. What it does lead to in this life when it advances sufficiently, as seems the case with Alonso and Prospero in "The Sea and the Mirror," is the awakening of man in his present divided condition as, in the terms of the poem's allegory, the existential reality of Caliban and the illusion-creating spirit of reflection, Ariel.

Prospero in his career as an enchanter has used Ariel's power in order to hide his real existence from himself. Now that that life is over — Auden's poem is a kind of epilogue to Shakespeare's *The Tempest* — he is able to know himself as he really is, an existing mortal: ". . . I am glad I have freed you, / So at last I can really believe I shall die. / For under your influence death is inconceivable . . ." (p. 352). He has used Ariel's power to suppress the uncomfortable awareness that existence hovers on the brink of nothing — "Sailing alone, out over seventy thousand fathoms" (p. 358) — and along with that awareness to suppress his real self generally so that it has remained undeveloped until this point. Realizing this, Prospero feels despair:

> . . . Caliban remains my impervious disgrace.
> We did it, Ariel, between us; you found on me a wish
>   For absolute devotion; result — his wreck
> That sprawls in the weeds and will not be repaired:
>   My dignity discouraged by a pupil's curse,
> I shall go knowing and incompetent into my grave.
>
> [P. 356]

Prospero's despair of Caliban is premature, however. When, in the last part of the poem, Caliban finally appears

22. Stoll, *W. H. Auden*, p. 6.

and addresses the audience in a long speech, he transforms during the course of it until at the end, after persuading the audience of his reality, he is speaking true wisdom that points beyond art to the new life of grace.

As Caliban describes the mechanisms of fantasy by which the members of the audience, like Prospero and men generally, try to hide their reality behind illusions of personal grandeur, he says that eventually one becomes bored with Ariel's play and tries to dismiss him, but only to discover that he has become so habitual he will not go away. Finally, striding up to him in anger, one sees in his mirroring eyes, the reflection of one's real self in its crude, neglected state:

> . . . a gibbering fist-clenched creature with which you are all too unfamiliar, for this is the first time indeed that you have met the only subject that you have, who is not a dream amenable to magic but the all too solid flesh you must acknowledge as your own; at last you have come face to face with me, and are appalled to learn how far I am from being, in any sense, your dish; how completely lacking in that poise and calm and all-forgiving because all-understanding good nature which to the critical eye is so wonderfully and domestically present on every page of your published inventions.
>
> But where, may I ask, should I have acquired them, when like a society mother who, although she is, of course, as she tells everyone, absolutely *devoted* to her child, simply *cannot* leave the dinner table just now and really *must* be in Le Touquet tomorrow, and so leaves him in charge of servants she doesn't know or boarding schools she has never seen, you have never in all these years taken the faintest personal interest in me? [Pp. 387-88]

By the end, however, perhaps because to listen to him as the audience is now doing is no longer to ignore him, Caliban is no longer the "gibbering fist-clenched creature" whose vision is limited to "secular stagnation. . . . a straight and snubbing stare to which mythology is bosh, surrounded by an infinite passivity and purely arithmetical disorder which is open only to perception" (p. 395), existence experienced as meaningless surface. Rather he is one who can speak not just for man at his undeveloped crudest, but for the whole of man — for himself, for Ariel and all the characters of the play, and even for the audience — and can state the meaning toward which the work as a whole has been moving:

> Now it is over. No, we have not dreamt it. Here we really stand, down stage with red faces and no applause. . . . Yet, at this very moment when we do at last see ourselves as we are, neither cozy nor playful, but swaying out on the ultimate wind-whipped cornice that overhangs the unabiding void — we have never stood anywhere else, — when our reasons are silenced by the heavy huge derison, — There is nothing to say. There never has been, — and our wills chuck in their hands — There is no way out. There never was, — it is at this moment that for the first time in our lives we hear, not the sounds which, as born actors, we have hitherto condescended to use as an excellent vehicle for displaying our personalities and looks, but the real Word which is our only *raison d'être.* [P. 402]

This does not mean, he says, that we ever in this life become altogether free from our tendency to egocentric illusionism; rather it means that although we remain "born actors," with all of "our shame, our fear, our incorrigible staginess," we also participate in the life of the real world under grace:

> . . . only now it is not in spite of them but with them that we are blessed by that Wholly Other Life from which we are separated by an essential emphatic gulf of which our contrived fissures of mirror and proscenium arch — we understand them at last — are feebly figurative signs, so that all our meanings are reversed and it is precisely in its negative image of Judgment that we can positively envisage Mercy; it is just here,

among the ruins and the bones, that we may rejoice in the perfected Work which is not ours. Its great coherences stand out through our secular blur in all their overwhelmingly righteous obligation; its voice speaks through our muffling banks of artificial flowers and unflinchingly delivers its authentic molar pardon; its spaces greet us with all their grand old prospect of wonder and width; the working charm is the full bloom of the unbothered state; the sounded note is the restored relation. [Pp. 402-3]

To put it in the terms Auden used later, the terms of primary and secondary worlds, man, the born actor and illusionist, normally lives only in the secondary worlds he makes up himself, and in this life he never leaves them altogether, but when he discovers the reality of his life, the neglected Caliban beneath his posing, he begins to live to a certain extent the life of the primary world, the real world of God's creation.

This brings us back to the problem we began with, the problem of the true and false forms of the sacred, and it points toward the solution. The normal world of human experience may seem profane — which is to say, boring and meaningless — or it may seem enchantingly beautiful, but in a way that mistakes something finite for God, treating a limited and relative good as though it were of unlimited and absolute value or considering one's personal ego as though it were the ground of being. Either way the experience is an illusion. The real world is grounded in God's creative act, and therefore, whatever it may seem, it is in actuality sacred, but not in a way that puts it in competition with its source.

To see this accurately, however, is for man in his fallen condition extremely difficult, though not entirely impossible. As Auden described it, it is difficult even for a Christian, because there is a sense in which, for most people who follow the path of the Christian religion, the state of being a Christian fully always lies ahead; he said, for example, in his introduction to Kierkegaard, ". . . nobody except Christ and, at the end of their lives perhaps, the saints *are* Christian. To say 'I am a Christian' really means 'I who am a sinner am required to become like Christ.' "[23] Still, to the extent that a person can participate in Christianity's vision of truth, the Christian religion does have the effect of dissolving false enchantments and of admitting one into the universe of the true sacred. Auden says of the mission of the apostles in "The Twelve":

> . . . They did as the Spirit bid,
> Went forth into a joyless world
> Of swords and rhetoric
> To bring it joy.[24]

And they accomplished this not by bringing a new enchantment, but by demythologizing the universe:

> Children may play about the ancestral graves: the dead
> no longer walk.
> Excellent still in their splendor are the antique statues:
> but can do neither good nor evil.
> Beautiful still are the starry heavens: but our
> Fate is not written there.
> Holy still is Speech, but there is no sacred tongue:
> the Truth may be told in all.

As Simeon puts it in "For the Time Being," when Christianity brings the message that in Christ "the Word is united to the Flesh without loss of perfection," it simultaneously redeems reason from "incestuous fixation on her own Logic" and transforms the universe from a "public illusion" into an authentically exciting realm of existential truth:

23. *Living Thoughts,* p. 20.

24. The poem appears in *City Without Walls and Other Poems* (New York: Random House, 1969), pp. 105-6.

For the Truth is indeed One, without which is no salvation, but the possibilities of real knowledge are as many as are the creatures in the very real and most exciting universe that God creates with and for His love, and it is not Nature which is one public illusion, but we who have each our many private illusions about Nature.[25]

Or as Caliban said, when man awakens from the egoistic dream that has falsified his picture of the reality God created, "its spaces greet us with all their grand old prospect of wonder and width."

The profane vision and the false sacred are both products of sin; and sin, though it is very real itself, is only an attempt to believe an illusion — that man and the universe are not God's creation but an ungrounded chaos of floating relativities. Auden's Simeon says of the Fall: ". . . his as yet unfallen will could only rebel against the truth by taking flight into an unconscious lie; he could only eat of the Tree of the Knowledge of Good and Evil by forgetting that its existence was a fiction of the Evil One, that there is only the Tree of Life."[26]

The way out of this illusion lies in disentangling the true sacred from the false ,and this involves purifying one's vision of all traces of either pagan or pantheistic conceptions of deity. A statement by Leslie Dewart that Auden has quoted at least twice, once in his commonplace book and once in *Secondary Worlds,* makes an important point about this: "The Christian God is not *both* transcendent and immanent. He is a reality other than being Who is present to being, by which presence He makes being to be."[27] Before one can know the true immanent sacredness of God's creation, one has to free oneself from the false

25. *Poetry,* p. 454.

26. Ibid., p. 450.

27. *A Certain World,* p. 176; *Secondary Worlds,* p. 135. The quotation is from Leslie Dewart, *The Future of Belief.*

vision of immanent sacredness that springs from man's habitual tendency to look upon the world or something in the world as itself the very presence of God. There is a passage in Kierkegaard's *Concluding Unscientific Postscript* that speaks directly to Auden's point:

> All paganism consists in this, that God is related to man directly, as the extraordinary is to the astonished observer. But the spiritual relationship to God in the truth, i.e. in inwardness, is conditioned by a prior irruption of inwardness, which corresponds to the divine elusiveness that God has absolutely nothing obvious about Him, that God is so far from being obvious, that He is invisible. It cannot immediately occur to anyone that He exists, although His invisibility is again His omnipresence.[28]

God is not any finite being, but the ground of being as such, and His invisibility is a function of His omnipresence as the transcendent ground of every being. When one sees this, then the genuine beauties of this world are freed from the fallacious burden of having to be God and are able to point beyond themselves to their Creator and to be what they always were in reality, the gifts of God's love. Auden's poem "The Prophets," written around the time of his conversion, presents this idea very beautifully:

> Their lack of shyness was a way of praising
> Just what I didn't know, why I was gazing,
> While all their lack of answer whispered "Wait,"
> And taught me gradually without coercion,
> And all the landscape round them pointed to
> The calm with which they took complete desertion
> As proof that you existed.
>   It was true.
> For now I have the answer from the face
> That never will go back into a book
> But asks for all my life, and is the Place

28. *Kierkegaard Anthology*, ed. Bretall, p. 224.

Where all I touch is moved to an embrace,
And there is no such thing as a vain look.[29]

When this is understood and grasped in faith, then, as Auden put it in *Secondary Worlds,* "the primary phenomenal world" can be seen as "a realm of sacred analogies."[30] When the world is no longer taken as a self-contained ultimate, in other words, and no longer has parts of it inflated into finite gods, then finite being becomes a sacramental sign speaking analogically of the infinite Being that is its ground. In the words of a recent poem, "In Due Season":

. . . Stones, old shoes, come alive, born sacramental signs,
Nod to us in the First Person of mysteries
They know nothing about, bearing a message from
The invisible sole Source of specific things.[31]

Poetry, as was mentioned earlier, was in Auden's view a kind of magic, and it shared in the ambiguity of the sacred; it could seduce one with false enchantments, or it could serve to "exorcise the Gentile in you." One of the reasons art has such powerful appeal, according to Auden, is that the true sacred in reality is so difficult to see:

Timeless fictional worlds
Of self-evident meaning
Would not delight,

Were not our own
A temporal one where nothing
Is what it seems.

A poem may function as a lie, or it may function as an invitation or even an enticement to truth:

29. *Shorter Poems,* p. 148. The poem was first published in *Southern Review* (Autumn 1939).
30. P. 144.
31. *City without Walls,* p. 83.

A poem — a tall story:
But any good one
Makes us want to know.[32]

Poetry's power of enchantment can make it seem sacred in itself, but when the poet can understand that "to a Christian . . . both art and science are secular activities, that is to say, small beer,"[33] he is in a position to respond to a poet's true calling: "The poet has to preserve and express by art what primitive peoples knew instinctively, namely, that, for man, nature is a realm of sacramental analogies."[34]

To do this is to become what Auden called, in an image that was central to his conception of the Christian life, a translator. In the prologue he wrote for the Christ Church College *son et lumière* in the summer of 1968, he speaks of "Dame Philology" as presiding over that portion of the realm of Truth "where to hear is to translate and to know is to be known" and goes on to praise her for, in effect, translating the appearances that could so easily be falsely sacred into true sacramental analogies:

> Except Her grace prevent, we are doomed to idolatry,
> to worship imaginary gods of our own childish making,
> creatures of whim both cruel and absurd.
>
> For She it is, and She alone who, without ambiguity
> or palter, can teach us to rejoice in the holy Providence
> of our Creator and our Judge.[35]

To be a translator in this way is to participate as a creaturely and secular instrument in an art of translation that is intrinsically supernatural — the miracle of Pentecost. Auden spoke in several places of the Christian

32. *About the House,* pp. 11-12.
33. *Dyer's Hand,* p. 456.
34. *Secondary Worlds,* p. 131.
35. *City without Walls,* pp. 115-16.

Pentecost as not a gift of tongues, in the sense of the ability "to make verbal noises which nobody else could understand," but a gift of ears, "a miracle of instantaneous translation": "The curse of Babel, one might say, was redeemed because for the first time, men were willing in absolute fullness of heart to speak and to listen, not merely to their sort of person but to total strangers."[36] As he put it in "Whitsunday in Kirchstetten":

> Rejoice: we who were born congenitally deaf
> are able
> to listen now to rank outsiders. The Holy Ghost
> does not abhor a golfer's jargon,
> A Lower-Austrian accent, the cadences even of my own
> little Anglo-American
> musico-literary set (though difficult, saints
> at least may think in algebra
> without sin): but no sacred nonsense can stand Him.
> Our magic syllables melt away,
> our tribal formulae are laid bare: since this morning,
> it is with a vocabulary
> made wholesomely profane, open in lexicons to our foes
> to translate, that we endeavor
> each in his idiom to express the true *magnalia* which
> need no hallowing from us. . . .[37]

Before we receive this gift that redeems and disenchants, "each of us," in the words of "Horae Canonicae," "Prays to an image of his image of himself,"[38] isolated from God, from the natural world, and from other men, locked in the solipsism that Auden said in his commonplace book was the essence of the sin of pride.[39] The way out of it is the act that is at the same time man's leap

36. *Secondary Worlds,* p. 139.
37. *About the House,* p. 83.
38. *Shorter Poems,* pp. 324-25.
39. *A Certain World,* pp. 344-45.

toward God in faith and the descent of the dove[40] into the renewed life of man. The necessary prerequisite to this is the acceptance of finitude, both one's own and the world's. In the "Ode to Terminus" it is the disenchanted and translated Roman god Terminus, a symbol of secular finitude,

> By whose grace, also, every gathering
> of two or three in confident amity
>   repeats the pentecostal marvel
>   as each in each finds his right translator.[41]

Still, this gift, welcome and rejoicing as it may be, remains in this life only partial — a glimpse or foretaste of what the Christian hopes for. It does not free one here from the effects of Original Sin, but prepares for a complete liberation to come. The last lines in *City without Walls* are a prayer that God will continue to "translate" for a new audience the poet's own efforts to translate in his verse sacramental analogies that speak now darkly of the glory into which he hopes all will eventually be translated by God's grace:

> Can Sixty make sense to Sixteen-Plus?
> What has my camp in common with theirs,
> with buttons and beards and Be-Ins?
> Much, I hope. In Acts it is written
> Taste was no problem at Pentecost.
>
> To speak is human because human to listen,
> beyond hope, for an Eighth Day,
> when the creatured Image shall become the Likeness:

40. Charles Williams, *The Descent of the Dove: A History of the Holy Spirit in the Church* (London: Longmans Green and Company, 1939) was one of the more powerful influences on Auden's theological thinking during the period of his conversion. Williams' emphasis on the immanent activity of the Holy Spirit in the world was an important counterforce to the influence of Kierkegaard and Niebuhr.

41. *City without Walls*, p. 99.

Giver-of-Life, translate for me
till I accomplish my corpse at last.[42]

The intervening period is a time of tension. In the words of the Narrator at the end of "For the Time Being," "To those who have seen / The Child, however dimly, however incredulously, / The Time Being is, in a sense, the most trying time of all."[43] One reason it is trying is that in the present life the true sacred and the false are always so difficult to keep distinct. If it were only a matter of affirming the transcendent glory of God it would not be so hard, but an essential part of the Christian life is "remembering the stable where for once in our lives / Everything became a You and nothing was an It" (p. 466). The last lines of the oratorio are: "He is the Life. / Love Him in the World of the Flesh; / And at your marriage all its occasions shall dance for joy." If one could simply reject the immanent sacred as a pagan illusion or exalt the transcendent at the expense of the immanent, the task would be much easier, but this would only be to replace a false sacred with a false profane. Instead, the true vocation is to simultaneously fend off enchantments and pray with the "Horae Canonicae": "God bless this green world temporal."[44]

Auden said that this is one of the distinctions between his own view of the Christian life and Kierkegaard's. In an essay on his conversion, he wrote:

Much as I owe to Kierkegaard — among many other virtues, he has the talent, invaluable in a preacher to the Greeks, of making Christianity sound bohemian — I cannot let this occasion pass without commenting upon what seems to be his great limitation, a limitation which characterizes Protestantism

42. "Prologue at Sixty," pp. 120-21.
43. *Poetry*, p. 465.
44. "Lauds," *Shorter Poems*, p. 338.

generally. A planetary visitor might read through the whole of his voluminous works without discovering that human beings are not ghosts but have bodies of flesh and blood. . . .[45]

Whereas Kierkegaard made the aesthetic level of existence, the life of pleasure and passion, seem something to be left entirely behind when one ascended to the religious level, much of Auden's poetry since he became a Christian involved an attempt to remind Christendom that the flesh, too, has its redemption. "In Praise of Limestone" is a particularly effective example of this effort. It describes the aesthetic life in its purest form — a gentle landscape of rounded slopes, fragrant with thyme, and watered by chuckling springs, and a people whose lives resemble this habitat:

> What could be more like Mother or a fitter background
>   For her son, the flirtatious male who lounges
> Against a rock in the sunlight, never doubting
>   That for all his faults he is loved; whose works are but
> Extensions of his power to charm?[46]

Such people are "unable / To conceive a god whose temper-tantrums are moral / And not to be pacified by a clever line / Or a good lay," and both the best and the worst, saints-to-be and intendant Caesars, shun their world. But, the poem concludes, their life too will have its place in the life to come, and it too, even now, can serve as a sacramental analogy pointing toward the joy that the flesh will share with the spirit:

> . . . But if
> Sins can be forgiven, if bodies rise from the dead,
>   These modifications of matter into
> Innocent athletes and gesticulating fountains,

45. James A. Pike, ed., *Modern Canterbury Pilgrims* (New York: Morehouse-Gorham, 1956), p. 42.

46. The poem appears in *Shorter Poems*, pp. 238-41.

Made solely for pleasure, make a further point:
The blessed will not care what angle they are regarded from,
Having nothing to hide. Dear, I know nothing of
Either, but when I try to imagine a faultless love
Or the life to come, what I hear is the murmur
Of underground streams, what I see is a limestone landscape.

In the journey through the present life there is no easy choice that can exclude either the *via positiva* or the *via negativa;* rather, the Christian calling requires that both be maintained in tension and, as far as possible, in balance until the end, when all false enchantments will vanish and the truth be known in its fullness. One of the first poems Auden wrote as a Christian affirmed this principle, and all of his subsequent work, whatever its specific subject matter, religious or secular, Good Friday or the poet's house in Austria, was an effort to practice it:

. . . Let . . .
The positive and negative ways through time
Embrace and encourage each other
In a brief moment of intersection.

That the orgulous spirit may while it can
Conform to its temporal focus with praise,
Acknowledging the attributes of
One immortal, one infinite Substance;

And the shabby structure of indolent flesh
Give a resonant echo to the Word which was
From the beginning, and the shining
Light be comprehended by the darkness.[47]

47. This was originally the epilogue to *The Double Man* (USA) and *New Year Letter* (UK). It was subsequently included in *Collected Poetry* as "Autumn 1940" (pp. 101-3) and in *Collected Shorter Poems* as "The Dark Years" (pp. 176-78), in both cases with modifications. I quote the passage as it appeared in *New Year Letter* (London: Faber and Faber, 1941), pp. 187-88.

CHAPTER IX

Conclusion

> Now it is understood that a critic resembles a poet to a hair; he only lacks the suffering in his heart and the music upon his lips. Lo, therefore, I would rather be a swineherd from Amager, and be understood by the swine, than be a poet and be misunderstood by men.
>
> KIERKEGAARD, *Either/Or*

> Poi s'acose nel fuoco che gli affina.
>
> DANTE, *Purgatorio,* XXVI, 148

In the case of a study that has opened with the paradox of the sacred and ended with its ambiguity, it may seem that to attempt a conclusion of any clear and definite kind must be paradoxical at best, or at worst, foolish. The subject of the sacred is so complex and so subtle in the forms it can take and in their transformations that perhaps only the kind of particular studies that the preceding chapters have presented can do justice to it. Nevertheless, there are a few final reflections I would like to offer.

In the first chapter I said that what the modern crisis of the sacred — the popularly termed "death of God" — means must depend on what one means by the language in which traditional attitudes of belief are expressed. And it is necessary to remember that although the conceptual content of that language is not negligible, it is not the whole of it — nor, in many cases, may it be the most important part of it: there is also the experiential aspect, the sense of the sacred, a force that gives rise to the concepts and that may even break their boundaries. When this happens, the traditional language no longer fits very precisely, and to use it is clumsy and probably misleading.

This is very much the case with the writers this book has been discussing. Although at first glance, because of the harshness of their criticisms of traditional religion, Nietzsche, Beckett, and Stevens would seem to be certainly atheistic, it becomes much more difficult upon close examination to distinguish so simply between their "atheism" and the pantheistic and theistic attitudes of Yeats, Rilke, Joyce, Mann, Eliot, and Auden.

One line of approach that can help to clarify this problem is to consider it in terms of its experiential aspect. From this point of view one of the ways in which theism of the orthodox kind, pantheism, and atheism may be distinguished is in terms of their relation to the sense of the sacred. Orthodox theism in its Hebraic form had a strong sense of the sacred as transcendent; in its Christian form, at least ideally, it is characterized by a strong sense of the sacred as simultaneously immanent and transcendent, with the two poles in balance. Pantheism, in comparison, is characterized by a definite sense of the sacred, but with a relatively strong predominance of the immanent pole; the sense of the transcendent sacred has to remain to some extent, or else there would be no sense of sacredness at all, but in pantheism it usually seems almost eclipsed. When it is fully eclipsed, there is no longer any sense of the sacred, and the consequent vision may then appropriately be termed atheistic.

Considered in this light, none of the three writers I just mentioned as possible candidates for the term "atheistic" would seem to qualify, and the only writer I have discussed who would is Ibsen, and then primarily on the basis of the vision presented in *Hedda Gabler*. And it must not be forgotten that Hedda's way of seeing the universe is not necessarily Ibsen's, or at least not the whole of Ibsen's. What seems more the case is that, as is also true to a large extent of the other authors we have considered, Ibsen saw at least two possible modes of vision, and his own alternated between them and always felt their tension.

From a conceptual point of view, the problem of the distinction between atheism, theism, and pantheism is an aspect of the problem of the relation between beings and being, perhaps a mystery that is not susceptible to analysis, or at least susceptible only in a very limited way. Considered in this respect, the dialogue among the three camps may be best understood as an aspect of the older dialogue between the cataphatic and apophatic approaches to theology. From this point of view, the problem is actually one of how best in limited and inevitably inadequate images to describe something that lies past the reach of all of them — *Ipsum Esse*[1] — and the debate is actually not an argument about the existence or nonexistence of a conceptually defined deity, but a critique of analogies, an argument only about the best, or perhaps least inadequate, means to a goal that each is seeking.

All of the writers this book has discussed have been touched in some manner by the sense of the sacred, and all have also been affected by the sense of its absence. Even Eliot and Auden, though they later became Christians, passed through the desacralized Waste Land on their journey to faith; and one might say the same of the others — for none of them simply sat down to die in the

1. See Aquinas, *Summa Theologica,* vol. 1, q. 3, a. 4.

wilderness. Each saw something up ahead drawing him onward, whether a shining light or a "darkness shining in brightness," and each responded in his own way, on the basis of the insights emerging from within his own authentic vision, to its calling and its challenge.

Even to speak in this way, however, of a response to a challenge, may be to oversimplify and perhaps to distort what has been taking place. This, too, is "an image, like any other." The movements of man's thought and sensibility do not happen only through the deliberate efforts of individuals; nor do developments even in the lives of individuals necessarily take place altogether consciously or through effort. A person may choose to seek or to reject the sacred, but he cannot, precisely speaking, choose to find it or to lose it; one might with greater appropriateness say that it finds or abandons him.

It is also true that just as ideas may have a life of their own, developing according to the laws of their own logic in the thought of a given period quite independently of what the individuals who work with them might wish, so also do images.[2] As experiences change, the images they give rise to change with them, and our thoughts take shape around their transformations.

It may also happen — and we have studied some examples — that just as in a primitive culture the natural symbolism of heights continues to function even after the creator has become a *deus otiosus,* so too the traditional imagery of the sacred, when used by a modern nonreligous

2. Cf. Austin Farrer, *A Rebirth of Images: The Making of St. John's Apocalypse* (Boston: Beacon Press, 1963), p. 14: "The images [of the Bible] are not through all ages absolutely invariable, and there is no historical study more significant than the study of their transformations. Such a transformation finds expression in the birth of Christianity; it is a visible rebirth of images." See also Austin Farrer, *The Glass of Vision* (London: Dacre Press, 1948).

writer in a secular context, brings with it a sense of the transcendent that can have the effect of resacralizing man's world.

Because it lives in analogies, and analogies must always limp and, to remain effective, must always be criticized, there is a sense in which the sacred will always be dying. But it will never die. We can flee it or, what is more likely, just wander away from it, but though we may leave it, it will not leave us for long — because its call is something in us, in the very heart of our being. To attempt to live permanently without it is to claim that being has no depth, and the cost of this is to lose the possibility of depth in one's own life. When it touches us, as it must when we read with our whole selves authors like those we have been examining, it can never leave us unchanged; as Auden says in "Nones,"

> . . . we have time
> To misrepresent, excuse, deny,
> Mythify, use this event
> While, under a hotel bed, in prison,
> Down wrong turnings, its meaning
> Waits for our lives.[3]

It waits for us in the failures of our attempts to live without it, and it also waits for us, fortunately, in poems like this one, in novels and plays, wherever there is an image that can serve as its vehicle. Images of the sacred may die, and become like "old stones that cannot be deciphered," but they may also rise again, light bursting from the stones; and when that happens, then we may say also with Auden:

> Perhaps I always knew what they were saying:
> Even those earliest messengers who walked
> Into my life from books where they were staying. . . .[4]

3. *Collected Shorter Poems,* pp. 331-32.
4. "The Prophets," ibid., p. 147.

Many may live without it all their lives, and whole generations may appear to have lost it or been abandoned by it, but again and again it breaks into our lives to call to us, even out of old stones, and to issue its challenge — to tell us, like the Archaic Torso of Apollo of Rilke's sonnet:

> . . . there is no place
> that does not see you. You must change your life.
>
> [. . . da ist keine Stelle,
> die dich nicht sieht. Du musst dein Leben ändern.][5]

5. "Archaischer Torso Appollos," *Translations from the Poetry of Rainer Maria Rilke,* trans. M. D. Herter Norton (New York: W. W. Norton and Company, 1938), pp. 180-81.

Bibliography

This bibliography is not intended as a list of books referred to — since these are already indicated in the notes — but rather as a list of works that would be of interest to a person desiring to explore further the general topic of the present book: the concept of the sacred and its relation to secular culture, with special reference to modern literature and its background.

Altizer, Thomas J. J. *Mircea Eliade and the Dialectic of the Sacred*. Philadephia: Westminster Press, 1963.

Becker, Carl L. *The Heavenly City of the Eighteenth-Century Philosophers*. New Haven, Conn.: Yale University Press, 1932.

Beja, Morris. *Epiphany in the Modern Novel*. Seattle: University of Washington Press, 1971.

Bellah, Robert N. *Beyond Belief: Essays on Religion in a Post-traditional World*. New York: Harper and Row, 1970.

Berger, Peter L. *The Sacred Canopy: Elements of a Sociological Theory of Religion*. Garden City, N.Y.: Doubleday, 1967.

Burtt, Edwin Arthur. *The Metaphysical Foundations of Modern Physical Science*. London: Routledge and Kegan Paul, 1932.

Campbell, Joseph, ed. *Man and Time: Papers from the Eranos Yearbooks*. New York: Pantheon Books, 1957.

———. *The Masks of God: Creative Mythology*. New York: Viking Press, 1968.

———, ed. *Spirit and Nature: Papers from the Eranos Yearbooks*. New York: Pantheon Books, 1954.

Cohn, Norman. *The Pursuit of the Millennium: Revolutionary Millennarians and Mystical Anarchists of the Middle Ages.* New York: Oxford University Press, 1970.

Cox, Harvey. *The Secular City: Secularization and Urbanization in Theological Perspective.* New York: Macmillan, 1965.

Eliade, Mircea. *Birth and Rebirth.* Trans. Willard R. Trask. New York: Harper and Row, 1961.

———. *The Myth of the Eternal Return.* Trans. Willard R. Trask. New York: Pantheon Books, 1954.

———. *Patterns in Comparative Religion.* Trans. Rosemary Sheed. New York: Sheed and Ward, 1958.

———. *The Quest: History and Meaning in Religion.* Chicago: University of Chicago Press, 1969.

———. *The Sacred and the Profane: The Nature of Religion.* Trans. Willard R. Trask. New York: Harper and Brothers, 1961.

———. *The Two and the One.* Trans. J. M. Cohen. New York: Harper and Row, 1965.

Eliot, Thomas Stearns. *The Idea of a Christian Society.* New York: Harcourt Brace, 1940.

———. *Notes toward the Definition of Culture.* London: Faber and Faber, 1948.

Ellmann, Richard. *The Identity of Yeats.* New York: Oxford University Press, 1954.

———. *Ulysses on the Liffey.* New York: Oxford University Press, 1972.

Erikson, Erik. *Young Man Luther: A Study in Psychoanalysis and History.* New York: W. W. Norton, 1958.

Fadiman, Clifton, ed. *I Believe: The Personal Philosophies of Certain Eminent Men and Women of Our Time.* New York: Simon and Schuster, 1939.

Farrer, Austin. *The Glass of Vision.* London: Dacre Press, 1948.

Feder, Lillian. *Ancient Myth in Modern Poetry.* Princeton, N.J.: Princeton University Press, 1971.

Fedotov, George P. *The Russian Religious Mind: Kievan Christianity — the Tenth to the Thirteenth Centuries.* Cambridge, Mass.: Harvard University Press, 1946.

Gardner, Helen. *Religion and Literature.* New York: Oxford University Press, 1971.

Gay, Peter. *The Enlightenment: An Interpretation. The Rise of Modern Paganism.* New York: Alfred A. Knopf, 1966.

Gilkey, Langdon. *Naming the Whirlwind: The Renewal of God-Language.* Indianapolis and New York: Bobbs-Merrill, 1969.

Guardini, Romano. *Rilke's Duino Elegies: An Interpretation.* London: Darwen Finlayson, 1961.

Hartshorne, Charles. *The Divine Relativity: A Social Conception of God.* New Haven, Conn.: Yale University Press, 1948.

Howarth, Herbert. *Notes on Some Figures behind T. S. Eliot.* Boston: Houghton Mifflin, 1964.

Jung, Carl Gustav. *Aion: Researches into the Phenomenology of the Self.* Trans. R. F. C. Hull. New York: Pantheon Books, 1959.

———. *Psychology and Alchemy.* Trans. R. F. C. Hull. London: Routledge and Kegan Paul, 1953.

———. *Psychology and Religion: West and East.* Trans. R. F. C. Hull. New York: Pantheon Books, 1958.

———. *Symbols of Transformation: An Analysis of the Prelude to a Case of Schizophrenia.* Trans. R. F. C. Hull. New York: Pantheon Books, 1956.

Kirk, G. S. *Myth: Its Meaning and Functions in Ancient and Other Cultures.* Cambridge: Cambridge University Press; Berkeley and Los Angeles: University of California Press, 1971.

Kitagawa, Joseph M., and Charles H. Long, eds. *Myths and Symbols: Studies in Honor of Mircea Eliade.* Chicago: University of Chicago Press, 1969.

Kojecky, Roger. *T. S. Eliot's Social Criticism.* London: Faber and Faber, 1971.

Krieger, Murray. *The Tragic Vision: Variations on a Theme in Literary Interpretation.* Chicago: University of Chicago Press, 1966.

Lawall, Sarah N. *Critics of Consciousness: The Existential Structures of Literature.* Cambridge, Mass.: Harvard University Press, 1968.

Leeuw, Gerardus van der. *Sacred and Profane Beauty: The Holy in Art*. Preface by Mircea Eliade. Trans. David E. Green. New York: Holt, Rinehart and Winston, 1963.

Lewis, Richard W. B. *The American Adam: Innocence, Tragedy, and Tradition in the Nineteenth Century*. Chicago: University of Chicago Press, 1955.

———. *The Picaresque Saint: Representative Figures in Contemporary Fiction*. Philadelphia and New York: J. B. Lippincott, 1956.

Lossky, Vladimir. *The Mystical Theology of the Eastern Church*. London: James Clarke, 1957.

Löwith, Karl. *Meaning in History: The Theological Implications of the Philosophy of History*. Chicago: University of Chicago Press, 1949.

Luckmann, Thomas. *The Invisible Religion: The Problem of Religion in Modern Society*. New York: Macmillan, 1967.

Macquarrie, John. *God-Talk: An Examination of the Language and Logic of Theology*. New York and Evanston: Harper and Row, 1967.

Marcel, Gabriel. *The Mystery of Being*. Chicago: Henry Regnery, 1960.

Maritain, Jacques. *Creative Intuition in Art and Poetry*. New York: Pantheon Books, 1953.

———. *The Situation of Poetry: Four Essays on the Relations between Poetry, Mysticism, Magic, and Knowledge*. Trans. Marshall Suther. New York: Philosophical Library, 1955.

Mascall, Eric Lionel. *Theology and Images*. London: A. R. Mowbray, 1963.

———. *Via Media: An Essay in Theological Synthesis*. London: Longmans, Green, 1956.

May, Rollo, ed. *Symbolism and Literature*. New York: George Braziller, 1960.

Mazzeo, Joseph Anthony. "Some Interpretations of the History of Ideas." *Journal of the History of Ideas,* 33, no. 3 (July-Sept. 1972): 379-93.

Miller, J. Hillis. *The Disappearance of God: Five Nineteenth-Century Writers*. Cambridge, Mass.: Harvard University Press, 1963.

———. *Poets of Reality: Six Twentieth-Century Writers.*

Cambridge, Mass.: Harvard University Press, 1966.

Molnar, Thomas. *God and the Knowledge of Reality.* New York: Basic Books, 1973.

Nicolson, Marjorie Hope. *The Breaking of the Circle: Studies in the Effect of the "New Science" upon Seventeenth-Century Poetry.* Revised edition. New York: Columbia University Press, 1960.

———. *Mountain Gloom and Mountain Glory: The Development of the Aesthetics of the Infinite.* Ithaca, N.Y.: Cornell University Press, 1959.

Ong, Walter J. *The Barbarian Within, and Other Fugitive Essays and Studies.* New York: Macmillan, 1962.

———. *In the Human Grain: Further Explorations of Contemporary Culture.* New York: Macmillan, 1967.

———. *The Presence of the Word: Some Prolegomena for Cultural and Religious History.* New Haven, Conn.: Yale University Press, 1967.

Otto, Rudolph. *The Idea of the Holy: An Inquiry into the Non-rational Factor in the Idea of the Divine and its Relation to the Rational.* Trans. John W. Harvey. Second edition. London: Oxford University Press, 1950.

Reeves, Marjorie. *The Influence of Prophecy in the Later Middle Ages: A Study in Joachimism.* Oxford: Clarendon Press, 1969.

Richardson, Alan. *History Sacred and Profane.* Philadephia: Westminster Press, 1964.

Scott, Nathan A., Jr., *The Broken Center: Studies in the Theological Horizon of Modern Literature.* New Haven, Conn.: Yale University Press, 1966.

———. *Craters of the Spirit: Studies in the Modern Novel.* Washington, D.C.: Corpus Books, 1968.

———. *Modern Literature and the Religious Frontier.* New York: Harper, 1958.

———. *Negative Capability: Studies in the New Literature and the Religious Situation.* New Haven, Conn.: Yale University Press, 1969.

———. *The Wild Prayer of Longing: Poetry and the Sacred.* New Haven, Conn.: Yale University Press, 1971.

———, ed. *The Climate of Faith in Modern Literature.* New

York: Seabury Press, 1964.

———, ed. *Forms of Extremity in the Modern Novel.* Richmond, Va.: John Knox Press, 1965.

———, ed. *Four Ways of Modern Poetry.* Richmond, Va.: John Knox Press, 1965.

———, ed. *The New Orpheus: Essays toward a Christian Poetic.* New York: Sheed and Ward, 1964.

Stark, Werner. *The Sociology of Religion: A Study of Christendom.* London: Routledge and Kegan Paul, 1966.

Tavard, George H. *The Quest for Catholicity: A Study in Anglicanism.* New York: Herder and Herder, 1964.

Tillich, Paul. *The Courage to Be.* New Haven, Conn.: Yale University Press, 1952.

Vahanian, Gabriel. *The Death of God.* New York: George Braziller, 1961.

———. *Wait without Idols.* New York: George Braziller, 1964.

Wilder, Amos Niven. *Modern Poetry and the Christian Tradition.* New York: Charles Scribner's Sons, 1952.

———. *The New Voice: Religion, Literature, Hermeneutics.* New York: Herder and Herder, 1969.

———. *Theology and Modern Literature.* Cambridge, Mass.: Harvard University Press, 1958.

Willeford, William. *The Fool and His Scepter: A Study in Clowns and Jesters and Their Audience.* Evanston, Ill.: Northwestern University Press, 1969.

Zaehner, R. C. *Matter and Spirit: Their Convergence in Eastern Religions, Marx, and Teilhard de Chardin.* New York and Evanston: Harper and Row, 1963.

Index

Note: Boldface numbers refer to the principal discussion of an author.